# BAYARD TAYLOR

*Laureate of the Gilded Age*

OTHER BOOKS BY RICHMOND CROOM BEATTY

*William Byrd of Westover* (Boston, 1932)

*English Dramas: A Critical Anthology*, co-editor
(New York, 1935)

*Bayard Taylor, 1878*

RICHMOND CROOM BEATTY

# BAYARD TAYLOR

*Laureate of the Gilded Age*

1936

UNIVERSITY OF OKLAHOMA PRESS

NORMAN

TO JOHN DONALD WADE

# PREFACE

THIS study is the result of an unprejudiced effort to understand the life of one of the most colorful and popular American authors of the nineteenth century. It attempts to answer what seems to me a decidedly significant question: the question, namely, of how it has happened that the once widely esteemed writings of Bayard Taylor are now almost completely forgotten. What was the nature of his work, that it was able to arrest so remarkably the imagination of his countrymen? Wherein has that imagination changed since? Moreover, with time's perspective to assist one, what conclusion can be reached about the intrinsic value of what the man did, regardless of its present popularity? What is there in it which at least *deserves* attention still?

The imperfect solution here presented to these questions naturally involved some examination of Taylor's way of life, and on this point there soon became apparent a remarkable circumstance: His way of life had a typicalness about it that, in America, appears characteristic not only of his own age but of the present as well. His biography, in other words, soon took on a symbolic character which was almost thunderously alive and contemporary. Thus, while it is evident that a taste for what he wrote has waned, it is equally evident that the tendency to live as he lived has not waned at all, but waxed. And this problem stood plainly in the wake of such discovery: Since Taylor's work was (as I believe is amply demonstrated in these pages) largely the product of his harassed manner of living, could there not conceivably be something in that manner which militates inevitably against the achievement of the artist who follows it? Does not his career assume, in brief, what one may term a genuine moral significance?

I think, devoutly, that it does, though—this book being a biography, not a treatise—I have not attempted to labor the point. But Taylor's story tends to establish, at least to my satisfaction, that the study of a "minor" figure in literature can upon occasion be fraught with conclusions very far from minor; indeed, such a study might possibly indicate that an age may often be better seen through those men who are more completely a part of it and thus more completely representative, than can readily be the case when one investigates its greatest figures only—figures who in general tower above it or move beyond it.

A good deal of the present discussion of Taylor's works has had of necessity to reflect my own judgment. No one of his previous biographers (see bibliography) saw fit in any real sense to examine them critically. They completely ignored the contents of his lectures; except for reference to titles and incidental comment, they ignored also his stories, dramas, and articles. His travel books, now out of print, likewise received scant treatment at their hands.

I have tried to present the flavor and spirit of all these things. Emphatically is it true that my excerpts have at no time been supercilious, in any conscious way. I have looked, rather, for what was representative. And if what appeared to be representative appears also rather extraordinary today, at times ridiculous even, then I am afraid one must blame a changed set of literary values, rather than a malice toward Taylor which I have never felt at all.

Already, by one of the gentlemen who were good enough to read this study in manuscript, a question has been raised which I feel certain will be raised again. It is this: Do I mean to imply that Taylor was, irretrievably, a second-rate artist, or do I mean to suggest that he was a great artist frustrated by the American way of life? Now there is nothing, in sober truth, that would please me more than the ability to answer this question. But I cannot answer it, even tentatively. Let me explain. In the Foreword to a recent book by Miss Babette Deutsch, *This Modern Poetry*, appears the following statement: "If we have no one equal to Shakespeare, surely a modern Shakespeare would outdistance his great ancestor by as much as the mentality and the sensibility of the twentieth century are richer than the mentality and sensibility of the sixteenth."

Perhaps the whole matter depends upon one's point of view. But this much is certain: Shakespeare, were he living in the twentieth century, would not be the Shakespeare we know. To suggest what he would be, moreover, seems to me entirely doctrinaire. Personally, I am happy that he is not our contemporary. If he were, the temper of our time being different, we might find him—to our distress—a sociologist, perhaps even an advertising manager. At all events, the issue is academic.

So it is with Bayard Taylor and his possibilities. Taylor, in my judgment, did not write a single work which was not influenced in one way or another by his age. This was his fate, his dark compulsion. Apart from this compulsion I am unable to think of him. Indeed, apart from it he does not exist.

A word ought to be added about the title of this book. "Laureate of the Gilded Age" may be a misnomer: nobody appointed Taylor laureate. I prefer the phrase because of its modern implications. Those implications *are* modern, I believe; for in its dominant attitudes the Gilded Age may be said to have differed only slightly from our own, if it differed at all. More specifically, I mean to imply that in his way of living Taylor was a modern (in spite of his romantic poetry), perhaps one of the first American moderns, in the special sense in which I prefer to use the word. Let us consider: Modernity was of course a characteristic of Benjamin Franklin; more broadly the term may be used to describe Francis Bacon, even Leonardo. But not even Franklin, I believe, can with fairness be described as a *modern*, as we of the present generation have come to construe the word. Franklin was up-to-date, surely; he was interested in science, and he took his religion mildly. Yet he was also a good deal more than this: he was economically secure, for one thing, and for another, he had a way of looking at life which gave to the scene about him something close to an ultimate meaning and significance. He was secure in his position. He saw life steadily, if he did not see it whole.

But on Taylor there fell the shadow of our great distrust. He knew what he wanted, no doubt, and mightily did he labor to win it. But the basis of any possibly satisfying achievement in the direction of his ambitions was lost to him. Rootless, in practice godless, eternally restless, harassed by debt and the sense of a fading, outraged purpose, he rushed through life seemingly aware of one unshakable certainty only: that the peace he sought was always ahead of him, the elusive rabbit that baited his race, but that never tired or faltered. In this sense, I suspect, his story is not yet obsolete.

Dr. John Donald Wade and Dr. Edd Winfield Parks, both formerly of Vanderbilt University, first stimulated my interest in Taylor. Drs. Frank Owsley and Daniel M. Robinson, of Vanderbilt University, have given me indispensable help. I am also indebted to Mr. John Oldham, of State Teachers College, Memphis, and to Dr. Howard Mumford Jones, of the University of Michigan, for reading through the manuscript, patiently and critically, and to Dean J. R. Schultz, of Allegheny College, for permission to examine his forthcoming edition of the Taylor letters in the Huntington Library. My major indebtedness, however, is to my wife, Floy Ward Beatty, without whose assistance the entire study would long ago have been abandoned.

R. C. B.

*University of Alabama,*
*April, 1936.*

# TABLE OF CONTENTS

# LIST OF ILLUSTRATIONS

# BAYARD TAYLOR

*Laureate of the Gilded Age*

*"So I have traveled,*
*Feasting on alien glory until I am*
*Myself no longer."*—DONALD DAVIDSON, THE TALL
MEN.

*"I shall gain far more by taking my own quiet*
*independent course, satisfied if the general tend-*
*ency of all I do is in the direction of a broader*
*and higher human culture."*—BAYARD TAYLOR to
an unknown friend, April 11, 1870.

# HERITAGE

## I

DR. ENGLISH fingered the young lad's head deftly. There was no flatness behind but a tapering prominence which aroused his interest anew. He had made his stock predictions about the prisoners the deputy had led out; he had lectured in West Chester on Mesmer and Spurzheim before enthusiastic, even amazed, audiences; he had fairly exhausted his anatomical vocabulary in describing the cranial peculiarities of the townsmen, and so he turned to the father and remarked quite simply, for he was now rather tired of exaggerations: "Sheriff Taylor, this boy of yours has all the marks of a poet." The sheriff spat and looked pensively at the young phrenologist from Philadelphia. "And what's more, Sheriff, you'll never keep him at home; he'll ramble about the whole world before he's old."[1] The boy himself said nothing, but stared out of the window across rolling fields now heavy with the midsummer afternoon and felt the wind from the distant Atlantic brush his face ever so lightly.

Now, plague it! this was an upsetting prophecy. For the sheriff knew, as Ben Franklin's father had known long before, that poets are generally beggars and, being so, scarcely even within the precincts of respect-

1. A. H. Smyth, *Bayard Taylor*, p. 20.

ability. Yet he remembered too many things to take the bright Dr. English in jest: It was 1839, Bayard was fourteen and the eldest living son, but around the house he was still practically useless. When he was sent to the mill for flour and a sack of it fell off his horse, he would mope along the roadside, helpless, until help chanced by, or come home without even a clear notion of where the sack lay. And when his mother set him to rocking his infant sister's cradle, he would do it automatically and viciously with his foot, absorbed in a book, while the child cried lustily.[2] And at night, moreover, he would copy out poems from ornate and essentially feminine looking albums—lines on "Hope," "On the Death of a Child at Daybreak," on "The Slave Ship," decorating his pages in crayon with scroll work that looked remarkably like lace and filing them away in his "Verse Book."[3] Naming him after the famous Senator Bayard from Delaware[4] had apparently accomplished nothing.

Or if not busy with this business of verses he was usually reading in one of that series of magazines—endless they appeared to the sheriff—which kept coming down from Philadelphia. There was Charles Alexander's *Every Bodies Album*, with its monthly allotment of "humorous tales, essays, anecdotes, and facetia"[5] and, the editor might have added, "costly

2. *Ibid.*, p. 12.
3. West Chester Library Mss., 1833.
4. This was, of course, the elder Bayard (James Ashe[e]ton) 1767-1815, ardent Federalist, and senator from 1805 to 1813.
5. F. L. Mott, *History of American Magazines*, pp. 622-3.

but absurd engravings." There was *Graham's Magazine,* with its positively queer stories by a person named Poe. There was the new *Pennsylvania Freeman* with its editorials by the stirring Quaker, John G. Whittier. There was *Peter Parley's Magazine*— not bad but, again, effeminate, thought the sheriff —filled with accounts of travel, fables, Bible narratives, and didactic little tales showing how Catherine and Martha were punished for disobedience, or how dear little Henry gave reading lessons to the drunkard's neglected boy, little William.

And finally, of course, there was *Godey's Lady's Book,* edited by that militant apostle of respectability, the widow Hale, who was to find immortality in her own account of Mary and the little Lamb, who was to blot out the word *female* from the name of Vassar college, who was to make Thanksgiving a national holiday, preserve Mount Vernon, perfect day nurseries for working mothers, discredit feather beds, popularize picnics, and rear to completion that Bunker Hill Monument which the eloquence of Webster had been able to fling heavenward only a little way,[6] and who even now, in 1839, was well started in her editorial policy of "the improvement of woman's status." James A. Godey, bald and effusive—the "prince of publishers," he termed himself—was supporting her. He planned to have his magazine in every home, and women already

6. Ruth E. Finley, *The Lady of Godey's: Sarah Josepha Hale* (J. B. Lippincott, Philadelphia), pp. 40 ff. Miss Finley gives Mrs. Hale major credit in carrying out the above movements and fashions.

were finding it indispensable because of its always reliable fashion plates and ennobling fiction and poetry.

Young Bayard fed amply on one writer of these ennobling gems, and sadly, for him, she was another woman of eminent literary purity. If fame is to be measured in quantitative terms, Mrs. Lydia Huntley Sigourney, "the sweet singer of Hartford," was perhaps the most famous writer of her generation. "She and George Washington were beyond criticism."[7] Born in 1791, she had made her father's shirts and socks before she was twelve; and though the old man never thanked her, the solemn intonation of his "my child" brought "the sweetest tears" to her eyes. After all he *was* old, and what young lady of her generation could contemplate white hair without weeping? "Melting"[8] the females of her generation termed it, lovely, unreasonable, bewilderingly tender "melting." At twenty, she began teaching school, rewriting Roman history for her children, in order that the lives of the emperors might illustrate appropriate virtues and vices. Four years later she published the first of some fifty volumes, *Moral Pieces*. She moved to Hartford and continued to teach, and the way from her room to the school soon proved fraught with a heavy significance. It led her past the home of a widower, Mr. Sigourney, "a gentleman of striking physiognomy and the elegant manners of the olden school." A year before, his wife had died, leaving him with a son and two daughters. Miss Huntley looked

7.  E. Douglas Branch, *The Sentimental Years*, p. 135.
8.  Gordon Haight, *Mrs. Sigourney*, pp. 5 ff.

her sympathy, while "his deep set and most expressive black eyes" spoke of things that were unutterable. A letter soon came from him—"a letter of touching eloquence and the fairest chirography," and resistance thereafter was useless. They were married.

Mr. Sigourney was a literary stylist himself, ever watchful, says his lady, "against new coined words and innovations of the language, referring constantly to the large edition of Dr. Johnson's Dictionary for etymology and shades of signification." The imputation of pedantry deterred him not at all. He took his bride to Virginia, where she saw Jefferson, and Madison, and Washington's tomb, and Jamestown, and where she wrote constantly, and always morally, about the sights of this colorful land of the Cavaliers. Her reputation was spreading even in the 1820's. The Gift Book and Annual editors implored her for contributions. Was not she the author of that immortal sentiment: "If there be a spot on earth which angels might long to visit, and where they might fondly linger, it is the loving Christian family?" Here was something which Americans would pay for. Give them these glowing platitudes, illustrated, when possible, by the colored engravings of Mr. Sartain, and the volume which contained them was certain to sell. In appearance these albums were all but ravishing to contemplate. Their bindings were ornate, frequently gaudy, but always glittering with floral designs inlaid with mother of pearl. If of leather, these bindings were invariably embossed; if of cloth, the dress was of water silk. And inside were the colored plates, twenty-five or thirty at times, and stories, essays, and selected poems, all redolent of tenderness, innocence, and sentimentality.

What was the reality even of Scott or Byron, compared with this more dazzling reality? Young Bayard had to read the English authors in cheap, pirated editions. Moreover, they were dead now, and not many people in West Chester talked about them. But Mrs. Sigourney and Mrs. Hale were living and vital—how vital one rather hates to remember. There was the glamor of newness about each volume which brought out their successive achievements; and, besides, how pleasant it was to sit before a fire when it rained or was cold and copy those engravings and floral designs and to try to imitate by hand the illuminated type such as printers used! What could be finer than to become an engraver one's self,[9] or to be a poet like Mrs. Sigourney and have one's work done out so handsomely!

It was a sad diet to set before any youngster, this pabulum of the "gemmiferous" school. Douglas Branch's description of it, though damaging, rings true: Ephemeral little sketches were the rule—sketches which "conjured a mood, fondled it, and let it trickle away, leaving a few jelly-like paragraphs about love, the landscape, sympathy, virtue, or death stranded on the flabby narrative."[10] Even among contemporaries there were protests. Poe, for example, had the

9. Smyth, *op cit.*, p. 19. Taylor, in 1839, applied to Sartain for a position as apprentice.
10. *Ibid.*, p. 138.

following to say on the subject in the *New World* (March 4, 1843). "The mass of matter appearing in the periodicals," he declared, "can only be designated as sentimental, love-sick, or fashionable stories, and unmeaning rhymes. Who can deny," he continues, "that an exceedingly bad influence is exerted by our magazine literature? Thousands of articles are published which instead of instructing the youthful mind 'please with a rattle; tickle with a straw;' instead of instilling a sound morality, they inculcate a neglect of everything that is valuable; instead of making the poor contented with their condition, they descant upon the luxury of fashion and wealth, causing a thousand hearts bitterly to ache for an imaginary want. . . . Let every man who believes that the tendency of this literature is bad refrain from purchasing the magazines which publish it. As to those who tax their brains to produce this literature, let them enjoy their only legitimate reward—the flattery of fools, foolish men and foolish young women." "Such matter," he concludes, "is almost without a single redeeming quality."[11]

Of course, young Taylor was coming to know other writers who, though romantic also, were not quite so vitiating. For example, Dr. Robert Montgomery Bird of Philadelphia was such a person. Almost everybody in the country knew about him. He had written *The Gladiator,* and that overwhelming actor Forrest had played in it as Spartacus ("Ye call me chief, and ye do well to call him chief who for twelve long years has met in the arena every manner of man or beast that

11.  Algernon Tassin, *The Magazine in America*, pp. 148-9.

the broad empire of Rome can furnish and who never once has lowered his aim," etc.). What ecstasy it would be to behold him, young Taylor doubtless thought, "in naked fighting trim, the muscles of his great form polished and hard"[12]—standing in splendid majesty upon the stage, while the crowds at the opera house rose and cheered tumultuously! The papers that came down to West Chester were all but filled with accounts of his performances. Indeed what boy, at least once, had not gone into his room when the family was away and declaimed, himself, the great speech of Spartacus to the gladiators? It was part of one's education.

Then there were the travelers. Washington Irving, in Taylor's opinion, was certainly the Washington of American prose. How many times had he read this genial author's account of the Alhambra and of the Conquest of Granada, lost in his pictures of crumbling palaces and sleepy sentinels and Arabian astrologers! And there were his narratives about England, about the stout gentleman and how he insulted the maid at the inn on that dull, wet Sunday, and about his broad expanse of breeches, and his umbrella and his pomposity. And again there was the picture of Christmas Eve in England, at Bracebridge Hall—the jovial squire and the merrymaking "where everything was done conformably to ancient usage;" where even the servants took part in the games—shoe the blind mare, bob apples, hot cockles, and hoodman blind—after the Yule log was brought in and the wine drunk and life had

12. E. P. Oberholtzer, *A Literary History of Philadelphia*, pp. 249-52.

grown pleasant to contemplate. What could be comparable to going to England one day and actually knowing such an old bachelor as Master Simon, who could imitate Punch and Judy, sing the old songs, dance the rigadoon and the heel and toe, and who still had a shrewd eye for the young wenches of the country?

Finally, there was the dazzling N. P. Willis, another traveler, famous even when he finished at Yale, and only now in his early thirties. No book which young Taylor ever read quite fascinated him like *Pencillings By the Way*, which had come out in 1835. Here was a born "foreign correspondent,"[13] who knew what his public wanted, who could grow rapturous at the sight of the proper cathedrals, who delighted in strange dress and manners, in gay throngs flooding ancient streets, in changing landscapes, in pretty women at balls, and who was never tiresome with serious information. To him Europe was a glittering holiday, a place where, it seemed, any young American with a pleasant address might go and shake the hand of the venerable Lafayette, talk with Tom Moore about Byron, or hear General Bertrand speak in sadness of the last days of Napoleon at St. Helena. What did it matter if the sour, carping Lockhart had labeled *Pencillings* "a goose of a book," containing no idea "beyond which might germinate in the brain of a washer woman." What did it matter, even, if this benighted traditionalist had called Willis himself "a lickspittle, a beggarly skittler, a jackass, a ninny, a haberdasher, a Namby-pamby writer in twaddling albums, a fifty-

13.  Henry A. Beers, *N. P. Willis*, pp. 10 ff.

fifth rate scribbler of gripe-visited sonnets, a windy-gutted visitor?" The point about Willis was that he was a young man, as Taylor would be soon, who had gone abroad and written a gloriously colorful book, and who was still sending letters to the New York *Mirror* which five hundred newspapers in the country were copying. Lockhart, if Taylor ever heard of his criticism, must have seemed merely a jealous foreigner, one who envied younger men of large talent. Was not *Godey's Lady's Book* paying Willis forty dollars for four page articles, and was not *Godey's* eminently respectable? And finally was not the great Senator Daniel Webster openly enthusiastic about *Pencillings?* "Góethe?" a certain Bostonian had asked, "No, sir, I haven't heard of Góethe, but I suppose he's the N. P. Willis of Germany."

So complete was Taylor's surrender to Willis that there was no place in his thinking for even the temperate inspiration of Longfellow. *Outre Mer* had also appeared in 1835, and Taylor had read it. It is a travel book in the more solid tradition of Irving, representing the effort of an American to steep himself in an older culture—a search after something spiritually satisfying but impossible of achievement in the new world. It is a leisurely book, containing a number of rambling stories which Longfellow purports to have heard from his innkeeper. There are few details about hotel service, "faithless stewards," exorbitant transportation rates, gratuities to natives, and chronology. Longfellow was not writing a guide book.

One feels, in consequence, that his volume is legitimate, a reflection of a rather moving and prolonged experience. He was not a tourist keeping a diary, as was Willis often, and as Taylor unfortunately became, almost always. One sees in Longfellow, to put the issue another way, the reflection of a mind unusually sympathetic toward an environment' steeped in rich associations, a mind which lacked the glitter of Willis but which contained nevertheless a far finer inspiration. Yet the way of Longfellow and Irving was to prove too long and tedious for Taylor. Their way called for a man's staying in a country until he had acquired the ability to think in its idiom.

But how could one buy a vast estate in this fashion, or become an eminent lecturer and novelist? Taylor began early to feel, it seems, that all these things were possible, and could be achieved without compelling a compromise with his art; they might be looked upon as so many serviceable steps which one used to mount to an eminence. One, in brief, could pay homage to Mammon without forgetting, even for an instant, that this homage was *enforced,* and in a later spring could be directed again skyward, toward poetry or, at any rate, toward *something* not really earthy at all.

It was a point of view remarkable in a great many ways—remarkable and astonishingly modern. For what it meant was that man is a creature without moorings, without tradition, without roots. He can turn as readily to one thing as to another: He can work with desperate energy, acquiring wealth and position, until the age of, say, sixty; then he can retire and seek culture, with an almost equally desperate resolve. The valves of his attention can be oiled to an infinite smoothness, may be turned on and off with an infinite ease. All these perplexities were in the future for Bayard Taylor; at sixteen he was still a home-loving boy. But soon they will reach out and seize him. And the imperious demands of them for Energy, Energy, shall beat without ceasing upon the reservoirs of his strength until, great as was their size, they shall have been drained, dried up, and rotted. His is the story of a man who lived from his youth to his premature death within a maelstrom.

# YOUTH

## II

BAYARD TAYLOR was born in Kennett Square, some forty miles southwest of Philadelphia, January 11, 1825, "the year the first locomotive successfully performed its trial trip."[1] Seven generations back, in 1684, Robert Taylor, of Cheshire, had come over with Penn and settled near the Brandywine Creek. This first Taylor was, naturally, a Quaker, and Quaker the family had remained until Bayard's grandfather John married a Mennonite lady of Swiss extraction and was turned out of meeting for not repenting. The rift widened with the years. Sheriff Taylor, John's son, never went back into the Society. Nor did Bayard go back.

Bayard's mother was Rebecca Way, granddaughter of Rebecca Mendenhall Way, who was related, uncertainly, to the distinguished family of Mendenhalls, of Mildenhall Manor, Wiltshire. The first Mendenhall, Benjamin, had also come over with Penn, and had given his daughter Anne as a bride to John Bartram, "the greatest natural botanist in the world."[2]

There was only one other important hereditary influence: Both of Bayard's grandmothers were of South German descent. His paternal grandmother knew little

1. A. H. Smyth, *op. cit.*, p. 12.
2. *Ibid.*, p. 14.

if any English, speaking always to her children in the dialect now termed Pennsylvania Dutch.

It ought to be admitted at once that there was very little in Taylor's immediate background which, in a purely literary sense, was capable of chastening the viciousness of Mrs. Sigourney, the album books, and Willis. His age, that is, was a sentimental age, and his family read, mostly, what the age produced. But in this respect he was doubtless no less fortunate than would have been the case were his century our own. The general quality of our popular magazines seems little improved, and the fact is true, now as then, that the average young man who aspires to a real literary prominence has to set himself against the ideals of the widely circulated publications. Those of his time were plastic enough to publish Poe and Hawthorne. One can scarcely say more, if as much, for their successors. This consideration, however, is true: The periodicals of his day influenced Taylor to a greater degree than seems common now, in the case of young men of his merit. He was more at their mercy, because of the relative inadequacy of libraries. To this extent one might suggest that he would have been more fortunate had his family inheritance included, for balance, a rather formal literary tradition.

Yet to say that it did not does not indicate that his family was ordinary. For generations it had played a quiet but respected rôle in the life of its section. A sensitive boy found it easy, in spite of the expansive temper of his age, to feel a sense of identity with such a family, an identity with something that was larger and stronger and more enduring than himself, yet made of the substance of which he was made. Taylor was never family conscious in the Brahmin sense, in the sense that, for example, Henry Adams was family conscious; but this, on the whole, was a minor handicap, if a handicap at all. What he *was* conscious of always, and what he seems to have remembered always, no matter how far from home, was that somehow, regardless of how well he liked a foreign place, that place was foreign. It could not hope to claim him for long. London might have appeared, to a Virginian of the eighteenth century like William Byrd, as the ideal city in which to live. But not to Bayard Taylor. After a while he would leave London or any other city and go back to Kennett Square. And when the time came to think of building a house of his own, there that house must be. He never once imagined it as existing anywhere else. And what doubtless prevented the intrusion of such a thought was the fact that his mother and father—the closest and most tangible links with his family—were there also, growing old wisely and happily in the village of his birth. But he was cursed with a restlessness and a necessity which likewise prevented him from ever being at peace, even after his house was built. Always there was this curse.

In spite of John Taylor's break with the Society, his grandson fell heir to a point of view that was predominantly Quaker. Kennett Square was a Quaker community; the attitudes of the sect were everywhere about him. Nearly all of his early companions belonged to it, as did the lady he first married. And there was at least one interesting and important influence which, it seems, may be traced very simply to this environment, and which deserves mention in any study of his life: One of the most significant tenets held by the Quakers was that which affirmed the existence between God and every man of a personal and peculiar relationship. It was the responsibility of the individual to discover, for himself, exactly what this relationship was, exactly also what God desired him to do, and how He wished him to do it. No minister could answer these questions—there *were* no ministers in the sense of professional or "acknowledged" clergymen—and the "exhorter" who took the minister's place could only suggest an answer in the light of some experience of his own. In Bayard's community there existed, in other words, a quiet earnestness, an attitude of self-reliance, an inborn aversion to surrendering to adversity, and the memory of unnumbered martyrs who had died courageously for the faith. It is probably questionable whether the general philosophy of this sect—complete faith in one's self, and such incidental doctrines as its opposition to slavery—would have flowered out so richly in Taylor had it not been re-emphasized: by Emerson on the one count, and by Dickens and the Abolitionists on the other. But it can be said with certainty that when Taylor first encountered the social message of Dickens, and the transcendental message of Emerson, he looked upon both enthusiastically, but naturally. They appeared merely as classic statements of convictions which he had come to share in childhood.

Bayard's mother taught him to read, and after he had learned, at six, sent him to Ruth Anne Chamber's log schoolhouse at Kennett Square, where he copied poems and memorized poems and thought of the day he would write them. The environment of the place was Quaker, as we have seen. Bayard said *thee* and *thou* naturally, learned that one must love peace and a quiet life, that one should avoid profanity, and that one should be kind to one's neighbors. He studied next with Friend Samuel Martin. They would walk together long evenings through the woods, collecting odd looking stones. One should always interest himself in natural science, taught Friend Martin, should keep a cabinet filled with curiosities, washed and polished for admiring visitors.

By this time he was reading in earnest—*Thaddeus of Warsaw*, all of Scott that he could find, and, of course, Byron, Shelley, and Wordsworth. In 1837 his father was elected sheriff of the county and moved to West Chester, then a bustling cattle town a dozen miles away. Bayard attended Bolmar's Academy there. Three years later, when the sheriff's term was out, the family moved back to Kennett Square, having sent Bayard four miles farther on to Unionville Academy to complete his education.

At Unionville he was progressing remarkably! By March, 1840, he had "completed astronomy" and was "studying the languages." He was reading Voltaire in the native French—not his "atheistical works," he wrote his mother, "but his tragedies, which are among the best writings in the French language."[3] He was also, he added, far along in his Latin.

Now, after listing his achievements as modestly as his enthusiasm would permit, he suggested earnestly to his mother a plan which was to bring him perhaps the first of his many disappointments. A cousin, Franklin Taylor, a student in a New England boarding school, had recently talked to Bayard about going back with him in the fall.

There were so many advantages! "The opportunities for learning are greater:" board is only $1.25 a week, one could pay tuition and live for $97.00 a year; even counting traveling expenses the cost was no more than at Unionville! And during vacation time, in August, "the scholars form into companies and travel, usually on foot, through Vermont and New Hampshire, and they thus have an opportunity of viewing the most romantic and sublime scenery in New England—Lake Champlain, Lake George, the White and Green Mountains, which afford a fine field for the labors of the artist, and if I get a box of *craeta laevis* [crayon] you will see the hills and rocks of New England glowing upon paper with all the beauty they really possess." Also he could build up his mineral collection, and learn much, much more than it was possible to learn at Unionville, and his father could take him there and see the wonderful landscapes himself, and his mother could go along and visit New York

3.  Marie H. Taylor and Horace Scudder, *Life and Letters of Bayard Taylor*, I, 17. To his mother, March 18, 1840.

and Boston. A new world was offering itself to young Taylor, and the lad knew it, and perhaps his mother knew it.

But he didn't go. Even if Jonathan Gause, at Unionville, did charge more, thought the sheriff, that was endurable, because Jonathan Gause was his friend, was safe, and Bayard would be near home.

The boy didn't grieve outwardly about his father's decision; his spirits were too high, the future too bright for that. Instead, he continued his studying, and his writing in a diary which he had kept for months. He also continued to compose poems—poems that, as nearly always with the youth of his day, reflected the borrowed splendors of the English romanticists only dimly beneath the muddiness of many album books. And he would visit, at times, the historic scenes of his section, and write about them for the West Chester *Register*. Brandywine Battlefield he had thus commemorated, and on week-ends there had been trips to Valley Forge, a good way beyond West Chester, where the bodies of nameless heroes slept unendingly on quiet hillsides, and where ruined huts and cannon impotent in rust proclaimed his country's immortal beginnings.

In 1841 his first poem was printed in the *Saturday Evening Post*. He called it, appropriately, "The Soliloquy of a Young Poet," and in it he spoke of the way the stars moved him, of the haunting sight of birds, of cooling rills, and of a thin moon curtained by dawn. And afterwards he made an open confession:

*High hopes spring up within;*
*Hopes of the future—thoughts of glory—fame*
*Which prompt my mind to toil and bid me win*
*That dream—a deathless name.*[4]

In the summer of 1842 he finished his course at Unionville and came home. There was no chance of going away to college, no talk of it even. The time was at hand for young Bayard to set about achieving his long-dreamed-of reputation by work, the only agency he knew.

Yet it was plain that as a farmer his time would be wasted. Besides, the family place was not large, only some 150 acres; he was hardly needed at home. He tried to get a school, but only half-heartedly, partly because he felt no genuine interest in teaching, and partly because he had been thinking of other employment far more attractive.

Why not become a printer, perhaps in time the owner of a thriving journal? He enjoyed books and writing; anything connected with publication fascinated him. Moreover there was Henry Evans in West Chester, who owned the *Village Record* and who knew his family. And there was that fine library in the town, which had flourished since 1818 and where he had spent so many pleasant hours when his father was sheriff of the county. He went to see Mr. Evans, and before the interview was over he had signed papers of apprenticeship which bound him for four years.

The step which he thus took so briskly brought him into a world of great glamour and infinite bustle. To

4.  *Ibid.,* p. 21.

be a printer meant that one must, at all costs, keep up with the times, know about the important personages of the day, and be able to quote their opinions on current matters. And this meant, in 1842, that young Taylor was immensely interested in the doings and sayings of Mr. Charles Dickens, beyond doubt the country's most distinguished guest.

Think, for example, of the way Boston had received this man of letters—how six newspaper editors had rushed out to wring his hand when he arrived, how the painter Francis Alexander hurried him to his home "through cheering throngs" to do his portrait, how an "official" banquet was tendered him, how the Jonsonian plays Dickens had acted in were performed nightly at two Boston theaters, and how the very name of the city had been changed, said facetious but envying New York journalists, from dignified Boston to "Boz-town"![5] Though this gentleman's brilliant green waistcoats offended the ladies, they were always anxious to meet him, to hear him talk, and to ask for his autograph. He was fêted in New York, as in Boston, and his popularity did not waver amid the ballrooms and drawing-rooms of genteel Philadelphia.

And how brave he was in his utterances, Bayard must have thought. At first there had been his invectives against the lack of copyright laws in America. England, he said, had done her part; the products of American authors could not be pirated there; and yet in this country the works of every important foreign

5. Ralph Straus, *Dickens* (London, 1928), p. 166.

writer were published without any royalties reaching him. It was a matter of simple honesty, said Mr. Dickens, a condition which all decent citizens should deplore. And he kept on saying this before distinguished audiences in our most distinguished cities.

Nor was this all. The people of Philadelphia had been "lovely" to him, and yet one condition there had filled him with infinite sadness. He had been taken out to see a prison in which solitary confinement was practiced. He wrote about this in great detail, and he lectured about it as well. He had talked to these miserable wretches himself; he had looked into their lustreless eyes, shaken their cold hands, pitied their slow and broken bodies. They lived on bread and water only, and there was never a fellow unfortunate to talk with, and never a friend to bring them news of home; there was nothing but interminable, empty hours of semi-darkness and stone walls.

And with what courage and candor he had denounced the crime of human slavery, as practiced in the South. There were, he declared, three types of slaveholders. The first type was made up of moderate owners, who deplored the institution but who felt that the slave represented more capital than they could afford to dispose of. Then, there were the buyers and breeders of slaves, who denied that the condition was horrible and who were willing to provoke war rather than give them up. Finally, there were those arrogant and pampered aristocrats who had come to be entirely dependent upon the slaves' services and whose vanity was consoled only through their constant, enforced ministrations.[6]

Consider, Mr. Dickens would continue, the usually offered defenses of the practice. There were those who said the slaves were always treated well, because if they were not their efficiency was impaired. It was bad business to abuse them, it was argued, just as it was bad business to beat one's horse to death. This argument was entirely specious. Read the advertisements for runaway slaves that blanketed the newspapers daily: "Run away, the negro Manuel, much marked with irons." "Run away, the negro Daniel, shot through the hand a short time since, several shots through left arm and side." "$100 reward for negro named Pompey, 40, branded in left jaw." "Run away, the negro wench Mary, many teeth missing. Letter A branded on cheek." What the gentlemen who advanced this argument forgot was the melancholy fact that human beings are not entirely rational, that they are alarmingly inclined to heavy drinking, to gambling, to murder and a thousand other excesses, any one of which can be economically destructive.

And there are others who said that public opinion prevents cruelty and unfairness to these unfortunates. But how can that be, asked Mr. Dickens, when we realize that public opinion is *slavery*, when even a freedman can be arrested on the merest suspicion and sold to pay the jailor? So ran the wisdom of this visitor, at that time called the greatest of living English

6. Charles Dickens, *American Notes* (London, 1928), pp. 197-205.

writers, who though manifestly ignorant of the nature and history of slavery as an institution in America, and of the constitutional guaranty of it, was daily becoming more and more popular with the Abolitionists. On this last question he probably made no more thorough convert in the country than young Bayard Taylor, who a decade later was to take to the lecture platform, as had Dickens, repeating his arguments before audiences even wilder and blinder, and whose happiest day in West Chester came when the postmaster handed him a letter from the great novelist, containing the autograph he had humbly requested.[7]

There were many other lecturers, of course, wise Americans with burning messages, and Bayard kept up with what they were saying. Indeed, this lecture or lyceum idea was one of the major institutions of the decade. In 1843, it had been seventeen years since the first course of lessons had been given under the sponsorship of the Mechanics of Millsbury, Massachusetts. Josiah Holbrook, the most active of its founders, saw in the movement a cure for practically all the educational ills of the country. In his pamphlet, the *American Lyceum*,[8] he had outlined ten important blessings which would soon result were his ideas adopted: Ly-

7. Taylor, in later years, lost his interest in autograph hunters. The following letter is typical of his general attitude: "Dear Sir: I do not attach any value to Ms. written merely for the purpose of being an autograph, but if you do so, this is mine. Very truly yours, Bayard Taylor." 8-2-65, to an unknown admirer. *Unpublished Letters of Bayard Taylor* (Huntington Library Pub.), J. R. Schultz, ed.

8. First published in Boston, 1829. He had previously sketched his plans in *Barnard's Journal*, in 1826.

ceum courses, he pleaded, would improve conversation, direct the young toward safe amusements, reduce the cost of education (a year's course for $2.00!), call neglected libraries into use, provide a seminary for teachers, encourage experimentation, foster charters for district schools, lead to the writing of town histories, to the making of maps and agricultural surveys, and, finally, to the augmenting of the state's collection of minerals. Incidentally, Mr. Holbrook had special apparati for sale which, if bought, would enormously assist any town in its program. Boston citizens were enthusiastic, and at a meeting distinguished by its presiding officer, Senator Daniel Webster, resolutions were passed recommending that these ideas be supported, and equipment bought.

The movement spread rapidly. Ralph Waldo Emerson was among the first professional lecturers. Willing to speak, in his early days, for "$5 and four quarts of oats for my horse," he eventually regarded $500 as a reasonable fee for only a night's services. In the forties these speakers were usually recommending reforms. Young James Russell Lowell, not yet the Bramin of his Harvard days, directed polished platitudes against the evils of slavery. Wendell Phillips fulminated on the same theme. Theodore Parker and William Ellery Channing, before his untimely death, pictured eloquently God's surpassing love. Margaret Fuller denounced man's subjugation of her sex; Thoreau commended a vigorous individualism; and Bronson Alcott, in rambling sententiae, fused Kant and Plotinus into enraptured incandescence.

These apostles on their sweeping circuits came often, we may be sure, to West Chester. With them came other, more tenuous, apostles, lecturing on phrenology (as had Dr. English), on animal magnetism, and on the spirit world which almost everyone in a Quaker community had come somehow to regard as half real at least, and with which certain favored mortals could at times establish transcendent communication. Bayard Taylor attended these lectures. He heard the country's wisest men tell hushed hundreds about the glories of education, how in a democracy boundless progress was inevitable, how any man with a will and industry could succeed beyond his farthest imaginings, how science was slowly, but with surpassing sureness, lifting the race out of ageless bondage.

And he was inspired. Had not Waldo Emerson declared that God was in everyone, a Light crying out against the blindness which kept it hid? Had he not said, this eloquent philosopher, that the iron string to which all hearts vibrate is self trust, really identical with trust in Deity? It was a doctrine which lifted men out of despair, unchaining the fettered Prometheus within, freeing a great and righteous force in a land where righteousness was desperately needed. Bayard Taylor, in short, believed, in common with most of his generation in the North, that the world would soon become immeasurably better than ever before men had dreamed it could be.

In addition to attending lectures and continuing with his work, he was also writing much, and reading still more, now that books were easily accessible.

"What do you think of Bryant as a poet, and especially of Thanatopsis?" he inquired of a friend. "For my part, my admiration knows no bounds. There is in it an all prevading love of nature, a calm and quiet yet deep sense of everything that is beautiful. And then the high and lofty feeling which mingles with the whole! It seems to me when I read his poetry that our hearts are united, and that I can feel every thought of his answered back by mine."[9] Tennyson's 1842 volume had reached America, and to Taylor it was like "the first sight of a sunlit landscape through a prism," a volume he read and reread until his aching eyes would assimilate no more.

Meanwhile, his own verses were being more than occasionally published. Since the "Young Poet's Dream," several other poems had appeared in the *Saturday Evening Post*, and through them he had come to be noticed by that gentlemanly editor, Dr. Rufus Griswold. Griswold was connected slightly with the *Post*, and he was made editor of *Graham's Magazine* after Poe had resigned. A former itinerant printer, Baptist preacher, and opponent of Jeffersonianism and the Papacy, since 1842 he had become the object of no little flattery from young writers, thanks to the publication of his anthology, *Poets and Poetry of America*. Taylor wrote him, naïvely, that his "highest ambition" was "to appear in *Graham's Magazine*." Griswold answered pleasantly: He had enjoyed his lines "To the Brandywine"; he would publish another of Taylor's pieces in *Graham's*, he should be glad to have

9.  Taylor-Scudder, *op. cit.*, I, 24-5.

him call when in Philadelphia. Taylor walked to the city from West Chester—only about thirty miles—the great man had by this time read his "Rosalie," a poetic romance renamed "Ximena," and "strongly advised me to publish it, with my other poems, in a volume!"[10]

To do this meant, of course, that he would have to get subscriptions to meet the charges of printing. But the fame he dreamed of in his first poem was not his only reason for wishing the book brought out. "My principal motive," he wrote a friend, "is to gain a small sum toward defraying the expenses of preparing for my voyage to the West Indies. I also wish to obtain the critical judgment of some of the best literary characters, which can be had in no other way. I do not dread condemnation, for if I have to bear it, I would rather do it now than at a future time, for errors would now be attributed to youth and inexperience which would then have no excuse."[11]

The thin volume appeared in February, 1844. *Ximena, or The Battle of the Sierra Morena*, ran the title page. "By James Bayard Taylor." The James he had added gratuitously, "because it sounded pleasant." He was later to regret it. He sent copies to "the best literary characters"—to Longfellow, notably, and to Lowell, whom he wrote in all humility:

"Will you receive the offering of a bard unknown to you, as a small return for the spiritual enjoyment you have given him? I am but a youth, and have a life of toil before me, and whenever I weary of my

10. *Ibid.*, p. 27.          11. *Ibid.*, p. 28.

28

burden, the voice of the poet, prophet-like, bids me 'suffer and be strong.' I dare not as yet call myself a brother-bard; but I send you the first breathings of my soul, with the ardent hope they will find a response in your own."[12]

This work, later entirely repudiated, was notable for its celebration of native subjects and for its lusty echoes of Scott and Mrs. Felicia Hemans. It hardly created a ripple critically, and it brought its author next to nothing in money. But for all that, grand dreams were shaking him. He remembered Willis' success with *Pencillings*, and he had since read George Putnam's *The Tourist in Europe*, a guide book, and Howitts' *Rural Life in Germany*, which convinced him that the continent might be visited cheaply on foot. All that was glamorous in his imagination poised itself upon the thought of a journey there. But a reluctant family had to be converted. And there was a young lady, Mary Agnew, hardly seventeen, whom he had known since childhood, and with respect to whom absence was desolation. And how could he meet the cost?

He would try it, at any rate. With the few dollars *Ximena* had given him, he bought the remainder of his apprenticeship time from Mr. Evans and went to Philadelphia to talk to the publishers. Fortune favored him. Peterson, of the *Post*, gave him fifty dollars in advance for twelve travel letters. J. R. Chandler, of the United States *Gazette*, made a similar offer.

12. A. H. Smyth, *op. cit.*, p. 32-3.

Graham bought several poems. He reached home with $140, and the family's protest dwindled away.

A new difficulty then presented itself. Travelers to foreign countries, men said, must have a passport from Washington. He did not delay long. Washington was only one hundred miles away; he set out on foot with his cousin, Franklin, who had arranged to go abroad with him for study in Germany. From Fort Deposit to Baltimore they traveled by boat. Arriving at Baltimore after the taverns had closed, they walked the remaining forty miles to their destination, tortured by thirst, "forced to drink from ditches and standing pools, closing our teeth to keep out the tadpoles and water beetles."

But that morning they reached the city. They called first upon their Congressman, through him met Secretary of State John C. Calhoun, and listened to encouragement from former president John Quincy Adams, now a Congressman again. By the end of June they were in New York, having been met by still another friend, Barclay Pennock. "The three wise men," they called themselves. Certainly they were three unusually brave men.

Before sailing, Taylor visited Willis, who received him with all kindness, and gave him a specific letter to his brother, Richard, then a music student in Germany, and another glowingly general letter of recommendation to all printers the world over. Finally, he went to see Horace Greeley of the *Tribune*. Greeley advised him to settle down in Germany, learn something real about the people with whom he stayed, and then write. Perhaps by that time, the publisher added, your letters will be worth buying. "But no descriptive nonsense. Of that I am damned sick."

The three left New York July 1 on the *Oxford*, bound for Liverpool. They paid ten dollars apiece for passage "and the privilege of finding our own bedding and provisions."[13] Denied a university education, Bayard Taylor expected this trip, so far as possible, to take the place of one. It would be his grand tour, seriously entered into and courageously prolonged until his last resources were exhausted, and until there was no hope of more. What, as he saw it, did the start one had been granted in life ever really amount to in terms of cold realities? The wise man of Concord village sang in eloquent reassurance. Greatness, even God, was in him. And was he not young and eager? Was not poetry a divine thing to him, as long ago it had been to John Milton?

The *Oxford* pushed quietly through a wide and dazzling sea, bringing him to the world which from childhood he had pictured as endlessly beautiful. He would write about it, in honesty, as he saw it. He would keep himself fresh and keen for it, as ladies did for absent lovers. And who could prophesy but that out of such devotion would come the fruits of his earlier dream—"the deathless name," about which he had never for an instant really forgotten?

13.  Bayard Taylor, *Views Afoot* (1885 ed.), p. 29.

# EUROPE

## III

A TALL, pale youth in his twentieth year, with a knapsack and one hundred and forty yet unearned dollars in his pockets, with no family to write to for more, out to absorb European culture, to stay "at least eighteen months abroad!" It could hardly have happened except in the 1840's, in a decade whose last years were to see the lusty romantic movement acting out its faith across an unpenetrated continent on the other side of which gold lay and freedom from the thousand ills that for centuries had made heavier the heavy lot of man. A youth going, not West, but East, seeking not gold, but a thing which to him seemed less tangible yet infinitely more enduring than gold—the illusion of a traditional culture which Irving and William Byrd and many another had looked for before him, which many others were to look for later—a dream as truly typical of America as the democratic dream or the dream of its own peculiar destiny.

Let us come closer to him. Already he is fully six feet in heighth, rather thin, but straight, even athletic in appearance. His eyes are brown, his hair a very rich brown, flowing carelessly, a trifle longishly, down to his neck. His forehead is high and broad, his nose and mouth finely modelled. Certainly one would call him handsome. But the eyes recall us—eyes in which, as it were, melancholy and eagerness appear by turns to usurp the usual placidity of his face.[1] They are remarkably heavy-lidded. His friends call them magnetic, remembering, perhaps, how successful Taylor has already proved himself as a practitioner of the new "science" of mesmerism.[2] He has hypnotised scores of persons. He can hypnotise almost anybody! And always he does it by having the subject stare for some moments fixedly into his eyes. Instinctively, it seems, when one looks at him once, one turns to look again.

The "three wise men" landed at Liverpool for a day, and then set out by boat for Scotland. London they could visit perhaps on the way back, but Loch Katrine, Loch Lomond, Ben Lomond, the Vale of Menteith, Ben Nevis, and Bruce's and Rob Roy's caves were not for an unnecessary instant to be neglected. Taylor sketched the famous lakes, climbed the famous mountains, heard the natives sing ballads in Gaelic, and finally went to Ayr to attend the Burns festival.

What he saw at this celebration did not entirely please him. Someone pointed out the cottage where the greatest poet of the country passed his first seven years. But behold the sign over the door, the work of a later and villainous occupant: "Licensed to retail spirits, to be drunk on the premises." If there was any propriety in the nature of this bold announcement, it was not apparent to young Taylor. "The rooms were crowded full of people, all drinking.... The hostess looked toward us as if to enquire what we would drink,

1. Taylor-Scudder, *op. cit.*, I, 42.
2. A. H. Smyth, *op. cit.*, p. 29.

but I hastened away—there was profanity in the thought."[3]

There were other things which saddened him, and with greater justice. The sons of Burns were there, within a place fenced about and guarded. But no one who had not bought a fifteen shilling ticket to the grand dinner could meet them, or see the festival which was being enacted before the favored gentry inside the enclosure.

He went to Edinburg and to Abbotsford. He saw Scott's library and study, "the walls of which are covered with books." The great man had walked there, had read there, had written there his immortal stories! "His books and inkstand are on the table and his writing chair stands before it, as if he had left them but a moment before. In the little closet adjoining, where he kept his private manuscripts, are the clothes he last wore, his cane and belt, and his sword. . . . The silence about the place is solemn and breathless, as if it waited to be broken by his returning footstep. I felt an awe in treading these lonely halls, like that which impressed me before the grave of Washington— a feeling that hallowed the spot, as if there yet lingered a low vibration of the lyre, though the minstrel had departed forever."[4]

The three friends traveled next to London, with plans for a week's stay. But it was Westminster Abbey that Taylor most desired to see, and as soon as possible he went there. "Oh [sic] Rare Ben Jonson," carved beneath a bust of the dramatist, he read upon entering.

3. *Views Afoot*, p. 59.    4. *Ibid.*, p. 69.

"Nearby stood the monuments of Spenser and Gay, and a few paces further looked down the sublime countenance of Milton." It was probably Taylor's first visit to a church with stained windows, his first consciousness of dead saints drinking in a blinding light while he, alive, stood pensive in dimness. And it moved him, as before it had moved Addison and Irving. He walked on to see the majestic head of Dryden, to contemplate the image of Gray, "full of the fire of lofty thought." And there were the gentle feminine countenance of Thomson, the monument to Garrick, and farther on, the tablet to Shakespeare. His imagination, he said, was fettered by these spirits; he tried to recall the day when first their names became symbols of fire to him, his mind ran off into childhood's channels and lost itself among other new world names, now strangely empty and meaningless.

He went into the side chapels, filled with the tombs of knightly families, where numberless earls stared in grim effigy, where Elizabeth lay and Mary and Darnley. He saw the chair in which the rulers of England had been crowned for four centuries, the hall in which the Knights of the Bath met. "Over each seat their dusty banners are still hanging, each with its crest, and their armour is rusting upon the wall."

This still place of the deathless dead was life to him. He was here no conventional tourist, saying the expected thing. The visit made permanent his allegiance to the desire to write, one day, poems that would not be unworthy of the gentlemen who slept before him, the wise fine gentlemen who even in death rebuked apostasy and a careless art. If he failed in this, it would not be for lack of trying, but only because he misjudged the way, or was denied the strength.

He went elsewhere in London, down the Thames to Wapping, to the parks, from the Strand through Regent Street and Picadilly Circus. Not everything in the historic city was commendable. "If London is unsurpassed in splendor, it has also its corresponding share of crime. Notwithstanding the large and efficient body of police, who do much towards the control of vice, one sees enough of degradation and brutality in a short time to make his heart sick. Even the public thoroughfares are thronged at night with characters of the lowest description, and it is not expedient to go through many of the narrow by-haunts of the old city in the daytime."[5]

He spent his entire visit in sightseeing. "I have neither made a single acquaintance, nor obtained the least insight into the social life of England. Having a plan mapped out for the day, I started from my humble lodgings at the Aldergate Coffee House, where I slept off fatigue for a shilling a night, and walked up Cheapside or down Whitechapel, as the case might be, hunting out my way to churches, halls, and theatres."

The travelers left England for the continent. They passed through Belgium hurriedly, but in Heidelberg they planned to spend an entire month. Franklin Taylor meant to study there, now that Gervinius and

5. *Ibid.*, p. 86.

Schlosser, former Göttingen liberals, were numbered among the faculty. Such modest prices prevailed! For twelve dollars a month they obtained separate rooms, food, and lights with a prominent family. Opposite their windows rose the Heidelberg, which they would climb on early fall mornings to visit the castles. And they were taking lessons in German, from a tutor who dined with them, that the native language might be spoken even at meals.

The Germans were such happy people, even the poorest of them! They would meet at the pavillion in the afternoon and drink beer under the shade of ancient linden trees, and listen to a band which played Beethoven and Bach. Or they would walk through the Odenwald in parties, or visit the Castle of Trifels, where Richard the Lion-Hearted was imprisoned by the Duke of Austria six centuries before. No one was exempt from these outings, and everyone was friendly.

Taylor visited the Heidelberg library: "You walk through hall after hall, filled with books of all kinds, from the monkish manuscript of the middle ages to the most elegant print of the present day. There is something to me more impressive in a library like this than in a solemn cathedral. I think involuntarily of the hundreds of mighty spirits who speak from these 300,000 volumes—of the toils and privations with which genius has ever struggled, and of its glorious reward. As in a church, one feels as if he were in the presence of God; not because the place has been hallowed by His worship, but because all around stand the inspirations of His spirit, breathed through the mind of genius, to men."[6]

The month out, Taylor went on toward Frankfort. During the journey he saw a Bavarian family, bound for Texas. The idea of leaving so lovely a country for a new world wilderness seemed madness to him. "I endeavored to discourage the man from choosing such a country for his home, by telling him of the climate and the Indians, but he was too full of hope to be shaken in his purpose. I would have added that it was a slave land, but I thought on our country's curse and was silent."

In Frankfort he met the brother of the famous N. P. Willis, Richard Storrs. For more than two years this young man had been studying music there. He had played for the great Mendelssohn, who listened "with the warmest approval." Willis helped Taylor find a place to stay. He moved into a house more than two hundred years old and for ten dollars monthly received all the privileges of home. He was already far advanced with his German. "The difficulties of the language are at last overcome, and all the more familiar phrases of the hearty German tongue come as naturally to my lips as the corresponding English ones.... I now read Hauff, Uhland, and Schiller, without difficulty, and look forward to a winter of much enjoyment in the study of the great German authors."[7]

He carried out this purpose in earnest, varying the routine of reading by frequent evening walks with Willis and by one trip back to Heidelberg, where he

6. *Ibid.*, p. 113.        7. *Ibid.*, p. 126.

saw a duel, drank beer with hundreds of strikingly handsome students ("the beer was a weak mixture, which I should think would make one fall over from its weight, rather than its intoxicating properties"), and heard speeches extolling "a strong, united, regenerated Germany"—speeches which in his own lifetime he was to see transformed into flaming realities.

Taylor did not leave the city until late April, but his progress thereafter was rapid. He walked alone through the Hartz, lured by Goethe's witches, delighted with several storms in the mountains, intrigued by German students whom he talked with about their native poetry.

At Leipzig he met his friend, Pennock, who had traveled a separate way for two weeks. They walked on to Prague through Bohemia, to Moravia, and finally to Vienna. Even more than it meant the university, Vienna meant Strauss to these travelers. They went to a large beer garden in the afternoon and heard the "waltz-king" and his band. The master came in, smiling, with his violin, and the music started. He never looked at the score in front of him. In the midst of a piece "he would wave his fiddle bow awhile" to subdue the brasses, and then "commence playing with desperate energy, moving his whole body to the measure, while sweat rolled carelessly from his brow.[8] Here was the man who had set the whole world talking, playing his slow, insidious music in his own glorious city of towers and palaces. How infinitely distant seemed Kennett Square with its neat Dutch farms, how drab and

8. *Ibid.*, p. 239.

desolate the barren hills of home. He would come back again, before always, to this land of gay ladies and open-hearted, laughing men. He visited the little cemetery where Beethoven was buried, where eternal restlessness lay at rest at last. "The perfection he sought for here in vain he has now attained in a world where the soul is freed from the bars which bind it in this: There were no flowers planted around the tomb by those who revered this genius; only one wreath, withered and dead, lay among the grasses, as if left long ago by some solitary pilgrim, and a few wild buttercups hung their bright blossoms over the slab. I could not resist the temptation to pluck one or two, while the old grave-digger was preparing a new monument."

They stayed for some days in the capital, sightseeing; then they walked on to Munich and Switzerland. All the attractions were carefully described. Taylor felt that he would have neglected his duty had he failed to catalogue for other less fortunate Americans the physical details of these lands so steeped in tradition. He climbed mountain after mountain, recording the ecstacy of his accomplishments methodically. He talked with farmers along the way. He treated all cathedrals with deference. What was there for him to see, except those things which met his eye? Of necessity his sketches became so much verbal photography, but even this implies that he was honest. He was also still very young.

The anniversary of their sailing date found the two friends in Italy. The architecture in Milan all but bewildered Taylor, the great cathedral, the Duomo, inspiring perhaps his first art criticism. Its hundreds of sculptured pinnacles resembled oddly, he thought, "the splintered ice-crags of Savoy. Thus we see how art, mighty and endless in her forms though she be, is in everything but the child of nature. Her divinest conceptions are but copies of objects which we behold every day. The faultless beauty of the Corinthian capital—the springing and intermingling arches of the Gothic aisle—the pillared portico or the massive and sky-pierced pyramid—are but attempts at reproducing, by the studied regularity of art, the ever varied and ever beautiful forms of mountain, rock, and forest. But there is oftentimes a more thrilling sensation of enjoyment produced by the creation of man's hand and intellect than is to be found in the grander effects of Nature, existing constantly before our eyes."[9]

He went on to Florence and Fiesole. All his talk was of beauty and art now, of leisurely strolls through galleries in which only the venerable masters had a place. The American sculptor Hiram Powers was at the former city with his family. Taylor met him and wrote a poem about his daughter and another about a statue, "Eve," which Powers had recently finished. The friendly artist was overwhelmed. "Who shall say," he wrote Taylor, "that your verses may not remain the only record of my statue of Eve long after it has returned in fragments to the earth from which it was taken?" Through him Taylor met Mrs. Trollope. This tart lady, no inconsiderable traveler herself, had asked to meet him after seeing the poem. "She read the first

9. *Ibid.*, p. 329.

stanza," Taylor wrote his cousin, "and then exclaimed, 'Very good!' The second was 'Charming! Delightful!' And so her admiration waxed with every stanza, so that it is fortunate there were only five, otherwise she might have been carried away."[10]

She gave Taylor a letter to her publisher, the famous Murray, in London. The sight of other artists in Italy, actually engaged in the business of creation, was unsettling. He wanted to get fairly started himself. News from home assured him that his letters were being rather widely read. "I tell you what, Frank, I am getting a real rage in me to carve out my own fortune, and not a poor one either. Sometimes I almost desire that difficulties should be thrown in my way, for the sake of the additional strength gained in surmounting them."

But these difficulties he desired were grandly imaginary—climbing up Parnassus in a cool morning mist (he was hoping to get to Greece before turning homeward), "sighing for fallen art beneath the broken friezes of the Parthenon" while the sun was somewhat warmer than one might relish. Genuine difficulties, it must be admitted, were as unromantic to him as to anyone. "I begin to get heartily tired of traveling in this manner," he had written Franklin. He deplored the fact that he was unable, because of lack of money, to leave Florence as soon as he desired. "Really it is disagreeable to be so circumstanced."[11] He had had to borrow from Powers. He was living on two meals

10. Taylor-Scudder, *op. cit.*, I, 63.
11. *Ibid.*, p. 59.

a day now, the better to economize, and then eating grapes mostly, because of their inexpensiveness. A small sum reached him from home. "I was obliged to get a new pair of pants for three dollars, as the others literally dropped in pieces from me." There is no trace of elation here over the fact that he was confronting definitely unpleasant, trying situations. The unimaginative nature of these difficulties robbed them of glamour and nourished disgust in him.

He went on to Rome. There were more cathedrals to see, more pictures and statues to whet wanly a curiosity now rapidly nearing surfeit. And one begins to feel in his rather desperately wrought enthusiasms a trace of the hollow conventionalized idolatry, the revolt from which was later to make Mark Twain's savage *Innocents Abroad* the most popular travel book of the century. "I absolutely trembled in approaching the Apollo Belvidere.... What shall I say of it? How describe its immortal beauty! To what shall I liken its glorious perfection of form, or the fire that imbues the cold marble with the soul of God..... I gazed on it, lost in wonder and joy—joy that I could, at last, take into my mind a faultless ideal of God-like, exalted manhood." And there were imposing statistics about St. Peters, and raptures added in gratuitous superlative: "It seems as if human art had outdone itself in producing this temple—the grandest which the world ever erected for the worship of the living God!"[12] He visited the graves of Shelley and Keats in the Protestant cemetery. "Glorious Shelley. He sleeps calmly now

12. *Views Afoot*, p. 414.

in that silent nook, and the air around his grave is filled with sighs from those who mourn that so pure a star of poetry should have been blotted out before it reached its meridian. I plucked a leaf from the fragrant bay, as a token of his fame, and a sprig of cypress from the bow that bent lowest over his grave."[13] He saw the Coliseum at sunset, a breathless scene, he pronounced it, though marred—shades of Mrs. Sigourney and Cotton Mather!—by "the shrines ranged about the place," redolent of "the pollution of paganism." When twilight had fallen he went to his rooms beyond the Forum, still eloquent in ruins.

Rome might be grand, but not the religion which had fed upon it in the waning years of its grandeur! Everywhere were beggars, who cursed or blessed you in the Virgin's name alternately as you were disgusted or sentimental with them. Of all this importunate tribe, the priests were the most vicious. "In every church are offering-boxes, for the support of the church or some unknown institution; the priests even go from house to house, imploring support and assistance in the name of the Virgin and all the saints, while their bloated, sensual countenances and capacious frames tell of anything but fasts and privations."[14]

He went on to Marseilles and to Lyons with Pennock. Their money was gone now, their shoes soleless, their patience all but exhausted. They walked the streets five days, lived at a French home on credit, and prayed for a letter with money. It came in time to prevent imprisonment for debt. Thank God, they could

13. *Ibid.*, p. 417.     14. *Ibid.*, p. 420.

now go on to Paris and to London—where there were sympathetic editors, and distinguished men to whom they had introductions. Taylor had written a poem of considerable length, *The Liberated Titan*. Murray, Byron's publisher, would surely bring it out!

He reached London alone—Pennock had remained in France—with a franc and a half, enough for one night's lodging. He tried to get work in the city as a printer. But there was no opening anywhere for a young man who lacked full apprenticeship papers. He was alone now, with but two pence in his pocket. He finally borrowed a sovereign from one publisher, in order to pay for a letter from America. It contained money. This publisher, Mr. Putnam, later gave him work filling orders and running errands. He was able to get some clothes, able to call upon the friends of his friends in Italy.

Lockhart he met first, through a note from Powers. This gentleman gave him a breakfast to which Murray came and also Bernard Barton, the Quaker poet who had known Lamb so well. But Murray didn't care for his version of the Prometheus legend. Another acquaintance, who read the work later, advised him to study more about his subject "and exacted from me a promise not to publish it within a year. At the end of that time I renewed the promise to myself for a thousand years!"

After six weeks, other funds reached him from New York. Frank Taylor and Pennock had also arrived. The three bought passage for home immediately. Taylor had been away, not eighteen months, but twenty-three. His total expenses, including amusements, guide fees, and incidentals, amounted to five hundred dollars. He had earned practically all of it himself, through his letters. And people who talked of literature in America were beginning to mention his name.

## 2

These letters which the *Tribune*, the *Post*, and the *United States Gazette* had been publishing should be collected into a book, advised the friends of the young traveler. He had thought so himself months before when penniless in Italy. He went to New York, after a short visit with his family in Kennett, to talk with the effusive Mr. Willis and the publishers. Mr. Willis was more effusive than ever: He would do a preface for the book himself. They would find a suitable title by writing out a dozen possible ones and showing them to a man of the streets. This nameless citizen would be certain to choose the one which was most reliably appealing. Willis had hit upon "Pencillings by the Way" in this fashion.

Taylor was delighted with the offer of a preface, disgusted with Willis' technique in selecting titles. Somewhat reluctantly he decided upon *Views Afoot*, but then only after further delay would not be tolerated by the publisher. Wiley and Putnam, with whom the book was placed, were to give him $100 for every thousand copies sold. It appeared in 1846. Within the decade, twenty editions were exhausted.

He sent copies around to his more famous contemporaries—Longfellow, Lowell, Whittier, Whipple, Emerson, James T. Fields, and to his friends abroad. The gentlemen of Boston were anxious to see him, and Taylor was fully as anxious to see them. Fields has written of his eventual visit: "We all flocked about him like a swarm of brothers. . . . When we told him how charmed we were with his travels, he blushed like a girl and tears filled his sensitive eyes."[15] They immediately made plans for a week's entertainment: suppers, theatre parties to see Edwin Booth in *Richard III*, visits to the University, trips up the river, and a long afternoon talk at Longfellow's.

But he could stay, he informed them, for twelve hours only. This was too regrettable! They took him then to Webster's Steak House and afterwards "handed him over to Longfellow. . . . who gave him such a welcome as he never forgot."

Boston had received him. He had passed delectable hours in talk with the man who, to his thinking no doubt, was the greatest poet of the country. He had heard him read, fresh from manuscript, immortal lines which twenty languages would echo, which millions of voices would quote in delight. Here was recognition not even imaginable before. What towering pinnacles there were in life which a man might climb to by industry alone!

But meanwhile, eminences being uninhabitable always, one must busy oneself with the prosaic problem of employment. He was not yet ready to risk a purely literary career. Besides, there was Mary, for whom he must soon get himself settled; a quiet, intense girl,

15.  Taylor-Scudder, *op. cit.*, p. 76.

twenty now, and still devoted to him, in spite of her family's censoriousness and his own long but now past absence.

Newspaper work seemed the wisest activity for him, because of his two year apprenticeship and because it would enable him to write. Frederic Foster, an interested friend, had proposed that they establish a weekly in West Chester. True, there were five other such papers already being published in the county, but they were all distressingly political. Taylor's paper would be predominantly literary, with non-partisan news letters inserted in proportion to the leanness of his muse.

When the two had all but decided upon West Chester—Kennett was only a village and therefore unsuitable—certain gentlemen from Phoenixville, a noisy industrial town nearby, came to them with offers to sell the *Phoenix Gazette*. It seemed a fine opportunity. Phoenixville was a booming city; already it had reached the size of West Chester. The neighborhood was "extremely beautiful," Taylor remembered. The new paper would be much better than the *Gazette*, larger and more attractive in style. Also, "we have facilities, through acquaintances with the principal editors in New York, Philadelphia, and Boston, for obtaining a far better exchange list than any of the present West Chester papers; and we can also, through the German, French, and English gazettes, make our own selection from foreign news without depending on other papers for them."

But would the citizens of Phoenixville object to paying two dollars yearly for subscription? This was an increase in price and, "though we should render a full equivalent for it,"[16] a cause for considerable misgivings. They were quickly assured that such fears were unwarranted. Though industrial, the town was already interested in culture, and there was talk of founding a library. Lyceum lecturers there had drawn hundreds to hear their messages. Taylor and Foster bought the *Gazette*. The first number appeared December 29, 1846, introduced by Taylor's poem "The Phoenix." It contained also Bryan's "O Mother of a Mighty Race," copied—as was usual, without permission—from *Graham's*. The name of the paper was now *The Pioneer*. It was well chosen.

Taylor had counted upon inheriting a circulation of a thousand from the *Gazette*. Here he met his first disappointment. And though it was soon plain that his paper was the best edited in the county, as it was certainly the most civilized, potential subscribers remained obstinately aloof. He consoled himself by long walks through the woods, and by climbing the nearby hills at dusk and watching the sky flame when the furnaces were opened or when slag was emptied down precipitous slopes. He also wrote verse almost constantly, and long letters to Mary, which recounted evidence in support of his faith that the world was watched over by benevolent spirits, and that certain mortals were by nature designed for more than mortal communion with one another.

Some of his evidence was obviously indisputable! "In Philadelphia I called one morning at Graham's

16. *Ibid.*, p. 79.

office. Just before entering the door, I thought involuntarily of T. B. Read, the poet and painter (thou hast, perhaps, seen something of his), and on going in I saw in the back part of the room a pale young man with tender blue eyes and a dreamy expression of countenance. I knew at once that this was Read, although I had never seen him. I went up, and we were introduced, when the first words he said were: 'The minute you entered the door, I knew you, although I have never seen you.' Was not this strange?"[17]

Again, in the same letter, he tells of being fully determined, when he retired, to go to a certain town the next morning. But for no accountable reason, he became desperately opposed to the plan when the train was due. He missed it deliberately, and lo! two important letters reached him before noon. Shortly thereafter he met a man who told him news which would have rendered his trip useless, had he made it. "I am glad of these things, because they seem to show that all this employment and commingling with the common affairs of the world need not dim the clear vision of the spirit."

"Sometimes," he added in another letter, " I feel as if there were a Providence watching over me, as if an unseen and uncontrollable hand guided my actions. I have often dim, vague forebodings that an eventual destiny is in store for me, that I have vast duties yet to accomplish and a wider sphere of action than that which I now occupy."

Perhaps one stimulus to these forebodings was a

17. *Ibid.*, p. 81.

mysterious note from Willis, which had come two days before he confessed them:

"Please write to me at Washington an account of your business arrangements at Phoenixville, what your views for the future are, what you would rather do, whether you wish to set up a paper or get printing materials, whether you are engaged to be married, or wish to be; what you think of your probable future under present circumstances, and how you would alter the view if you had means. Trust me, and do this frankly and I will tell you a good reason for it by and by."

He was lost in conjectures. It *must* mean that Willis wanted him as an assistant editor of the *Home Journal*. Should he accept? A melancholy reflection deterred him. The father and mother of Mary had contended all along that he was not reliable. To go with Willis would be to arm them now with a fresh instance of his "instability of purpose." But there were such limitless possibilities in the thought! His mind wandered off into realms unsanctioned in the quiet room where the two lovers had spent long winter evenings together, talking. "Mary and I would go to Europe together, and Greece would not be missed this time; and then we would build a beautiful homestead in Kennett, where life would grow to be like a sweet dream of poetry, for I would have no golden threads snapped, no fast-ripening fancies trodden underfoot, by contact with coarse and jarring natures. I would work ceaselessly and untiringly, for the poor and needy in spirit; I would speak for the silent soul and for the heart which has not found utterance."[18] All this might be, and more—much more, indeed, than a feverish fancy could at present commend to his soaring contemplation —if only money were forthcoming from somewhere out in Mr. Willis's dazzling world.

Money did not arrive, but an explanation did. Mr. T. H. Perkins, "a Boston Mycenas," had read *Views Afoot* and had asked Willis if financial aid would not put Taylor "upon good ground in his professional calling." Perkins' letter was cautious, tentative, even slightly suspicious, but to Willis his young Virgil was already provided for permanently. Taylor wrote out a frank account of his ambitions, which his friend sent on to Boston. No reply ever came. Willis finally was forced to confess that "the old gentleman," though of great wealth, was "getting very infirm." In sober truth the old gentleman needed a guardian.

The result of this episode was an increase in Taylor's dissatisfaction with Phoenixville. But he tried vigorously to educate the town. He formed a literary association and reviewed the latest books for its members. He published London literary letters in his paper. He published much of his own poetry. He did translations from the German poet Freiligrath. Phoenixville was unmoved; the clay in its citizens was too hardened to be modelled into an approximation of spirit. And his old Quaker friend Bernard Barton wrote him discouragingly that in his judgment journalists had difficult struggles to face, if they would also

18. *Ibid.*, p. 83 (Diary).

be poets. "We cannot of a truth," he concluded, "serve God and Mammon."

But if one could only get away to a free environment such as New York, thought Taylor, all these oppressive realities would be changed. He went to New York to talk with editors. He met Bryant—"calm and cold, as I had expected"—Seba Smith (Major Jack Downing) and his wife, Charles Fenno Hoffman, and Mrs. Kirkland, editor of the *Union Magazine*. Later he wrote other important personages about living there. "Write to every paper and everybody," advised Willis. "Be willing to go in at a small hole, like a lean rat, trusting to increase so much that you cannot be got out without destroying what took you in. This is fair play, where the property of an establishment is made by your underpaid industry."[19] Within two years, Willis then predicted, "you will have made a name for yourself, and be ready to marry and thrive."

Greeley told him to stay where he was. "All the aspiring talent and conceit of our country confront and crowd on our pavements, and every newspaper or other periodical establishment is crowded with assistants and weighed down with promises." Bryant, likewise, could assure him of nothing. But his old friend Griswold was able to suggest hack work on a series of literary bibliographies he was editing, and Hoffman offered him five dollars weekly for two months, for services in the miscellaneous department of the *Literary World*, his magazine.

19. *Ibid.*, p. 101.

He decided to go. Already he had wasted a full year in an intellectual desert; the thought of remaining there longer was intolerable. Yes, he would go up to the city, to the center of things, as young men before him, in Dr. Johnson's day, had gone up to towering London. He would not be provincial, backwards, ordinary. Had there not come to him, in still moments of transcendent peace, the premonition of a fame such as none of the verdant hills of his state could ever shut in? Let the city be filled to its limits with the aspiring talent and conceit of the country! It would yet make room for him. And after a certain not timeless interval his merit would be recognized, his genius known. He would bring Mary there. And they would explore together then the limitless sweet vistas of the future.

# CALIFORNIA

## IV

THE surly warning of Mr. Greeley proved meaningless. Taylor began working for Hoffman at once, and a
short time later he was augmenting his income to the extent of four dollars weekly by teaching literature for as
many hours in Miss Green's School for Young Ladies.
It required but one week for him to become irretrievably reconciled to his new condition. On Christmas
day he wrote Mary that "the gay crowds of the busy
city seemed familiar and homelike. Here is my sphere
of action," he concluded . . . . "my place of sorrow and
suffering, and unhappiness."[1] He had moved from a
town of 4,000 to a city of 400,000 as indifferently as
one might change trains in the darkness. Having no
roots that he was able to recognize, he could survive
anywhere, he thought. One was, purely, what one made
oneself. The day of the cosmopolite, of the intellectual,
had arrived.

Now that he was in New York, this same Greeley
who had at first been so discouraging was among the
first to give him genuinely attractive employment.
"Today, to crown the sum of my good fortune came
Greeley, and *of his own unsolicited accord* offered me
a situation as assistant editor, with a salary of $625 a

1. Taylor-Scudder, *op. cit.*, I 107.

year ($12 a week), and the prospect of its being soon raised to $800. This is a glorious chance. The duties of the place involve the severe discipline which I need, and it is a certain stepping stone to something better." Within six weeks of his arrival his future seemed assured. But it was the future of a journalist, not a poet's future, not the future of an artist.

He had come to work for an enterprising publisher. Greeley was thirty-seven, but already peculiar, even queer, almost entirely bald, given to carrying a fat umbrella on all occasions, compelled to wear thick spectacles, socially altogether lacking in the graces, shrill voiced, but immensely well-informed. He was a follower of Dr. Graham, believing with him that were it not for white flour the lot of mortals would be in little distinguishable from that of celestials. He regarded the use of tobacco as vile, but drank and swore regularly. Six years before, in founding the *Tribune,* he announced the editorial policy which was operative, largely, when Taylor joined his staff. "To print the information daily required by those who aim to keep posted on every important occurrence, so that the lawyer, the merchant, the banker, the economist, the author, and the politician may find whatever he needs to see."

Greeley's was not the oldest paper in the city. The *Evening Post* ran back to Federalist days, to 1801; and the poets Halleck and Drake had given it a distinctively literary flavor which Bryant, the editor from 1829 to 1878, was always careful to maintain. There was also the *Sun,* Charles F. Dana's sheet, "the poor man's paper," which sold for one penny and which had flourished since 1833.

But Greeley's greatest rival was probably James Gordon Bennett of the *Herald*, "the best journalist and worst editor in the country." Discharged from its political organ for offending certain Tammany officials, he distinguished himself the first year his journal appeared by his remarkable stories of the Great Fire of 1835. He often had important news printed and on the street hours before his rivals; and though he was many times accused of sensationalism—as Greeley was of radicalism—his business prospered. "It would be worth my while, sir, to give a million dollars," H. J. Raymond of the *Times* once said, "if the Devil would come and tell me every evening, as he does Bennett, what the people of New York would like to read about next morning."[2]

Largely because of Bennett's desire to preëmpt his rivals in news getting, journalism in New York, when Taylor began it, had become an enterprise not far from desperate in character. Allan Nevins has well stated several often-noted facts: "Expresses were used on election nights, and in times of great excitement the *Herald* and *Tribune* raced locomotive engines against each other, in order to get the earliest news. On one occasion, we remember the sharp reporter engaged for the *Tribune* [he was not Bayard Taylor!] appropriating an engine which was waiting, under steam, for the use of the opposition agent, and so beating the *Her-*

2. Callender, *Yesterdays in New York*, p. 227.

*ald* at its own game."[3] Carrier pigeons were often used to hasten the arrival of news from Europe, the ship's captain dispatching them from Halifax, his first port of call. When the legislature was meeting at Albany, before an all rail route from New York existed, Greeley installed typesetting machinery on a Hudson River steamer; and while correspondents wrote on the way down, compositors busily set up their copy. When the boat docked at New York, their stories were ready to be printed.[4] It was thus a busy business indeed that Taylor moved into, and though connected, formally, with the literary department of the paper, he was sent often to cover important news events: riots, which were frequent, fires, which were numerous, recitals, such as the one given in 1848 in the "memory of Mendelssohn," and shipwrecks, notably the one off Fire Island in 1850 in which Margaret Fuller Ossoli was drowned.

But of course Taylor's central interest was verse, and he began early to distinguish himself with his editor as the author—anonymous to the public—of the "Picturesque Ballads of California." They appeared both in the *Tribune* and in Greeley's other paper, the *Literary World,* a weekly, and were said to be translations from the Spanish "by a gentleman of St. Louis." "I am delighted," he wrote Mary, "with the idea of writing for once behind the curtain.... Please hold this secret."[5]

3. *New York Evening Post,* p. 160.
4. Don Seitz, *Horace Greeley* (Used by special permission of the publishers, The Bobbs-Merrill Company), p. 98.
5. Taylor-Scudder, *op. cit.,* I, 116.

He had but one worry about his poetry. It was a fear of Tennyson's influence:

"I had the misfortune to be deeply intoxicated yesterday—with Tennyson's new poem "The Princess," which I shall bring to thee when I return home. I dare not keep it with me. For the future, for a long time at least, I dare not read Tennyson. His poetry would be the death of mine and, indeed, a *pervadence* of his spirit would ruin me for the great purposes of life. His intense perception of beauty haunts me for days, and I cannot drive it from me."[6]

Meanwhile, he was, as he phrased it, meeting all the artistic lions worth knowing. Anne Lynch, a bluestocking lady devoted to fostering genius ("a perfect jewel of a woman," said Taylor), was inviting him regularly to her *soirées*. Fitz-Greene Halleck, Bryant, and Willis were frequent guests also, and the Seba Smiths, Mrs. Kirkland, Hoffman, and Mrs. Mary Hewitt. At her Valentine party Taylor was particularly honored; his hostess allowed him "to write a number of valentines to her more favored guests. I shall be kept busy in hammering out stanzas up to the eventful day, and I intend dipping into some book of metre for a variety in that line at least."

"Hammering out stanzas." His delight over being taken into Miss Lynch's rare and exclusive circle was all that mattered. Poets, so read the philosophy of this lady, should write appropriate birthday verses, soothing doggerel for the childish minded, and sugared couplets to grace album books. They should always be

6. *Ibid.*, p. 119.

eager to improvise, and to say bright odd things to dazzle one's visitors. After all, of what real value was a poet who could not render one's party a success?

Taylor was making a low courtesan of his "divine mistress," acquiring a facility that would later prove fatal; and the kind of thing Greeley was asking for in the *Tribune* was very far from a corrective. Poetry was becoming something which one "hammered out" in terms of newspaper columns. But at any rate, he was prospering in a way which to him seemed now vastly important. Within two years, at the splendid rate of his recent advancement, he could bring Mary to New York as his bride. Would not the fervor of that consummation fuse itself untraceably into all that he later should write, making it sacred, fine, and enduring, winnowing with infallible instinct all that was heavy with earth and mortality? He left the future to his flattering imagination. All things were working together to bless him.

Meanwhile, outside Miss Lynch's dazzling circle, Taylor had met two friends with whom he was to be intimate for life. Richard Henry Stoddard had called upon Taylor at the *Tribune* offices, anxious about the fate of some of his verses which he had sent to the *Union Magazine*. Mrs. Kirkland, during a trip to Europe, had turned over the editorship to Taylor. He announced to his visitor that he planned to publish the verses. Here were two poets, born brothers in spirit, talking to each other. They were of the same age. Regular Saturday night meetings were soon taking place. Stoddard worked in an iron foundry; Taylor confessed that during the week he was busy "fifteen hours a day, scribbling book notices, leaders, foreign news, reports—turning his hand and pen to everything that went to the making of a newspaper."[7]

Taylor lived in an attic, "a sky parlor," because "he liked a good view." It was poetry which had made us friends, Stoddard wrote years later, "and we never spent a night together without talking about it, and without reading the poems we had written since our last meeting. . . . I thought well of my attempts, no doubt, but never in my wildest moments did I dream of comparing myself with him. He had an imagination which surpassed mine, a command of the fervors and splendors of language, and an intuitive knowledge of rhetoric and of sonorous harmonies of rhythm." They conceived themselves as the poetic inheritors of Shelley's and Keats's inspiration. Was not the more prolific of these friends, "twin doomed," with Ariel, "to feel the scorn of wrong, to worship beauty as a thing divine?"[8] Their weekly meetings were, to both, bright intervals in a dark routine, hours in which their spirits found renewed courage to endure many, more extended hours of drabness and labor. If the criticism of each regarding the other's work was too tender, the praise of each for the other too indiscriminate, perhaps both faults are explainable on the score that they felt themselves alone—for all the incidental social acquaintances of the one—in a place where loneliness can be vast and

7. *Ibid.*, p. 133.
8. Taylor, *Poems*, "Ode to Shelley," p. 8.

sharp, and where indifference can be withering in its completeness.

Taylor's other important friend was George H. Boker, handsome son of a wealthy Philadelphia banker, who had early distinguished himself at Princeton by outsmoking the upperclassmen, who had married early, and who, in spite of a half-hostile family, was now devoting himself to the writing of plays. *He* would become the inheritor of Dr. Bird's renown. Boker was also interested in verse. He had published a slight volume, *The Lesson of Life,* which Taylor, probably at Greeley's request, had abused mildly in the *Tribune.* But that was before the two had met. T. B. Read introduced them in 1848 when both were guests at his New York studio. They were soon intimate.

Boker, back in Philadelphia, shortly proved himself a valuable person to know. He was on good terms with the editors of *Graham's* and *Sartain's,* and enthusiastic about the work of both Taylor and Stoddard. His interest took the form of efforts, nearly always successful, to sell the verses of his two friends to these magazines, to secure notices, however brief, of their volumes. The return he got was elaborate praise of his own poetry:

"Gods, my dear Boker, what a poem you have written [Taylor called it "The Song of the Earth"], by all we have sworn to do, it is magnificent. . . . I am sick of affectation and sentimentality and soulless cant and thank God from my heart at every token that tells me there are still true poets' hearts beating. We will resolve to worship poetry in a purer and more glorious sanctuary. I hope a great deal from you, Boker."[9]

Meanwhile he was increasingly cordial with the literary deities and near deities of New England. "Saturday [he wrote Mary in the fall of 1848], when there was a chance of escape for a few days, I jumped on board a boat, reached Boston Sunday morning, galloped out to Cambridge, and spent the evening with Lowell; went on Monday to the pine woods of Abington to report Webster's speech, got up early on Tuesday and galloped to Brookline to see Col. Perkins; then off in the cars to Amesbury and rambled over the Merrimac hills with Whittier, then Wednesday morning to Lynn, where I stopped awhile at Helen Irving's; back in the afternoon at Cambridge, where I smoked a cigar with Lowell, and then stayed all night at Longfellow's.... I find that I am better known in Boston than even in New York.... We shall go there together after a while, and thou shalt know them too....."[10]

And why should not New England be aware of him! His second volume of poetry was in the presses, and in December it came out. The title was *Rhymes of Travel, Ballads, and Poems*, "by Bayard Taylor," he wrote a friend, "without the *J*." These lines, he declared in a preface, were principally the expression of "thoughts and emotions inspired by my journey to Europe.... faithful records of my feelings at the time, often noted down hastily by the wayside," and aspiring merely to the favor of some pilgrim who might

9. Taylor to Boker (Feb. 28, 1849). *Cornell Univ. Mss.*
10. Taylor-Scudder, *op. cit.*, I, 135.

pass the same scene, and be moved by the same rap-tures. He also included a number of the "California Ballads," and oddly enough, the book was scarcely out before California became the focus of the world's interest.

He was sorely tempted to go West, with thousands of others, but a shred of prudence deterred him. "I am doing too well here to leave," he wrote Mary. "The gold fever is worse than the cholera; everybody has it, even the gravest and the wisest. Rufus Griswold is going; Osgood, publisher of the *Union Magazine*, and I don't know who else. I could easily go if I wanted, but the *Tribune* is my California just now. I console myself with thinking that I can go overland in five or six years, write a few California ballads on the spot, and come back with a new book, without having spent much time or run any risk."[11]

"Time" and "risk" were already becoming objects of grave importance to him. Here was the most stirringly romantic event of the century, unfolding itself before him. He had no attachments, and possessed considerable money, enough at any rate, to finance the adventure amply. It hardly even tempted him. Consider the uncertainty involved! There was Herman Melville, for example, who had gone to distant places, who had written absorbing stories, but what of the cost! Melville would probably be, before another decade had passed, adrift in the world, a derelict, forced to forgo the lovely quiet vision of a home and children and a safe fireside love. Why could not one be,

11. *Ibid.*, p. 139 (12-11-48).

at once, famous and also *of* the world, regarded as one regards the business men of one's city—naturally, not queerly? If he worked with diligence and saved with care, Taylor thought, perhaps in no mistily far future he would become an owner of a great paper, a force in his environment, a gentleman of no mean importance.

One need hold no brief against conformity to say these things about Taylor. The point is that his ambition, in spite of all his breathless enthusiasm on the subject of poetry, was becoming indistinguishable in character from that of millions of his countrymen. He was beginning to worship practical gods, gods in whose imperious decalogue Shrewdness and Common Sense were commandments not to be violated, ever, without shuddering penalties and long remorse. He was probably wise to stay out of the gold rush. But wisdom itself can at times become a drapery, like lead, for wings that, freed, might brush the sky. And Safety even, so unreasonable are life's complexities, can wed itself by slow degrees to Sterility.

What Taylor deemed it wise to forego at his own expense came to him a few months later as part of his duty on the *Tribune*. Greeley's regard for him had augmented. He was writing good editorials. He had bought stock in the company, was obviously a reliable young man. Why not send him to California, to report events in that land of miracles? He wrote engaging travel sketches which readers were willing to pay for; already *Views Afoot* had run to nine editions. Here was a chance, moreover, to build for the *Tribune* "a circulation on the Pacific."[12] Taylor was to go as a reporter only, was not to engage in any mining, was to regard himself merely as a commentator on far western society.

He was wildly enthusiastic! "The main thing to me is that I see all this not only without cost, but actually make money all the time. . . . Another consideration is that it will recruit my system completely. . . . If I go and successfully accomplish the journey, it will advance me more, as an editor, than five years of steady labor here. . . . God is great; let us trust Him. I am going to tell the truth, and I think I shall have a cheerful story to send home. . . . . Everything favors me. I have excellent letters to California. . . . . My friends here are delighted. . . . I am light and buoyant hearted . . . . Think of moonlight in the tropics. . . . Try and feel cheerful; be as happy as thou canst."[13]

There were, of course, four routes to California. One could go across the continent itself, one could sail to Vera Cruz and hazard a land journey through Mexico, one could take a boat to Panama or elsewhere in Central America and employ a guide to see him over to the Pacific, or one could make the all-water voyage around South America. Taylor decided on Panama. He could see, in this way, something of the tropics, and the danger was comparatively slight, if one escaped fever.

He left New York June 28, 1849, some eight months after the first news of gold had reached the East. His

12. *Ibid.*, p. 148 (To Mary, 6-13-49).
13. *Ibid.*, pp. 148-53 (Letters 6-13, 6-27-1849).

vessel sailed first to Havana, then to New Orleans ("a dull and healthy city, enjoying an interregnum between the departure of the cholera and the arrival of yellow fever")[14] to pick up other passengers. Those who boarded the *Falcon* at this last city hardly pleased Taylor. They were "tall gaunt Mississippians and Arkansans, Missouri squatters who had pulled up their stakes yet another time, and an ominous number of professed gamblers.... There were among them some new varieties of the American—long, loosely-jointed men, their faces lengthened, with an expression of settled melancholy. These men chewed tobacco at a ruinous rate and spent their time either in dozing full length on the deck or going into the fore cabin for drinks. Each of them carried arms enough for a small company and breathed defiance to all foreigners."[15] Eight days after leaving New Orleans they were in Chagres, trying desperately to get across the country. "Life and death were small matters compared with immediate departure from the city. Men ran up and down the beach, shouting, gesticulating, and getting feverishly impatient at the deliberate habits of the natives." A returning Californian had just reached the place with a box containing $22,000 in gold dust, and a four pound lump in one hand. The sight of such tangible evidence of wealth brought on a fresh panic. Food was bad and scarce, the natives naked and laconic, the sun fiendishly hot, their progress slow.

He was five days, in fact, crossing the isthmus. He saw men die of cholera, he saw fights over guide fees,

14. *Eldorado*, p. 6.    15. *Ibid.*, p. 8.

he saw swart beauties dance in the moonlight, he saw heavy rains and dazzling lightning. In the city of Panama were women who were attempting the journey alone, who had waded waist deep through torrential waters. He saw three hundred passengers draw lots for fifty tickets to San Francisco. He saw a number of these tickets sell for $600 each. He saw many other travelers set out in sailing vessels, a seventy day journey; but it was good to leave this place. Cholera "had already carried off one-fourth of the native population," and was "making havoc among the Americans."[16]

Fifty-one days after leaving New York, Taylor found himself tipping a porter two dollars for ordinary services. "There was no longer any doubt of our having actually landed in San Francisco." His fellow passengers were soon busily engaged in speculation. One had brought out 1,500 copies of the *Tribune*, which he sold in two hours at one dollar apiece. Taylor bethought himself of a dozen copies he had used in packing. He sold them, to a news dealer, for the same price. Other rates seemed proportionate: rental for his hotel, the Parker house, a two-story frame structure, was $110,000 yearly, "at least $60,000 of which was paid by gamblers, who held the second story.[17] A canvas tent, fifteen by twenty-five feet, the Eldorado, was rented by gamblers for $40,000." Cellars twelve feet square brought $250 monthly. Servants were paid fifty dollars a week. Barley for mules sold at one dollar a quart, grass at one dollar a handful.

16. *Ibid.*, p. 30.                    17. *Ibid.*, p. 57.

All indebtedness was discharged promptly. The population of the place was now six thousand. By day many people scraped about in the street and collected gold dust worth from five to fifteen dollars. At night virtually the entire population crowded into gambling dens, playing monte and faro for immense stakes.

He pushed on to "the diggings," pausing on the way long enough to meet Colonel Fremont and to send off a flattering account of his person and achievements. The first scene of actual operations Taylor visited was the Mokelumne River settlement, and he was soon writing with authority about successful mining technique. Those who worked singly were fortunate, for the most part, only when the land had not previously been exploited. Unless one had the good fortune to find such virgin territory, the labor involved was severe and called for concerted enterprise. "Of all classes of men, those who pave streets and quarry limestone are best adapted for gold diggers."

But let not the man who is industrious be discouraged! If certain people fail to find gold in California, they have only themselves to blame. There are those who compare the gold rush to a lottery (one Henry David Thoreau, for example), in which people grow rich only by accident or luck. This is false. "There is no such thing as accident in Nature, and in proportion as men understand her, the more sure a clue they have to her buried treasures. There is more gold in California than ever was said or imagined: ages will not exhaust the supply."[18] Let men but have the courage

18. *Ibid.*, p. 90.

to discipline their resources for the task. Let them but match the incisiveness of Mind against Matter's ancient reluctance and inertia. God, Who *is* Intellect, will win out inevitably. His faith in human nature's perfectibility soared heavenward like the lark of the poet who first inspired him! He was billowed about from cloud to cloud, mellow with Emersonian vapor and mist. What did the other side of the story matter —the spectacle of mad, desperate men, of degeneracy, depravity, of constant drunkenness and gambling? These darksome things, when one was forced to notice them, only made more evident the eloquent possibilities of mankind for good. They were but occasional crumbling steps on the way to God's temple, placed there, purposely, to try the rightness of our discernment.

He recounted story after story about "gold hunting," all of them alike in pointing the moral of persistence."I saw a man who came to the river to dig in a dry gulch, three weeks before my visit, without money. Being very lazy, he chose a spot under a shady tree and dug leisurely for two days without making a cent. He then gave up the place, when a little German jumped into his tracks and after a day's hard work weighed out $800.... The largest piece found in this rich gulch weighed eleven pounds—more than $1,000!"

Methods of punishing theft were summary. Offenders were "whipped and cropped, or maimed in some way, and one or two of them hung.... Two or three who had stolen largely were shot down by the injured party.... We met a man whose head had been shaved and his ears cut off, after receiving one hundred lashes, for stealing 98 pounds of gold." Usually, Taylor declared, a brief but fair trial preceded any action. The extreme nature of many punishments seemed justifiable, to him, because no other security existed. He stated that major offenses were rare because of it.

Men seriously intent upon the business of mining almost uniformly respected the rights of others. "Among the hundreds I saw on the Mokelumne and among the gulches, I did not see a single dispute or hear a word of complaint. . . . A man might dig a hole in the dry ravines, and so long as he left a shovel, pick, or crowbar to show that he still intended working it, he was safe from trespass. His tools might remain there for months without being disturbed. . . . Abundance of gold does not always beget, as moralists tell us, a grasping and avaricious spirit."[19]

Taylor went about to other diggings in the territory and then rode over to Monterey, where a constitutional convention was shortly to be held. One of his important assignments was to report the action of this assembly for the *Tribune*. While the deliberations were in their early stages, he wrote descriptive sketches of the country, made a study of the history of Monterey before the Americans came, recounted the conflict between the Catholic *padres* and the Mexican government, and pointed out the unfortunate consequences of depriving the former of civil power. He observed that the natives of California were openly hostile to the unheard of immigration of recent months, but expressed

19. *Ibid.*, p. 103.

the hope that a reconciliation would soon take place. This reconciliation seemed likely, he added, because of "the constant and impartial kindness" of the United States civil authorities.

He did not fail to list, if only briefly, the more melancholy phases of life in California. One third of the miners were suffering from agues—caused by sudden change from the intense heat of midday to cold nights —or from diarrhea, the result, usually, of bad water. When camping out, moreover, one might possibly encounter bears; Taylor himself met four one morning and was forced to acknowledge that "they seemed the more unconcerned of the two parties." Voting was often done in a spirit of unintelligent jest. Some voted only for those whom they knew personally. Others followed the opposite practice, justifying their action, as one did to Taylor, in the following way: "I was determined to *go it blind*. I went it blind in coming to California, and I'm not going to stop it now. I voted for the Constitution, and I've never seen the Constitution. I voted for all the candidates, and I don't know a damned one of them. I'm going it blind all through."[20]

But the rising city of Sacramento—"it will one day be the New York of the Pacific"—more than atoned for those incidental shortcomings. Here was located the Eagle Theatre, the only playhouse in the territory, a large canvas structure behind a prominent barroom. An orchestra of five pieces added zest to the performances, the most popular of which was the *Spectre of*

20. *Ibid.*, p. 253.

--{ 72 }--

*the Forest.* Of course the important element in any presentation of this work was the appearance of the leading lady, a genuine "live female," who rushed in when ghosts were about to prevent the rescue of a "captive maiden and, wholly without reason, threw herself into an attitude in the middle of the stage." The miners regarded this as a blessed, if dim-remembered, sight and "applauded vehemently." Music was also deeply esteemed. "A musical gentleman was paid $96.00 for singing 'The Sea! The Sea' in a deep bass voice."

Taylor remained in California for four and a half months, and shortly before leaving he attempted to arrive at certain characteristics of the people of the country. Most of these people were hopeful, men who found their greatest satisfaction in activity, respecters of a blunt good fellowship "infinitely preferable to the ordinary forms of courtesy. I was constantly reminded of .... the stout Vikings, who exulted in their very passions and made their heroes of those who were most jovial at the feast and most easily kindled with the rage of battle."[21]

Drinking and gambling were the usual vices of the Californians. "I say drinking, rather than drunkenness, for I saw very little of the latter." Indeed, he witnessed but one instance of drunkenness during his entire stay. "The man's friends took away his money and deposited it in the hands of the Alcalde, then tied him to a tree where they left him until he became sober." Gambling flourished "in spite of universal pub-

21. *Ibid.*, p. 312.

lic sentiment against it." Sadly, he was compelled to declare that many of these gamblers were "orderly and respectable" citizens when in the East. "I have heard them frankly avow that nothing would induce them to acquaint their friends and families with the nature of their occupations." They were all looking, wistfully, to the time which would allow them to go home again to honorable living. "But alas! it is not so easy to wash out the memory of degradation. Unless depravity has altogether seduced them, every coin which they bring away will awaken a shameful consciousness of the base and unmanly business in which it was obtained."

Finally, let us rejoice, said Taylor, in the universal respect with which work is regarded. "Lawyers, physicians, and ex-professors dug cellars, drove ox teams, sawed wood, and carried luggage; while men who had been army privates, sailors, cooks, or day laborers were at the head of profitable establishments.... To sum up all in three words, *Labor is Respectable*: May it never be otherwise, while a grain of gold is left to glitter in California soil."

### 3

Taylor reached New York in March, 1850. He busied himself with revising for publication in book form his notes and the letters he had sent the *Tribune*. He had written attractively about California, "a cheerful story" as he had predicted; and even if some of his conclusions appear now at variance with other accounts, certainly no one can charge that he misinterpreted deliberately. As he saw life in the West, he put it down. Whatever the defects of his record, they were defects of insight which run far beyond the subtleties of analysis, down into the inherent optimism of his nature.

But these defects were present, if other more intimate and more scholarly works on the subject are trustworthy. Perhaps a few of them ought to be noticed.

*Eldorado* suffers, principally, because of a certain indefiniteness. Should every man who was industrious and persevering have gone West, for example? Taylor, in effect, says Yes. Go and work intelligently, and no inconsiderable amount of that limitless treasure, hidden only from the slothful, will become yours. A Philadelphia teacher and contemporary thought otherwise. Daniel B. Woods spent sixteen months there, and he returned with the advice (given by many other travelers) that only unmarried men, with no family responsibilities, "strong constitutions and stronger moral courage" should venture the experience. And let not even these men go, unless their prospects at home are entirely worthless.[22]

For in the prosperous year of 1849-50, said Woods, after some reckoning with statistics, the highest average earnings of miners ran to only $3.26 a day. In July, 1850, before Taylor reached San Francisco, Woods wrote in his journal a significant thing: "One of the conclusions at which we are rapidly arriving is

22. Daniel B. Woods, *Sixteen Months at the Gold Diggings*, pp. 18-20. Stewart Edward White, *The Forty-Niners* (Vol. 25, *The Chronicles of America*, copyright Yale University Press), p. 108, is added authority for the same average earnings and for the statement, amply supported, that men with families were advised to stay away.

that the chances of our making a fortune in the gold mines are about the same as those in favor of our drawing a prize in a lottery. No kind of work is so uncertain."[23]

Prices were not merely a source of naïve amusement to Woods. He went on to list the cost of the more necessary articles: coal, one hundred dollars a ton; eggs, twenty dollars the dozen; flour, sugar, and coffee, four dollars the pound; picks for digging ore, eighteen dollars each. Going to California, as Woods conceived it, was an economic problem primarily, one which called for accurate information if one were to solve it with intelligence.

Charles Pancost, a Quaker who went to the mines, had similarly discouraging stories about women, pointing his moral by a specific case: A man, his wife, and two daughters, fifteen and seventeen, came over from Missouri. "The father had not finished putting up his tent before several young miners were hanging about the girls and making love to them. Before they had been there three days, a young fellow ran away with the youngest daughter and married her, and a few days later the other daughter ran away with another fellow. The father, having poor luck in finding gold in that locality, went off with a prospecting party, and when he came back home found that his wife had also eloped with a gay suitor."[24]

In his digest of a number of diaries of miners, Stewart Edward White is also considerably less buoyant than Taylor regarding the promises of Eldorado.

23. *Ibid.*, p. 56.     24. *A Quaker Forty-Niner*, p. 274.

There was the overland journey, for example, of five months, which almost crushed out of even the noblest travelers anything which one might in the larger sense term human. Instances of depravity were overwhelming—men, maddened by fresh stories of wealth, burning the grass behind them so that those who came later would perish or lose their horses; attempts to poison water; flour or sugar abandoned, that loads might be lightened, but ground into the dirt, lest others should find it; clothes cut to tatters through the same fear; false directions given stragglers; families left to die when a horse would fall in his traces.

And beyond all this—cholera, which claimed one among every ten who started, and scurvy and immense boils, from months of dieting on meat. And far westward on the trail, when it seemed that all further endurance was futile, the Humbolt Sink itself—long white fields of alkali with ash drifts across them so soft that cattle sank halfway to their bellies. And the fine light dust that rose chokingly and impotently toward a flaming sun. If wagons came to a full stop here they were abandoned, no matter who might remain inside to die.[25]

Yet, as has been implied, it is difficult to believe that Taylor in any deliberate way glazed over these unpleasant facts about California. Greeley doubtlessly wanted an enthusiastic account of the region, and this was exactly what he got. But there is no evidence to support the possible suspicion that he ordered Taylor to write as he did write. The probability is simply that

25. White, *op. cit.*, pp. 70-75

Greeley knew his man, knew the kind of thing this young traveler-reporter was given to writing, and felt safe in the assumption that anything as outwardly romantic as a gold rush would fascinate his imagination.

"The culture and refinement of such men [gold-miners]," said Thoreau, "are not worth the dust of a puff ball." Praise the pioneer as one will, the fact persists that as an individual he is far from leading the life of the spirit. His art is a travesty, his philosophy one of acquisitiveness alone; he has sold out to the future. One might suggest that Taylor would have done well to face his situation with possibly a more deliberate fairness; that he might have felt compelled in his book to ask and to answer the question: Would *I* care to live in California myself, during the years 1848-50? His reply, had it been honest, would also have been indicative of a good deal. One thinks that, forgetting Mary even, he would have answered negatively; that he would have been driven to acknowledge a longing after something which was partially satisfied when he stood before Shakespeare's tablet at Westminister, when he talked to Powers in Florence, or when he drank beer in Vienna and heard Strauss play. He must have known, that is, that life in Europe, even when intimate with poverty, was rich in a quality which life in California might, even yet, be regrettably without. And that being true, he might have confessed it.

But *Eldorado* was published, without this confession, in May, 1850. Two thousand copies were ordered before it was ready.[26] He had completed a successful journey, written another successful book. All that in his mounting enthusiasm he touched appeared to flourish magically before him. All that he touched, save one thing only.

26. Taylor-Scudder, *op. cit.*, I. 171 (Taylor to Fields, 5-10-50).

# MARY

## V

NEVER had Taylor been conscious of a time in which Mary Agnew was not alive, in a peculiar, personal sense that, even in contemplation, brought a vivid delight to him, They had played together when too young to know anything except that in some dim way spring was lovely when it came, showering the hills with white blossoms, autumn rich, riotous, and gusty, winter dazzling, yet strangely awful, like death. The same winds had brushed their faces, the same rains had kept them indoors, the same attitudes had shaped their natures. It would have been an anomaly worth marvelling at had these two not decided that one day they should marry.

It was simply a matter which both took for granted, and which, when later it seemed to them that all things must be rationalized, they began to look upon as having been, from the start, integrated unshakably with their destinies. And so indeed it was, in a fashion not to be destroyed by protests from the Agnew family on the score of Bayard's unusual profession, or by his poverty, or by Mary's illness, growing insidiously now into the resemblance of consumption, then an incurable disease.

Why had he walked across the continent of Europe, really, if not to earn a recognition which she might share? Why had he tried newspapering in Phoenixville, or gone to New York in the face of Greeley's warning? Why, indeed, had he traveled to California? Was it not plain to her, and to the world, that she was the motive behind his every ambitious gesture, that the good fortune he had so often met with seemed meaningless until she was informed of it? All that was fine in his nature, and that was much indeed, converged and blended into their foredesired unity which, if life was purposeful, appeared as certain to him as the tides and darkness.

"If thou were here—if we were but united—I could willingly prolong my stay. As it is [he was writing from California] the prospect of seeing thee in two months is a joyful one. How much we shall have to say to each other! How many memories to recount! How many happy anticipations to exchange! Ah, dearest Mary, let us not be kept much longer from each other's happiness: let us soon unite our fates. . . . I shall come back to thee with a more profound yet not a more sorrowing knowledge of human nature. . . . and with as true a heart, as loyal a constancy, as fervent a devotion as before. 'I trust in God; I trust in thee.' By that trust, my own dear Mary, I ask thee to wait for me with a brave and cheerful heart, and to welcome me back with a face on which the tears of absence have left no trace."[1]

But when he returned it was to find her, though hopeful, definitely victimized by the disease which for months had weighted their plans with misgivings, and

1. Taylor-Scudder, *op. cit*, I, 164.

pointed the bright imagery of their love toward frustration. "Thou wert so well, looked so well, and I thought would be so strong and happy; and now, the health and strength thou has been gathering for a year are gone at once. . . . I will stop my marriage preparations, if thou wishes it; but it will be a terrible disappointment if we should have to postpone the day. Still, need this be done under any circumstances? Even if thou shoulds't not be considered well enough to come here in June, could not the ceremony be performed on the 19th. . . . Could not at least the simple words be spoken?"[2]

They could not. She must wait somehow until her strength was normal, until she could go away with him. Again he saw spring return and prayed that its warmth would restore her, that life might revive again in her, as in all that lived. "I will wait calmly and hopefully."

But each letter which reached him from Kennett was more saddening. His mother wrote, in June, that Mary was worse; the weather had been "delightful," but had brought no delight to her. The physician "expressed but little hope." "I shall dare to hope against him."[3]

Respite, if brief, came to him in the form of an invitation to deliver the annual commencement poem before the Phi Beta Kappa Society at Harvard. It meant that he would be able to see his Boston friends again. The poem was duly read, was widely applauded,

2. *Ibid.*, p. 170.
3. *Ibid.*, 172 (to R. H. Stoddard, 6-27-50).

but publication shortly afterwards, he wrote Boker, "killed the tradition of its excellence." At Columbia College, however, it was thought well of; Taylor was asked to "redeliver" it there in the fall. He was encouraged by news of the reception of *Eldorado* in England. Bentley, "her majesty's publisher," had brought out an edition. Dickens had written about it in all kindness.

But now, in Mary's own mind, an ultimate question was shaping itself. What would be the end of this business, and of all else, all their fine, high imaginings, unrealizable unless the doctors restored her? These men of science would tell her nothing, except that she should not worry, but hope. And this advice was growing at length hollow and, when given, seemed mockery. Could it be that already they had ceased to hope themselves, had told her family that hope was futile, had told Bayard even? "When Sunday came it was a beautiful morning, and I thought I must take a ride. I went as far as thy father's, and against I got back I was so fatigued, and coughed so much, it was impossible to write intelligibly..... I cannot tell thee particulars, because it takes so much writing to tell so little. Thou wilt soon be home, dear Bayard; we can talk everything over, and thou canst tell me what is to become of me.... Why is it that we are so much apart? Sometimes I think there is a more cruel destiny yet awaiting us. God grant that it be not so."[4]

As often as possible he would come from New York

4. *Ibid.*, p. 178 (7-28-50).

to see her, engaging someone to do his work for the paper. In August he took her to a physician in Philadelphia. "He says there is no action in her right lung, and probably never will be again.... The only thing he could recommend was a visit to West Point, which would do more than medicine, or indeed any other course of treatment."[5] With her mother they went there, but Mary did not like the place at all. "The noise was too great, and the hotel was so crowded with visitors, many of whom knew me, that it was very unpleasant for her." They met the Willises there, and Willis suggested a quieter place nearby. Her health improved slightly, but within a few weeks the weather had become too severe for her to remain.

Now came another, more vexing irritation. Barnum, the showman, was bringing the great Jenny Lind to America and was offering a prize of two hundred dollars for the words of an original song which this lady might sing at her first appearance. Taylor had been put to considerable expense because of Mary's illness. His associate on the Phoenixville paper had absconded and left him indebted to former creditors. Here, it seemed, was an opportunity to right matters, at least to an extent. He entered the contest along with 752 others. Ripley, his associate on the *Tribune*, and Putnam, his publisher, were on the board of judges. This board was unable to decide between Taylor's verses and those of another contestant. Let Jenny herself decide then, said Barnum. Jenny read both, and an-

5. *Ibid.*, p. 181 (to his mother, 8-9-50).

nounced, imperiously: "I will sing Bayard Taylor's song, or none at all."[6]

It was a bitter day when the decision was made known. "Fraud and corruption," cried the disappointed rivals. "The judges were partial to their friend Taylor." Up and down the land they protested, appealing to the newspaper editors who had published their earlier lyrics to print their contest poems, beside Taylor's, that the public might judge between them. "Epigrams and epics" spotted the nation's weeklies. Taylor received abusive letters. He was vilified in editorials; Jenny Lind was *news*, and his name was linked grotesquely with hers. "I am undergoing a flaying at the hands of every six penny critic in the country," he wrote Boker. He stoutly affirmed his innocence before acquaintances; he attempted with friends, to treat the incident in jest. "Through the acceptance of the poem I have one less creditor." But he was definitely disgusted with so many unsavory press comments. Already, it seemed, he had been harassed more than he deserved.

He went to hear Jenny sing; he met her and was charmed by her delightful naturalness and simplicity, but even this occasion could not blind him to his grief. "The news from home is most dispiriting, and all joy, even of the intellect, comes to me under a cloud. Mary is much worse than ever. . . . I thank you most warmly, my dear friend, for your sympathy with me. God knows I shall need it in the desolation that is to come. I shall try to bear it like a man, but when I

6. *Ibid.*, p. 185 (Taylor to Fields, 9-17-50).

think of her—poor girl!—whose only dream for years has been a life shared with me, and now to be cut off just as our paths joined and our hands were meeting, no more to be divided—it quite unmans me."[7]

Summer had come and gone, leaving her not better but worse. "The dreary melancholy November days will soon be at hand, and what must I do?" Was she too weak to travel to New York? How could it be that she was ill, "when in all other respects Fortune is so gracious. Scarcely an hour passes but some pleasant recognition is given me." He had dined, one day, with Bancroft and Cooper, on the next with Sir Edward Belcher and Herman Melville. A library society in Philadelphia had offered him seventy-five dollars to deliver a lecture. His friend Boker had been "gloriously successful" with a play. "But these things seem like mockeries, sent to increase my bitterness of heart."

October 24 they were married in Kennett. "There were only three persons present—Mary's parents and my mother." She would die bearing his name. "I am no longer rebellious against God, as I have been, but try to yield to his will. I see now a thousand warnings to which I was always blind—warnings that our vision of love would never be fulfilled."[8]

A week later he was compelled to return to New York, leaving Mary at home. What could he tell her, while yet there was hearing, which would bring peace to her on her darksome journey? One could say so lit-

7. *Ibid.*, p. 187 (to Boker, 9-19-50).
8. *Ibid.*, p. 190 (to Stoddard, 10-22-50).

tle, less even than one could do. He wrote from New York:

"My dear wife, I am trying to look calmly on the future. I foresee that it will be stern and solemn, yet with God's blessing, not wholly dark. It remains for me to do what I have sworn to do, as a Poet and a Man, with a more true and conscientious aim—more than ever to subdue and correct the restless, unenlightened impulses of my nature, and so to strive with all that drag us down to the degrading level of the world that I may at least win a crown worthy to be worn with the blessing of thy love. Thou wilt ever be with me in this struggle, and I suspect it will not last very long. Forgive me for speaking of this. I would not add my sorrow to your own, and I wished to show the fountain whence I hope to draw that serene strength which purifies the heart under affliction. It is wrong for either of us to despair—nor do we. Never, never has God seemed so near, so kind, and so tender."[9]

At least from this bitterness would come one blessing. His poetry would flourish. "I see heights to reach which I once thought above my powers."[10] Yes, there was discernible, if dimly, God's hand at work to effect with sureness a compensation for all he was suffering. Mary was in one sense a sacrifice—virginal and pale and of infinite loveliness—but all that he lost in her would be restored. So it seemed to him at moments, moments wherein the vision of God's justice subdued his grief and by logic dissolved it.

When he visited her, during week-ends, he would sit

9. *Ibid.*, p. 191-92.        10. *Ibid.*, p. 193.

beside her bed, while she slept, and write his friends, "to lay a spirit of unrest" within his heart. And what did he think of the possibility of a soul's returning to earth, now that Mary's was soon departing? He was doubtful. "Greeley's boy has twice sent a message to me from the spirit-world. He lately rapped out on the floor a number of lines of poetry which were said to be quite good. In spite of all, I refuse to believe that intelligent souls pass their future in such trifling employment."

No—for what really persists is the inspiration of one's life which, in proportion to one's goodness, makes for good in those who live on. This would be his legacy from Mary, from one who was to die only as the body dies, who was going only "in mercy to herself" to rest, and peace, and to the preparation of that purer life which would follow his life on earth.

She died December 22, 1850. He buried her the following afternoon in a snowstorm of pitiless fury. He would lie, one day, beside her; eternity should find them together. If his heart seemed even now like dust, it was but an augury of their ultimate union, wherein dust is symbolic, alone, of pain and sorrow transcended.

# NEW ENGLAND

## VI

TWO months of despondency followed that dark end to a darker year, months in which even poetry appeared a futile matter designed for dabblers to play with, an inadequate business without pertinence to his grief. Ages before, when infinitely younger, he had wished that a sorrow of overwhelming proportions might come to him, giving motive to his tears. Now that it dealt with him, a familiar, he had no strength to transmute it into song. All that he had written before belonged to a different life. He had passed beyond it.

Yes, he decided at length, when time and action had dulled the memory of his love, he was entering a new amplitude as an author, a grander prospect was unfolding itself, an eminence higher, by far, than his dreams could lift him formerly, even in their most ecstatic soarings. "I am getting out of the age of sensations and short poems."[1] In time the epic element, even, would ring in his work. "I am working up to it gradually."

But that the past might not be laid away with seeming indifference—for it had brought him, though curtained with sorrow, the consummate blessing of mortals—he decided to bring out another volume of verses.

1. Taylor-Scudder, *op. cit.*, I, 209 (to Boker 5-1-51).

It would mark the end of his apprenticeship, the beginning of his immortality. And this immortality seemed assured without question when Ticknor, Reed, and Fields, publishers of the great authors of New England, consented to sponsor the book. He had arrived.

These authors of New England represented to Taylor all that was significant in the literature of his country. As a beginner he had coveted their praises above the praises of all others, and this attitude he never abandoned. Aldrich and Howells, his earlier friends who moved in among them and who became in time editors of the *Atlantic,* felt upon their acceptance by Boston that they had reached the loftiest eminence possible to writers anywhere in the country. In simple truth, it ought to be added, they would have been right about the matter had their coming been twenty years before it actually occurred. For whatever one might think now on the subject of New England provincialism, it must be conceded that it did represent a culture—a culture that was genuine at first and perhaps no more narrow than cultures are the world over. Taylor longed to identify himself with that culture, and in so far as this was possible for an outsider almost continually travelling, he succeeded. But before he succeeded he found it necessary to approximate a certain pattern.

(Now the author of this study is aware of the treacherous nature of generalizations about literature. He is aware that Thoreau cared scarcely at all for any of the conventional attitudes of New England; he is

aware that Emerson, with laudable, if later embarass-
ing, enthusiasm greeted the pagan Whitman "at the
beginning of a great career"; he is aware that Holmes
did remarkable work in medicine; he is aware that
Hawthorne thought John Brown "justly hanged"; he
is aware that Lowell, to Mr. Trent and other important scholars, was the greatest American critic of the
century. He is aware, further, of the often-cited distinction in point of view between the Concord Trans-
cendentalists and the Boston Brahmins, of the Platonic other-worldiness of the former, of the rather
complacent snobbishness of the latter. But he is also
aware—and most desirous of communicating his
awareness—of the fact that, in the mind of an outsider,
like Taylor, the philosophies of these two schools had
a confused way of merging with each other, that Taylor in part probably derived, for example, his optimism
from the one school, his conventionality from the
other. And he is aware, finally, of a certain dominant
moral attitude that made itself felt, in no uncertain
fashion, when younglings fled Canaan and came Bos-
tonward, or Concordward, to prostrate themselves before their elected holy of holies. It is this attitude,
primarily, which is described in what follows. The description, I feel, has the usual value of any universal.)

To the New Englander, one should primarily be genteel, both as man and artist. And there were always certain things which genteel people did not do. For one
thing, they rarely referred to sex, except in its early or
romantic stages. In other words, the body as such was
largely taboo as a subject for literature. Some interest-

ing consequences of this point of view have been suggested—notably De Voto's theory[2] that the ultimate denial of the physical (by Trancendentalism in its extreme stages) prepared the way for the syllogisms of Mary Baker Eddy and the rise of Christian Science. Emerson's attitude toward Whitman is a case in point. Whitman was saturated with transcendentalism largely derived from Emerson; but—strange anomaly—Whitman was also an apostle of the physical in life; he was positively lyrical about the felicities of the body. This inexplicable contradiction was what Emerson hoped to resolve when he took Whitman for their famous walk in Boston Commons. And the fact that he failed to convert his disciple—though Whitman acknowledged that he did convince him—was evidence of certain attitudes in the mind of the Good Gray Poet which New England was never to understand,[3] was evidence in turn of certain attitudes that Bayard Taylor would never entirely understand.

There were many other articles in the New England faith which one was expected to accept, before he could in turn be considered acceptable: One was that the frontier, and practically all life outside New England, was culturally of no significance. To Thoreau, for example, it was synonymous with barbarism; to Longfellow, Holmes, and Hawthorne it simply didn't exist.

2. *Mark Twain's America*, p. 184.
3. "It (*Leaves of Grass*) is a book I never looked into farther than to satisfy myself that it was a solemn humbug," wrote Lowell. He added that he would "take care to keep it out of the way of students"—Harvard students! *New Letters of James Russell Lowell*, M. A. De-Wolfe Howe, ed. (N. Y., 1932), p. 115.

Lowell could not see it because his head was turned in the opposite direction, toward Europe. To Emerson it appeared, apprehensively, as the breeding place of a political rabble that would in time engulf the few men of principle remaining in the country.

A second article had to do with slavery. The Brahmins thought the Abolitionists devoid of good taste, crude, and hysterical; and even Emerson refused to participate actively in their cause;[4] but the disagreement among classes in the section was merely one of degree or method. The section was, as a whole, notably hostile, the skeptic Hawthorne being practically unique in his conviction that if slavery agitation were stopped the institution would of itself die out before the end of the century. Of course, on this question it is obvious that Taylor was not called upon to readjust any of his former attitudes. He merely had them strengthened. It is equally obvious that Taylor, like practically all of his literary friends, was so blinded by the moral smoke screen of the Abolitionists that he failed entirely to see what was behind it—the conquest of the agrarian South by an industrial East that was demanding an ever expanding market for its surplus.

Taylor, in short, approximated the pattern of New England with very little effort. For instance, it is plain that the only valid difference between the New England writers and those who influenced him in youth (Mrs. Sigourney, Willis, Mrs. Hale, and Felicia Hemans) lies in the fact that the former group was more learned. Longfellow and Lowell were excellent schol-

4. See his "Ode to W. H. Channing."

ars, and even today belong among the most distinguished men who ever taught at Harvard. But both schools looked out upon the world under the compulsion of identical codes. Mrs. Sigourney was a fool, thought Boston, but a much safer companion than a person like Mark Twain. Willis was a scented fop, but somehow a truer judge of values than Melville. And they respected one another heartily. Longfellow's most ordinary moralizing far outshone the verses of Whitman and Poe. These two men were half-Bohemians; and if one cultivated them, he might be asked (as Holmes was once) to some cellar restaurant to drink beer or dine. They must see white robes before aware of angels!

Only once, indeed, did Taylor's respect for New England waver, and on that occasion it wavered only for four days. The circumstance had to do with the publication of his translation of *Faust*. This work had entailed much effort, as we shall see, and Taylor had brought it to completion with no great hope of consoling royalties. It represented probably the most disinterested labor of his life: his one ambition about it was that it be respected and praised by those critics and poets whose judgment he esteemed—in brief by the critics and poets of New England.

But when his *Faust* came out a grievous thing happened. It appears that a friend of Taylor's, Mr. Conant, was asked by Henry Adams, then editor, to do "an article" about it for the *North American Review*. Conant complied, but his twenty-five page manuscript was cut to ten pages and its "character destroyed."

Adams' action seemed to indicate a plain conspiracy against those authors not Boston born. Taylor was furious when he heard about it, and wrote his friend Osgood, without trying, in the least, to disguise his feelings:

"I must say, the course of the N. A. R. has been excessively clannish and narrow. Longfellow's *Dante* was hardly printed before it had a stately, *eulogistic* article. After Bryant's *Homer* had been published a year or so, an article in the body of the *Review* appeared, but it had to be prepared in the *Eve. Post* office. As for my *Faust,* I don't suppose it will ever be noticed in the exclusive society of the N. A. R. I don't ask such notice as a favor: I claim it as a right. I have worked for years in the interest of the N. A. R., urging the people everywhere to support it as the *best* of our periodicals, even introducing the subject into my recent lecture on Schiller, and preaching it to thousands of people. But if the N. A. R. is to represent the individual A. with his tastes and prejudices only, it is time to take another view of the matter. I never met A.[dams], so his course is dictated solely by *literary* taste or prejudice. Conant did not show me his article —in fact he barely mentioned it to me—but judging from the mangled remains, it could not have been excessive in its praise.

"I confess, this thing both annoys and disgusts me. I do not like to be compelled to look to England for almost the only intelligent criticism I receive; but there is no other alternative. However, if there is to be an exclusive Boston circle created in our literature, the sooner the rest of us know it the better."[5]

Osgood was justly alarmed and answered at once. He explained that the New England authors and critics certainly were without animus toward outsiders, that Longfellow had received added consideration simply because he was so truly identified with the section, and that it would grieve him exceedingly if Taylor continued to think as he had written.

Taylor was entirely disarmed, even apologetic:

"As for the N. A. R., I wrote to you (as I ought not to have done) *instantly,* and with the exaggeration natural to my feeling of annoyance. Aldrich, who knows me of old, can testify that I never keep fire—at least, of that kind—long. At present, I am comfortably indifferent to the whole matter. I presume the *nearness* of an author (as in Longfellow's case) is enough to secure prompter notice of his works. I certainly never meant to charge the *authors,* in your latitude, with any clannishness, for the best encouragement I receive, or ever have received, comes from them. Lowell, Longfellow, Holmes, and Whittier have all been as frank, hearty, and generously appreciative as possible towards me. But the editor (perhaps inevitably) is more inclined to notice an author whom he constantly meets in person, than a stranger at a distance. After all, that is about the substance of my grievance. The only work of mine which the N. A. R. has ever noticed was *The Picture of St. John* (1866), which Lowell reviewed in

5. *Unpublished Letters of Bayard Taylor (Huntington Library Publications),* J. R. Schultz, ed.

the kindest spirit. A Review of this character, however, would have been prompt to notice, however briefly, the appearance of a work which has more than a personal character—which is accepted, both in England and Germany, as one of the indications of our American culture. I think this ought to be done, independently of residence, and personal relations with the editor. When I examine my feelings dispassionately, I find that this is really what I meant. Please consider everything else *retracted!*"[3]

We have said that Taylor approximated the pattern of New England with very little effort. It would probably be more accurate to say that he approximated the pattern in all but one way. To the end of his life he was fond of talking about "the animal man," and a casual reader might be led in consequence to suspect him of a primitivism close to Whitman's. But this would be an error. Always, in Taylor's judgment, there were limits, beyond which one must never go. His hero in his novel, *Hannah Thurston,* for example, confesses to his bethrothed a past affection. She was a surgeon's wife, much abused, and the lover met her on board ship while crossing the Indian Ocean. Soon they were intimate. The story of her sufferings swept all his caution away. He proposed to her. They could flee to Java, "beyond the reach of pursuit." "What was wealth, or name, or station?"

"She heard me in fear, not in indignation. 'Do not tempt me,' she cried with a pitiful supplication; 'think of my children and help me to stand against my own

6. *Ibid.,* April 7, 1872.

heart!' Thank God, I was not deaf to that cry of weakness. . . . Thank God, I overcame the relentless selfishness of my sex! She took from my lips, that night, the only kiss I ever gave her—the kiss of repentance, not of triumph. It left no stain on the purity of her marriage vow."[7]

The validity of one's conclusions about an author's ideas is of course questionable, when those ideas appear in his fiction only. But Taylor, in his letters also indicated many times a similar regard for the tradition of respectability. He met Swinburne in April, 1867, and what he wrote Stoddard by way of a description of the poet constitutes one of his most revealing documents.[8] Swinburne's "shocking" *Poems and Ballads*, we should remember, had been published the previous year:

". . . . In all important respects except one I found him to be much what I had anticipated. The exception is, instead of being a prematurely blasé young man o' the world, he is rather a wilful, perverse, unreasonable spoiled child. His nature is still that of the young Shelley, and my great fear is that it will never be otherwise. He needs the influence of a nature stronger than his in everything but the imaginative faculty— such a nature as Byron's was to Shelley. Again, a clear headed and hearted woman would cure him of his morbid relish for the atrocious forms of passion. He has a weak moral sense, but his offences arise from a

7. *Ibid.* (1888 edition), p. 389.
8. The letter is dated April 24, 1867, from Lausanne. *Bayard Taylor Mss.*, Cornell Univ. Library.

colossal unbalanced affectation. This, or something like it, is the discouraging element in his nature, which quite obscures the organizing (that is artistic) sense. What I admire in him—yet admire with a feeling of pain—is the mad, unrestrained preponderance of the imagination. It is a god-like quality, but he sometimes uses it like a devil. He greatly interests my intellect, but he does not touch me magnetically. He could have no power over me, but on the contrary, I felt that I should be able to influence him in a short time. I had a letter from him the other day, which shows he feels an intellectual relationship between us. Now this is not a question of native poetic power, but of a certain diversity of qualities, and I don't mean to be egotistic in saying that I might perform somewhat the same service for him as Byron did for Shelley. I feel that (if it is not already too late) I could help him to some degree of poise, of system, of law—in short, art.

"In this case he moves my deepest sympathy, for I see now the matter that might be molded into a splendid poet relapsing into formless conditions. It is sad, it is tragic—and if this fancy of mine be foolish, there it is, nevertheless. Without this sense of giving assistance, a week alone with Swinburne would be intolerable to me, or to any other human being. The preponderance of some discouraging force in him gave us a constant keen sense of pain. I have urged him to join us in Italy next winter, but I doubt whether he will succeed in doing so. If he comes, and I find there is no hope of establishing any germ or central point of order in his nature, I shall really be forced to keep out of his way. He is, indeed, with all his wonderful gifts the most wretched man I ever saw.

"I said that he had a weak moral sense, but his English friends say that he has none at all. Here I don't agree with them, and moreover I don't think they quite understand his nature and therefore can't be of much service. One thing is certain—his aberration of ideas is horrible. He told me some things, unspeakably shocking, which he has omitted from his last volume. I very frankly expressed my opinion and he took it with a gentle sort of wonder. He is sensitive, hugely ambitious, and utterly self-absorbed—which things have wrought disease. If I did not think so, I should never wish to see him again.

"There, that's enough on this point, I'll to bed."

It appears rather plain that Taylor was unable to comprehend the significance of his new acquaintance as a poetic force. What was Swinburne's real significance? Gosse has written wisely on this "last volume," whose once possible contents had so astonished Taylor:

"We see the unquestioned genius of Tennyson in 1862 acting as a upas tree in English poetry, a widespread and highly popular growth beneath whose branches true imagination withers away. Propriety had prevailed; and, once more to change our image, British poetry had become a beautiful guarded park in which, over smoothly shaven lawns, where gentle herds of fallow deer were grazing, thrushes sang very discreetly from the boughs of ancestral trees, and where there was not a single object which could offer the very smallest discomfort to the feelings of the most refined gentlewoman. Into this quiet park, to the infinite alarm of the fallow deer, a young Bacchus was preparing to burst in the company of Maenads, and to the accompaniment of cymbals and clattering kettle-drums."[9]

The volume, in other words, was "a protest against the idyllic and tender optimism of Tennyson."[10] But how could one dream of wanting to turn away from England's Laureate? In all seriousness Taylor might have asked this question. Any conventional contemporary would have asked it.

How does one explain this conventionality, an attitude which was throttling the creative instincts of New England? At the risk of over-simplifying the problem, one might term it, broadly, the crystallization of a protest against the liberalism of the French Revolution, a protest which, though valid and vigorous in the thirties, had lost its validity in the fifties and become in effect hollow and formal merely. One sees it in England, of course, in the work of Tennyson. One sees it, pinnacled, in the commonplace and unblinking materialism of Macaulay. One sees it in George Eliot's emphatic moral earnestness. One sees it in the Oxford movement, in so far as that movement represented a distaste for the individualism of Wesley's followers and a return to the authority of the medieval church. One sees it in the docility of a burnt-out Wordsworth, fallen to seed, and to the sere and yellow leaf.

One sees it also in France: Mussett, Vigny, and La-

9.  Edmund Gosse, *Swinburne* (1917), p. 151.
10.  Harold Nicholson, *Swinburne* (1926), p. 106.

martine move aside for the St. Beuve of his second or "Portrait" period, for the author who judiciously defends truth and virtue, while he indicts romanticism, in *Chateaubriand et son groupe litteraire*. One sees it, later, in the work of de Lisle, Heredia, and other Parnassians, who disparaged subjectivism and the tendency to exploit one's personal passions verbally. One sees it in Hugo, subduing emotionalism and looking to history for material.

One sees it in political outline in America—first in the surviving Federalism of the Adams family; secondly, in the conservative defense of property by John Marshall in his supreme court decisions, and by Webster in his opposition to Jackson's war on the national bank and to the doctrines of Jefferson generally. Everywhere the desire for peace, stability, safety, the middle road, and for the establishment of an environment where tangible values alone deserve respect, an environment against the enthrallment of which an artist must either rebel or perish.

Taylor sought, rather, compromise. He would serve his age in all save poetry. There he must be free, as Shelley had been. What he blinded himself to was the cardinal fact that a sane and conventional romantic poet is an absurdity, and that the man who respects the moral values of a generation such as that which flourished in the mid-nineteenth century and who at the same time writes romantic verse inevitably seems foolish. A conventional Shelley is inconceivable, as is a conventional Burns. The adjective and noun are contradictory and neutralize each other.

Taylor had one other personal characteristic which set him apart from most of the New England brother-hood: Almost everyone who knew him spoke of a certain cordiality in his nature. It was, likely, his most obvious trait as a man. He made friends easily; he was enthusiastic about almost everything. Lacking an aristocratic family tradition himself, he was quick to recognize intrinsic worth in others. Largely as a re-sult of his travels, he acquired a democratic tolerance that destroyed whatever vestige of aloofness he might have absorbed from such men as Holmes and the later Lowell. Anyone who esteemed the moral values of New England—assuming, always, his major interest to be poetry—might readily hope to become his familiar.

But this tolerance was also certainly, in part, the result of his experience in New York, whose society has received its share of comment. Mrs. Elizabeth Oakes Smith (wife of Seba) had the fortitude to extol that society, even in the face of Emerson's demurrer:

"One evening Mr. Emerson said to me, 'How do you think Boston compares with New York society?' to which I am afraid I answered, almost impertinently, I must think New York far superior to Boston. If society represents humanitarian and progressive ideas, they are about equal; but it seems to me that society for genial, social purposes is almost lacking in Boston. They meet together to discuss; they utilize each other; they sound you, teach you, never enjoy you."

Emerson: "You think them more utilitarian than æsthetic?"

Elizabeth: "Perhaps that is the impression made

upon me. The women all seem propagandists and the men leaders in something or other. They all appear to have a specialty and go out to promote it. New Yorkers study at home and go into society to please and be pleased."

Emerson: "Perhaps for that reason society in New York is more shallow and its knowledge more superficial."

Elizabeth: "I have not thought so. New Yorkers have not the intense admiration for each other that Bostonians have; they are not cliquish; they are not pedantic. Their culture is rather to be inferred than defined, as seen in a pervading taste and elegance of manner."

Emerson: "I have thought that there might be something in their manner that at once puts a stranger at his ease."

Elizabeth: "New York men and women dress better, look better, and stand better. The women have a pleased elegant air; they are handsome and carry about them a harmless consciousness of the fact, which plain Margaret Fuller could never quite pardon."

"Mr. Emerson bowed acquiescence, and I went on, airing my vocabulary perhaps too much."[11]

Howells wrote on the same theme, but with considerable partiality toward the section which had adopted him. "I had found there [in New York] a bitterness against Boston as great as the bitterness against respectability, and as Boston was then rapidly becoming

11. Mary Alice Wyman, *Elizabeth Oakes Smith* (selections from her autobiography), pp. 143-4.

my second country, I could not join in the scorn thought of her and said of her by the Bohemians. I fancied a conspiracy among them to shock the literary pilgrim, and to minify the precious emotions he had experienced in visiting other shrines; but I found no harm in that, because I knew just how much to be shocked and I thought I knew better how to value certain things of the soul than they. Yet when their chief asked me how I got on with Hawthorne and I began to say that he was very shy and I was rather shy and the King of Bohemia took his pipe out to break in upon me with 'Oh, a couple of shysters!' and the rest laughed, I was shocked all they could have wished, and was not restored to myself until one of them said that the thought of Boston made him as ugly as sin; then I began to hope again that men who took themselves so seriously as that need not be taken very seriously by me." [12]

Aldrich, too, liked the "Hub" much better. In 1866 he wrote Taylor, contrasting the status of a young writer in the two environments: "I miss my dear friends in New York—but that is all. There is a finer intellectual atmosphere here than in our city. It is true, a poor literary man could not earn his salt, or more than that, out of pure literary labor in Boston: but then he couldn't do it in New York, unless he turned *journalist*. The people of Boston are full blooded readers, appreciative, trained. The humblest man of letters has a position here which he doesn't have in New York.... The luckiest day of my professional life was

12.  Ferris Greenslet, *Thomas Bailey Aldrich*, pp. 44-5.

when I came to Boston to stay. My studies and associations are fitting me for higher ends than I ever before cared to struggle for."[13]

Probably the real trouble with New York was the fact that it sheltered too many *poseurs* (five-dollar-a-week men, as Greeley called them) who lacked, primarily, the materials of creativeness—knowledge and imagination. A second-rate artist could win esteem much more readily there than farther East. The shifting fraternity which met at Pfaff's beer cellar, by way of example, was composed for the most part of cheap journalists, purveyors of eroticism, and parlor cynics—adolescent minds who had made a fetish of nonconformity. They lacked a sense of purpose, and their contempt for convention was rootless and without that motive which would excuse it. They were dabblers, to whom even the sterility of New England was preferable; and the important New York authors—except Whitman, if he may be so classed—met with them infrequently.

In Taylor's case, then, the foregoing comment should have suggested his position as midway between the alternatives of a very distressing dilemma. Safe impotence and vulgarity were about all the two schools of American literature were able to offer him; and as we have seen, he had formed in childhood, the attitude of dependence upon *some* force outside himself. Of the other writers of any moment, Poe had left no following in America, Irving was defunctive, Cooper cantankerous, and Melville incomprehensible. In spir-

13. *Ibid.*, pp. 81-2.

it Taylor turned gradually to Boston, with the reserva-
tions just noted. New York became to him, in time,
merely a place where one worked.

Yet in our literary history Taylor's position will
still bear some clarifying. It should be no great cause
for wonder that Boston received him so excitedly when
he first returned from Europe, for there had come to
them a sensitive young man whom the chaste Commons alone could never have nurtured. His blood ran
more swiftly than blood was wont to run in their city;
his gusto astonished them. He was a curiosity. What
he really possessed might be called, simply, vigor—
vigor and boundless ambition. He was a writer bent
upon making a stir in the world, a product of the new,
democratic America who yet seemed somehow to know
that the foundation of that democracy, the basis for
it (and indeed what crowned it) was in Boston, was
made up of that friendly fraternity whose minds had
been nourished within the sweet serenities of Harvard.
Taylor appeared to them, in other words, a tempered
wind from the barbarous provinces. In a subtle way
his deference was extremely flattering; it at least implied that his New England friends were still impor-
tantly alive.

But this innocent lad represented another force,
more subtle still, and sullenly ominous—a force which
his guests, in their splendid isolation, never for a moment suspected. For in a sense the rising importance
of Taylor was coincident with the decline of New England's domination in American letters: he foreshad-
owed, albeit imperfectly, influences which the leaders of

that section were incapable of absorbing, in their efforts to portray the life of a new country. The best writers of the group had, with few exceptions, already done their work, or were ready to do it. And by the time Taylor became really established, by 1860, Emerson, Hawthorne, Thoreau, Lowell, Holmes, and even Longfellow, if his *Dante* be excluded, might all have died on a single day without affecting, except for the better, their ultimate reputations. What Taylor saw then, when he visited New England in his middle years, was really not the most vital school in American literature, but "the grand decadence of the perished swans"—though even to have whispered such a thought to him would have been, one feels certain, a final anathema.

# THE EAST

## VII

BAYARD TAYLOR was getting along in his world of safe conventions and tangible objectives. Balancing his accounts in the spring of 1851, he found himself three thousand dollars ahead of his creditors. He was impatient to travel again, but disliked the notion of spending this surplus. He went to see the publisher Putnam. The result of their interview was that Taylor agreed to edit a *Cyclopædia of Literature and the Fine Arts*. It meant about three months of drudgery, but the reward would enable him to take a leisurely trip to Africa. By writing letters for the *Tribune*, as he had done before, he might even augment his fortunes during his absence. Of course this would involve more drudgery, but not for always, thank heaven. His stock in the paper was paying well. In a few years he would be able to forego any attention at all to vulgar, materialistic details. Freedom beckoned with dazzling wings now visible to him in a sky of blue serenity. Soon they would be abreast, soaring together. Romanticism's undying illusion.

After he had sailed, in the fall of 1851, his volume of poems was brought out by Ticknor, Reed, and Fields. *A Book of Romances, Lyrics, and Songs* was the title which finally won precedence over "Mon-da-Min, the Spirit of Maize" ("not corn brandy, but an

Indian divinity").[1] Although the pieces in this work belonged to what seemed now an earlier stage in his development, Taylor was concerned considerably about their value. "In studying over the plan of the book," he wrote Fields before it went to press, "I have resolved to exercise the severest judgment upon all my published poems, mercilessly casting out all that do not satisfy me, and to admit a greater number of unpublished poems. The book must have no half-way character; it must be either something or nothing. My very life's blood is in some of the poems I shall include."[2] He had said the same thing, in effect, to Boker. "I want to make a decent book—something, if possible, which shall put a stop to all this slang about 'promise'; for if I have yet performed nothing, I never shall. The volume, I am sure, will decide the question whether I am to be acknowledged as a true poet."[3]

Several of these pieces deserve notice. "Hylas" had been commended by all his friends. "Hylas—beautiful Hylas," exclaimed Boker when he first read it. "You do not know how you have advanced in *strength* and finish. There is a beautiful classic polish—a hard yet warm polish—which you have seldom attained to before. How it delights me to see you advancing, stride by stride, slowly yet certainly, in the paths of poesy— the pleasant paths. The boy poet is fading, the man poet is coming on, in majestic power, to take his station among men."[4] The story is concerned with the

1. Taylor-Scudder, *op. cit.*, I, 210 (Taylor to Fields, 5-2-51).
2. *Ibid.*, p. 214 (6-9-51).
3. *Ibid.*, p. 212 (5-29-51).
4. Boker to Taylor (10-18-50), *Cornell Univ. Mss.*

boy Hylas, beloved of Hercules, with how he found the song of the naiads resistless, and was drawn down into the water to die. The lines in places are movingly lyrical:

> Oh come with us beneath the emerald waters.
> We have no love: we have thee, rosy Hylas.
> Oh love us, who shall nevermore release thee.
> Love us, whose milky arms will be thy cradle
> Far down on the untroubled sands of ocean
> Where now we bear thee, clasped in our embraces.
> And slowly, slowly sank the amorous naiads;
> The boy's blue eyes, upturned, looking through
>     the water
> Pleading for help; but heaven's immortal archer
> Was swathed in cloud. The ripples hid his fore-
>     head,
> So warm and silky that the stream upbore them,
> Closing reluctant, as he sank forever.[5]

Of course this is conventional verse, the sort of thing which English poets from Spenser to Morris have done often. But granting the validity of the type, one must concede that it is well handled. The diction, though undistinguished, is fervent and simple. One can still read the poem with pleasure, rejoicing that the diffuseness which mars much of his work is, for once, refreshingly absent.

"Kubleh, a story of the Assyrian Desert," is a less fortunate exercise. The narrative treats of "Sofuk's wondrous mare" which he found "lean with thirst"

5. *Poems*, p. 36.

by "a lonely palm"; how, befriended, "she waxed strong," and bore her master "through many a battle's thickest brunt," "lithe as the dark eyed Syrian gazelle." After ten years, she died gloriously in battle against the "base Jebours," springing athwart "the javelins' points" which were meant for Sofuk.[6] "The Metempsychosis of the Pine" was another poem of which he was proud. The poet was once, he is convinced, a pine tree, "rooted upon a cape that overhung the entrance to a mountain gorge." Far below him stood "a many templed town." Whirlwinds beat about him, eagles slept in his boughs, armies marched by, and the music of numberless voices and storms was made vocal in him, "a harp for every wind." All that was in another life, of course; and yet, unaccountably except in the light of metempsychosis, these long wasted rhythms renew themselves in him, compelling him again to poetry.

Taylor is able to sustain his narratives well, except for a rather frequent weakness for pretty descriptions. One suspects him of a habit which Stoddard, writing in old age about his own early work, freely admitted. "I knew what I wanted to write and, within my limitations, how to write it. It was something outside myself, something healthier and larger, something that concerned the emotions of mankind and not my own petty feelings. If it was a river, and I wrote about a river, I described the stretch of country through which it flowed, and its human environments; if it was a wood, and I wrote about a wood, I described

6. *Ibid.*, pp. 37-9.

its shadowy leafage, the notes of its birds, and recalled the phantoms of its original inhabitants; if it was a cathedral, and I wrote about a cathedral, I described its massive architecture and its historic associations, peopling the long-drawn aisles with medieval worshippers, the festivity of their weddings, the solemnity of their funerals, and whatever else imagination suggested as proper to the place and time."[7]

One more than suspects Taylor, again, of a certain glibness, which makes for an indifference toward inevitable diction, of a proneness to fall into the comfortable ruts of earlier imaginations, imitating their pleasant figures and approaches. He writes surface verse, extrinsic verse laden with a content that is slight and always apparent. The explanation, in part, is that he wrote too hurriedly. But in fairness it should be added that "the sonorous, well balanced rhythm"[8] which Poe noted in the *Rhymes of Travel* is evident in this volume also, as in practically all that he ever published.

## 2

November found Taylor in Egypt. He had gone by way of London, meeting the Brownings and Robert Owen, notably, and visiting the World's Fair. He was dressing in native costume, smoking the fragrant Latakieh, "in order to taste the true flavor of the Orient," lost in the delicious sense of repose and inertia of the country. How distant and unbelievable seemed every-

7. *Recollections, Personal and Literary* (N. Y., 1903), pp. 48-9.
8. A. H. Smyth, *Bayard Taylor* (A. M. L. S.), p. 216.

thing in America! There, he thought, "we live too fast and work too hard: Shall I know what rest is, once, before I die?" He was ascending the Nile with a wealthy German, Bufleb, with whom he was fast becoming intimate. They had forgotten already "that Europe existed." Everywhere were sleepy natives, fishing in the sluggish water or shouting to the guides the two travelers had engaged, and wheat fields plowed by buffaloes, and acres of sugar cane and tobacco.

He visited the tombs of Memnon and Osirei I, "crawling through a hole barely large enough to admit my body, after which I slid on my back down a passage nearly choked with sand, to another hole, opening into the burial chamber. Here no impious hand had defaced the walls, and the figures were as perfect and the colorings as brilliant as when first executed."[9] He saw a mummy. His clothes were soon saturated with the strange odor given off by the body. This was the thing which Bayard Taylor was bringing to his tradition-starved countrymen—color, exotic mysterious orientalism, reflected by one who had seen the dark continent and come away from it an ardent lover of his own land still, a cheerful ordinary American, as unaffected as one's neighbor.

Farther on their way, Achmet, Taylor's guide, announced that two Almehs "or dancing women of the East," could be engaged to divert them. This raised an important question. The obliging ladies had been banished from one city, and Taylor could recall a number of his own friends "who will condemn our

9. *Journey to Central Africa* (10th ed., 1856), p. 121.

proceedings as indiscreet, and unworthy the serious aims of travel." But he excused his behavior by saying, courageously, that "the first end of travel is instruction, and that a traveler is fully justified in pursuing this end, so long as he injures neither himself nor others."[10]

And so it was that in the cool Nile evening he went with his party to see Apple Blossom and Orange Blossom dance the barbaric rhythms of Egypt. The ladies were not disappointing. They drank plentifully of arokee, tightened their shawls about their hips, and began a slow movement which was very remarkable to witness. Apple Blossom was especially interesting: "She was lithe as a serpent, and agile as a young panther, and some of her movements were most extraordinary. . . . she had the power of moving her body from side to side, so that it curved like a snake from the hips to the shoulders.[11] Later there was a dance to a strange accompanying song, whose burden was "I am alone, my family and my friends are all dead; the plague has destroyed them. Come then to me and be my beloved, for I have no other to love me." Throughout the performance Taylor smoked a native pipe vigorously!

He inserted considerable history in his volume [*Central Africa*], largely a rehash of other travel books and texts which he had studied before setting out. He described the ruins of Karnak in great detail, wishing for despotic power in order to "tear down some dozen villages and set some thousands of Copts and fellahs

10. *Ibid.*, p. 132.     11. *Ibid.*, pp. 132-7.

at work in exhuming what their ancestors have mutilated and buried." He crossed the Nubian desert. Every day he saw the mirage, finally deducing rules about its nature: "The color of the apparent water is always precisely that of the sky, and this is a good test to distinguish it from real water, which is invariably of a deeper hue." But how deceptive it all was, in spite of his analysis! "The waves ripple in the wind; tall reeds and water-plants grow on the surface." And how fascinating, in spite of the intense heat of midday and shuddering cold of the night! The air held the secret. You inhale its "unadulterated elements; there are no exhalations from moist earth, vegetable matter, or the smokes and steams which arise from the abodes of men." God's hand was directing it all, through a Providence "which leaves none of the waste places of the world without some atoning glory." He had "breathed upon the wilderness His sweetest and tenderest breath." To Taylor this breath was sublimely restorative, "giving clearness to the eye, strength to the frame, and the most joyous exhilaration to the spirit."[12]

He traveled on into Ethiopia, intrigued by the ever-recurring spectacle of ancient ruins. He sketched a number of the sights, planning to adorn his book with them. Here was a civilization profoundly moving to him, because fallen into decay. His reflections drifted to the contemplation of the ephemera Greatness, and he remembered Shelley's king of kings, Ozymandias, crumbled and forgotten, for all his brave boast,

12. *Ibid.*, p. 182.

amid the limitless unheeding sands. He was saddened, and for a moment—before the thought of its blasphemy could freeze him into silence—he seized upon one of the major mysteries of human life, and wrote it out in simple and moving prose:

"I walked slowly back to the boat, over the desolate plain, striving to create from these shapeless piles of ruin the splendor of which they were once a part. The sun, and the wind, and the mountains, and the Nile were what they had ever been; but where the kings and priests of Meroe walked in the pomp of triumphal processions, a poor, submissive peasant knelt before me with a gourd full of goat's milk; and if I had asked him when the plain had been inhabited, he would have answered me, as Chidhar, the Prophet: 'As thou seest it now, so has it been forever.' "[13]

Deeper into the continent he went, noting down all that he saw and did, the important and the trivial, indiscriminately. In Khartoum it was the society which impressed him, its rich variations and surprises. "On the same day, I have had a whole sheep set before me, in the house of an Ethiopian princess who wore a ring in her nose; taken coffee and tea with the Pasha; and drank tea, prepared in the true English style, in the parlor of a European." He met the Sultana, and was eloquent in his compliments: He had heard of her often in his native land; indeed her name was well known throughout the world. He had come to Africa especially for a glimpse of her! She received these speeches "quietly, as if they were her right."[14]

13.  *Ibid.*, p. 237.             14.  *Ibid.*, p. 295.

He writes often about topography. The course of the Blue Nile is traced carefully. Perhaps the reason for inserting this wearisome information is to be found in his statement that "until within a recent period, but little has been known of the geography of Central Africa." He looked upon this journey as something not devoid of interest to science; natural history of every sort should be indicated, for those who may come later. A travel book should thus contain an account of all that a ranging eye could comprehend, all that an attentive ear could make out. Ideas didn't matter, were to be inserted only when there was nothing material to be observed.

But this reverence for fact and incident becomes genuinely oppressive when Taylor extends it to encompass his private behavior. One can possibly excuse his habit of recording the temperature during every waking hour (before a curious native stole his thermometer); for Science must march on, no matter at what cost to one's patience. Yet this is merely the beginning of his zeal. "After half an hour's labor the boxes were repacked." "In the afternoon we passed another akaba." "I traveled on until after sunset." "On the fifth day I reached the large town of El Metenna." "I occupied the rest of the day filling water skins." "We left El Metenna at noon, February 10." "During the night the wind increased." "Toward evening the wind fell." Examples multiply staggeringly. His approach, in brief, is that of the reporter.

Native legends were a source of much entertainment to him: The Kyks and Baris, interior tribesmen, were "full seven feet in height." In the regions beyond Fozogl, thirty blacks had been captured "who were nine feet high and terrible to behold. They were brought to Haartoum in chains, but refused to eat, howled like wild beasts, and died in paroxysms of savage fury." Alexander the Great had constructed from Alexandria a subterraneous passage two hundred miles long. The sultan at Constantinople had an ape twenty feet high. The spirit of men slain in battle haunt the place of their death and groan hideously until the time of their natural, intended lives expires. God has ninety attributes, which every good Egyptian can catalogue from memory. So the stories went.

About the most original and lively passage in the *Journey* is concerned with Taylor's account of the Arab temperament. He begins it by describing one of his own guides, Mohammed, "the vainest and silliest Arab I ever knew." He braided his hair, keeping it in place with layers of mutton fat. He prayed at length before and after each meal "and always had a large patch of sand on his forehead, from striking it on the ground, as he knelt toward Mecca." His arms were ringed with bands of hippopotamus' hide, to which were attached leather cases, containing sentences of the Koran.

"The other man, Said, was a Shygheean, willing and good natured enough, but slow and regardless of truth, as all Arabs are. Indeed, the best definition of an Arab I can give is—a philosophizing sinner. His fatalism gives him a calm and equable temperament under all circumstances, and 'God wills it!' or 'God is merciful!' is the solace for every misfortune. But this same carelessness to the usual accidents of life extends also to his speech and his dealings with other men. I will not say that an Arab never speaks truth: on the contrary, he always does, if he happens to remember it, and there is no object to be gained by suppressing it; but rather than trouble himself to answer correctly a question which requires some thought, he tells you whatever comes uppermost in his mind, though certain to be detected the next minute. He is like a salesman, who, if he does not happen to have the article you want, offers you something else, rather than let you go away empty handed.... The people do not steal outright; but they have a thousand ways of doing it in an indirect and civilized manner, and they are perfect masters of all those petty arts of fraud which thrive so greenly in the great commercial cities of Christendom. With these slight drawbacks, there is much to like in the Arabs, and they are certainly the most patient, assiduous, and good humored people in the world. If they fail in cheating you, they respect you the more, and they are so attentive to you, so ready to take their moods from yours—to laugh when you are cheerful, and be silent when you are grave—so light hearted in the performance of severe duties, that if you commence your acquaintance by despising, you finish by cordially liking them."[15]

But here he was nearing the end of his travels in Egypt, and he had yet to indulge in one of the more engrossing sins of the country. He must purchase some

15. Ibid., pp. 396-7.

*Bayard Taylor in Arab Costume*

hasheesh, "for the purpose of testing it." A single dose proved without effect. He took another. "In about ten minutes I became conscious of the gentlest and balmiest feeling of rest stealing over me. The couch on which I sat grew soft and yielding as air; my flesh was purged from all gross quality, and became a gossamer filigree of exquisite nerves, every one tingling with a sensation which was too dim and soft to be pleasure, but which resembled nothing else so nearly. No sum could have tempted me to move a finger. The slightest shock seemed enough to crush a structure so frail and delicate as I had become. I felt like one of those wonderful sprays of brittle spar which hang for ages in the unstirred air of a cavern, but are shivered to pieces by the breath of the first explorer."[16]

A second stage followed in which the most ordinary situations became ludicrous in the light of his stimulated perspective. Achmet sitting upon a chest was outrageously comical. A turban was unbelievably so. Finally it seemed that his eyes were increasing in breadth. "Achmet, how is this? My eyes are precisely like two onions!" Mortal frame could stand no more! He laughed so vigorously at this original simile that he immediately became quite sober again. He sat down at once and began to record his impressions.

### 3

Now that Africa had been partly explored, there remained other lands to lure him, before he turned homeward. There was the Holy City, not far away, and no

16. *Ibid.*, p. 518.

true Christian has ever lived *really* until he has looked in rapture upon it, Taylor could not forego his opportunity. "It may never come again," he reflected; he might live to be a hundred without visiting Constantinople, without touching the continent of Asia. Three continents he had traveled in already, but another, the largest, had been so far denied him. No, he must not turn back. Who could tell but that yet another travel book, his fourth, might result from this trip? He went to Palestine.

The Dead Sea offered him his first temptation. He must bathe in it. His guide protested, but to no effect. "Soon we were floating on the clear bituminous waves. .... I kept my turban on my head, and was careful to avoid touching the water with my face.... It was impossible to sink; and even while swimming, the body rose half out of the water."[17] Before night they had crossed the Jordan and were camped at Jericho.

Jerusalem proved disappointing, and he had the courage to say so. "It is the last place in the world where an intelligent heathen would be converted to Christianity." Constant quarrels divided this city of the Prince of Peace. Notable among the offenders were the followers of the Latin and Greek churches. "Go into the Holy Sepulcher when mass is being celebrated, and you can scarcely endure the din. No sooner does the Greek choir begin its shrill chant, than the Latins fly to the assault. They have an organ, and terribly does that organ strain its bellows and labor its pipes to drown the rival singing. You think the

17. *Saracens* (Household ed., N. Y., 1886), p. 66.

Latins will carry the day, when suddenly the cymbals
of the Abyssinians strike in with harsh brazen clang
and, for the moment, triumph. Then there are Copts,
and Maronites, and Armenians, and I know not how
many other sects, who must have their share: And
the service that should be a many toned harmony per-
vaded by one grand spirit of devotion, becomes a dis-
cordant orgy, befitting the rites of Belial."[18]

It was "Christ the Man, not Christ the God" whom
he recalled, now that he saw this land. "As I toiled up
the Mount of Olives, in His very footsteps, panting
with the heat and the difficult ascent, I found it utterly
impossible to conceive that the Deity, in human form,
had walked there before me..... It would be well for
many Christian sects, did they keep more constantly
before their eyes the sublime humanity of Christ. How
much bitter intolerance and persecution might be
spared the world if, instead of simply adoring Him
as a Divine Mediator, they would strive to walk the
ways He trod on earth."[19] He was aware of his heresy.
"It is my misfortune if I give offense by these remarks. I cannot assume emotions I do not feel, and
must describe Jerusalem as I found it."

And yet, for one moment during his stay, he beheld
a sight which atoned for all his earlier unpleasantness.
While walking through the bazaars "I encountered a
native Jew, whose face will haunt me for the rest of
my life." It was Jesus—"the very face which Raphael
has painted." His eyes were overwhelming! "Large,
dark, unfathomable, they beamed with an expression

18.  *Ibid.*, p. 80.          19.  *Ibid.*, pp. 84-5.

of divine love and divine sorrow, such as I never before saw in human face.... There are still miracles in the land of Judea. As the dusk gathered in the deep streets, I could see nothing but the ineffable sweetness and benignity of that countenance, and my friend was not a little astonished, if not shocked, when I told him with the earnestness of belief, on my return: I have just seen Christ."[20]

He went next to Damascus, a city of undiscoverable age, and wrote at length of the legends which hallowed it. He saw the place where Saul was converted, the subterranean chapel in which Ananias hid from infidel wrath, the pillars which supported the Church of St. John. He bought a sword made in 798 A. D., when Haroun Al Raschid was caliph; and after much meditation he yielded again to the lulling seductiveness of hasheesh, appeasing for a second time "that insatiable curiosity which leads me to prefer the acquisition of all lawful knowledge through the channels of my own personal experience."[21]

This time he "swallowed enough for six men," and of course there was six times as much recorded in the way of impressions. He devoted an entire chapter to classifying, as DeQuincey had done, in terms of the pleasures and pains of the drug. "I was a mass of transparent jelly, and a confectioner poured me into a twisted mould.... I laughed until my eyes overflowed profusely. Every drop that fell immediately became a large loaf of bread and tumbled upon the shop board of a baker in the bazaar at Damascus." He was pos-

20.  *Ibid.*, p. 82.                    21.  *Ibid.*, p. 133.

sessed by a devil who desiccated him. "My mouth and throat were as dry and hard as if made of brass, and my tongue, it seemed to me, was a bar of rusty iron." Water was of no help. "The flesh fell from my bones; it was a skeleton head that I carried on my shoulders." A friend who was making the experiment with him had become, he believed, a locomotive "and for the space of two or three hours he continued to pace to and fro with a measured stride, exhaling his breath in violent jets, and when he spoke, dividing his words into syllables, each of which he brought out with a jerk, at the same time turning his hands at his sides, as if they were the cranks of imaginary wheels."[22] Other tortures followed, and were prolonged far past the stage of amusement. It required a day and a night's rest, and a Turkish bath, to restore him to his senses. He was thoroughly chastened. He had committed the greatest debauch of his life.

The ritual of the bath in the Orient intrigued Taylor considerably. He devoted another chapter to a detailed account of it. "No man can be called clean until he has bathed in the East." He was steamed, he was massaged, he was rubbed with towels until his epidermis fell off, he was beaten, he was manipulated, he was soaped, he was oiled, he was polished. "The skilful bath attendant has a certain æsthetic pleasure in his occupation."

"I envy those old Greek bathers, into whose hands were delivered Pericles, and Alcibiades, and the perfect models of Phidias. They had daily before their eyes the

22. *Ibid.*, p. 143.

highest types of beauty which the world has ever produced; for of all things that are beautiful, the human body is the crown. Now since the delusion of artists has been overthrown, and we know that Grecian art is but the simple reflex of Nature—that the old masterpieces of sculpture were no miraculous embodiments of a *beau ideal*, but copies of living forms—we must admit that in no other age of the world has the physical man been so perfectly developed. The nearest approach I have ever seen to the symmetry of ancient sculpture was among the Arab tribes of Ethiopia. Our Saxon race can supply the athlete, but not the Apollo."[23]

He continued his circuit of these lands washed by the Mediterranean, concerning himself with visits to ancient tombs and temples, with descriptions of the cedars of Lebanon, with accounts of cities which dated from Roman times. He apostrophized the Narghile, tobacco generally, and coffee, "the seal of purity." He was plagued with gadflies in Asia Minor, he explained the celebration of the fast of Ramazan, he recounted stories of Turkish harems, he saw the ruins of Troy, he climbed Mount Olympus, sacred to the gods. Many times, now, he was taken for an Arab, for some exalted Sheik, touring for culture's sake, and this pleased him highly.

His most significant achievement during these travels, he thought, lay in the deep intimacy he had formed with Nature. "All was resolved to me: the heart of Nature lay bare, and I read the meaning and

23. *Ibid.*, p. 154.

knew the inspiration of her every mood. . . . Would to Heaven I might describe those scenes [the piny hills of Phrygia, the beechen solitudes of Olympus] as I felt them." But though the communication of this rapture was denied, he could not pause to grieve about it. He traveled on to Constantinople and was ravished, once more, by the sight of countless minarets and mosques. And after wandering about this exotic city, enjoying with still unmitigated delight its strange charm and stranger revelations, he put down for his readers in America a statement of his purpose in traveling. Nor is it surprising that upon his reflectiveness at this particular moment of writing no base motives dared obtrude. Indeed, his spirit had been purged of baseness, as had been his body in the healing baths of Arabia.

"I set out, determined to be satisfied with no slight taste of Eastern life, but to drain to the bottom its beaker of mingled sunshine and sleep. All this has been accomplished; and if I have not wandered so far, nor enriched myself with such varied knowledge of ancient history as I might have purposed or wished, I have at least learned to know the Turks and Arabs, been soothed by the patience inspired by their fatalism, and warmed by the gorgeous gleams of fancy that animate their poetry and religion."[24]

Throughout his trip his attitude had been one of studious receptivity, and upon departing he had but one criticism to make, a criticism which reflected dishonor, not upon the Saracens but upon his own coun-

24. *Ibid.*, p. 355.

try: "The regulation of the American consular system, which gives the consuls no salary, but permits them, instead, to pay their way out of travelers, is a disgrace to our government. It amounts, in effect, to *a direct tax on travel,* and falls heavily on the hundreds of young men of limited means, who annually visit Europe for the purpose of completing their education."[25]

What, meanwhile, was happening to his literary reputation? He went back to London circuitously, by way of Spain and Germany, and on his way he picked up a copy of the *Westminister Review.* In it appeared the first notice he had seen of his *Book of Romances:* "Bayard Taylor has published a volume of Tennysonian imitations." He read no more. "Damn the reviewer! I said to myself. Before he dies he shall tell another story, and in two days I had conceived at least six new poems. This convinced me that the faculty was not dead, but only sleeping, and I shall never doubt it more. If God gives me life and health, I shall prove that I am something better than a mere traveler —a reputation which the world is now trying to force upon me."[26]

"What is there so humiliating," he had written Boker in August, "as to be praised for the exhibition of poverty and privation, for parading those struggles which I would gladly have hidden forever, when that which I feel and know to be true to my art is passed by unnoticed? For I am not insensible that nine-tenths

25. *Ibid.,* p. 449.
26. Taylor-Scudder, *op. cit.,* 1, 240 (to Boker 10-18-52).

of my literary success (in a publishing view) springs from these very *Views Afoot* which I now blush to read. I am known to the public not as a poet, the only title I covet, but as one who succeeded in seeing Europe with little money; and the chief merits accorded to me are not passion or imagination, but strong legs and economical habits."[27]

Yes, it was strange indeed that the world should forget "The Spirit of Maize" and remember him only as the lad who had walked through Europe, described the California gold rush, and who was even now probably in Constantinople, talking with the grand eunuch of the sultan's harem. It was strange, and greatly disappointing. Could not the blind world trace the hand of imminent compulsion in all that he wrote about travel? Must it cling only to what bespoke the necessitous baseness in his nature, the evil? The world was palpably unfair. It would judge a man in terms of his major occupation in life, in terms of that business which consumed most of his time. The world, in brief, had a way of thinking, quaintly, that if a man spends his days in traveling, he probably deserves the name of traveler. And yet, even the vilest of worlds should know better than to impute vileness to *him* into whose body the spirit of Shelley had descended, to give forth anew an ineffable music. He would show the world and its visionless critics! He would rededicate himself to "sacred poesy." And he did so, only to receive, simultaneously, a notice from the *Tribune* which ordered him, because of the success of his letters about

27. *Ibid.*, pp. 227-8.

the Arabs, to go across Europe another time, and on
through India and to China. He was to join Commodore Perry in Hong Kong, and to write for the paper,
in his inimitable way, an account of America's penetration of unpenetrated Japan, and of the beginning of the trade negotiations which would one day
westernize that country completely.

# THE FAR EAST

## VIII

FORCES which he could not foresee were riding him now, away from the pleasant green paths of his poetry, away from his ordered word, away from that Europe whose culture had first drawn him eastward, to other lands, older and more eastward still, to lands whose dark mysteries he would have been content to dream about before an undefined hearth in America, where peace was and a mellow domesticity cool and restful to contemplate. He had worn a turban and sandals for nothing; in vain had he taken hasheesh and sought atmosphere. There was something more to be done yet, tediously, for he was surfeited with travel. "I am led into these wanderings without my will; it seems to be my destiny." Directionless, far, and imperious, they summoned him; and he began to be aware of a thing which, earlier, he was not prepared to understand: weariness and a sense of waste, and the further sense of having suddenly become the throttled victim of a way of life that had promised him, in the beginning, kindness and love only.

By the end of November, 1825, he had passed Gibraltar and was sailing along the African coast, stopping at occasional ports, enjoying the antics of less experienced travelers, complaining about the food he received, and admiring the evident military genius of the English. The supremacy of the Anglo-Saxon race was everywhere reassuringly traceable. "Aden, the Gibraltar of the East," was especially well protected: "The fortifications are ably planned. The skill and genius exhibited in their design impressed me far more than the massive strength of Gibraltar. I never felt more forcibly the power of that civilization which follows the Anglo-Saxon race in all its conquests and takes root in whatever corner of the world the race sets its foot. Here, on the farthest Arabian shore, facing the most savage and inhospitable region of Africa, were law, order, security, freedom of conscience and of speech, and all the material advantages which are inseparable from these. Herein consists the true power and grandeur of the race, and the assurance of its final supremacy."[1]

India, he knew, was a land of much interest to his countrymen, and that interest he nourished amply by devoting one-half of his book on the Far East to an account of it. He began by telling of the Hindu divinities: Brahma, the Creator, Vishnu, the Preserver, and Shiva, the Destroyer. He next described the aloofness of the Brahmin caste, its remarkable belief that contact with inferiors was contamination. He was lusty in his praise of the bungalows built by the English for the comfort of travelers there. He spoke of the landscapes of India, contrasting them unfavorably with those of Mexico. And he reminded his readers of the peculiar opportunity awaiting America: We "need not envy England the possession of India; for if we

1. *India, China, and Japan* (1855 edition), p. 3.

were not a people obstinately opposed to the acquisition of new territory—if we were not utterly blind to 'manifest destiny,' and regardless of the hints which 'geography' is constantly throwing out to us— we might possess ourselves of Cuba and Mexico and thus out-rival her."[2]

He noted the important trees—the sycamore and the tamarind, with its delicate leaves, explaining that the *Koran* pictured hell as a place where sufferers were given, once in a thousand years, "just as much water as will lie upon one of these leaflets." He mentioned the costumes of the native servants, and their stultifying submissiveness, telling of how when one of them sought a favor he would "come to you with grass in his mouth, saying he is your beast."[3]

He visited Bombay first, then Akbar, then Delhi. Missionary work in the country was encouraging. The Taj Mahal was ravishing; he described it in detail, "reluctantly," but scrupulously "because the reader expects it." Later, he witnessed a "curious illustration of progress in India": While dining with one of the many courteous Englishmen who befriended him during his journey, a "Hindoo minstrel came along with his mandolin and requested permission to play for us." Taylor naturally expected native music, but to his "complete astonishment" he heard, instead, the American favorites "Get out of the Way, Old Dan Tucker," "Oh, Susanna," and "Buffalo Gals."

He noted frequent instances of misrule and corruption—petty monarchs duped by scheming servants,

2. *Ibid.*, p. 73.          3. *Ibid.*, p. 85.

laborers impoverished; he deplored the privilege of the East India Company to appropriate as a tax three-fourths of a farmer's crop. He would change this condition at once; no sluggard he. But when he complained to the English residents about it, he "was generally met by the remark (the same often used by Americans, apologetic of slavery): 'We did not make it—we found it so.' "[4] What could one do with such people? He passed on to Lucknow, to Allahabad, to Benares.

And finally, when he reached Calcutta, and after he had in deference described the temples of India, and the "sub-Himalayas," and the cart horses, and sanitation facilities, he attempted another thing which he had rarely tried in the past. He attempted an honest summary of his opinions about India, he ventured certain conclusions, he praised and he condemned; and for doing this he deserves respect. For he had been two months in the country, and his effort meant that he was trying to reduce a series of increasingly confused impressions to something like order and clarity.

He came there, he said, prejudiced against the English: Both American newspapers and the progressive journals of London had aided in shaping his opinion. But he was ready to recant. "I have seen enough to satisfy me that, in spite of that spirit of selfish aggrandizement which first set on foot and is still prosecuting the subjugation of India, the country has prospered under English government. So far from regretting the progress of annexation, which has been so

4. *Ibid.*, p. 194.

rapid of late years (and who are we that we should cast a stone against this sin), I shall consider it a fortunate thing for India when the title of every native sovereign is extinguished, and the power of England stretches, in unbroken integrity, from Cashmere to Cap Comorin."[5]

Yet he deplored the fact that the country was governed by a commercial corporation, The East India Company. He deplored the high salaries of civil service officials. He deplored the unwieldy nature of legislative machinery, its system of checks which made the introduction of progressive measures "extremely difficult." He deplored the relation of the government to "the laboring millions." "It is substantially that of landlord and tenant, the government holding all the land as its own property and leasing it to the inhabitants." Those laborers employed on government projects receive an annual wage of twenty-four dollars. He deplored, finally, the attitude of English officials toward the natives. "I have heard the term *niggers* applied to the whole race.... And this, too, toward those of our own Caucasian blood."[6]

But a layer of virtue coated these blemishes. The first virtue was that of peace. "Despotic as the Company's government is, it is a well regulated despotism, and its quiet and steady sway is far preferable to the capricious tyranny of the native rulers." The military service was commendable. It was composed, principally, of some quarter million Sepoys, or native volunteers, who were well fed and well paid. The Grand

5. *Ibid.*, p. 268.        6. *Ibid.*, p. 273.

Trunk road, from Calcutta to Delhi, a distance of nine hundred miles, "is one of the finest in the world." The Ganges Canal, almost finished, "will cover with perpetual harvests the great peninsula plain between the Ganges and Jumna, and render famine impossible in the north of India." Schools, colleges, and hospitals were in every large city. And as final evidence of the progress the English had brought, he reported that "the horrible practice of *suttee*, or widow-burning, had been totally suppressed."

By the middle of March he was in Hong Kong. He stayed there for one day and sailed to Macao on the U. S. frigate, *Susquehanna*. There he was invited to become a member of the Embassy, and to proceed with the American commissioner "to the seat of war in the north." He accepted immediately—Commodore Perry had not yet arrived—and boarded the frigate again to the thunderous salute of welcome for the commissioner. How inspiring it was, after long absence from home, to walk the deck of a vessel of one's native land! "I want no man for a friend whose heart will not beat more warmly at the sight of his country's banner floating on a distant sea."

But Taylor saw nothing of the "seat of war in the north." The native pilots they engaged had a way of running the *Susquehanna* on numerous reefs and shoals. A native chart of the water was found to be entirely unreliable, and it was soon apparent that "the only way in which the vessel could go up the river would be to survey and buoy out the channel—a work which could not be accomplished in less than two weeks."[7] They turned back, with lusty imprecations against Chinese treachery, and anchored at last, disgusted, in "our old position, in front of the American Consulate" at Shanghai.

Disappointed in his hope of seeing the battlefields, he turned to the recording of current newspaper reports of carnage and hostilities. After Nanking fell, "the city was given up to sack and slaughter," and 20,000 Tartars were massacred. "The viceroy was quartered and his remains nailed to the four gates of the city. Before his death, his veins were opened and his blood made to flow into a large vessel of water, which the conquerors drank. His daughter, a girl of nineteen, was stripped in the public square, bound upon a cross, and her heart cut out. Many of the Tartar officers were thrown into boiling oil, or tied to stakes surrounded with bundles of oiled straw and slowly roasted to death."[8] . . . . Foreign residents were not molested if they gave security not to carry on the opium trade. The Chinese government was utterly incompetent. Generals were made governors after their death. Others who fled from the scene of battle but who died afterwards were "absolved" from the condemnation due them because of cowardice. The emperor declared himself so alarmed over the conflict that he could neither eat nor sleep! "So imbecile and absurd a court as that of China never before governed a great empire."[9]

He discussed the social customs of the Chinese. Their reverence for the dead was incomprehensible, since it

7. *Ibid.*, p. 302.    8. *Ibid.*, p. 308    9. *Ibid.*, p. 311.

was not in keeping with his idea of progress. Often land of great value went unused, out of respect for the dust of nameless hundreds who were interred in it. He visited a Baby Tower. "All infants who die under the age of one year are not honored with burial, but done up in a package, with matting and cords and thrown into the tower." A "pestilential effluvium" made these places naturally far from attractive.

He visited a camp of Chinese gypsies. "Their degradation is almost without parallel, and I doubt if there be anything in human nature more loathsome than their appearance..... Their lairs—for they cannot be called tents—of filthy matting are not more than four feet high, and barely large enough to contain two persons.... As we approach, a wild head, with long, tangled hair, and deep-set glaring black eyes, is thrust out from each of these lairs. Some lie still, merely following us with their gaze, like a beast surprised in his den; others crawl out, displaying garments that are dropping to pieces from sheer rottenness, and figures so frightfully repulsive and disgusting that we move away, repenting that we have disturbed this nest of human vermin."[10]

Ths sight was typical of the city. Even near the tea gardens one found wretched streets bordered by ditches "filled with black stagnant slime from which arises the foulest smell. Porters carrying buckets of offal brush past us; public cloacae stand open at the corners; and the clothes and persons of the unwashed laborers and beggars distil a reeking compound of still more

10. *Ibid.*, p. 325.

disagreeable exhalations. . . . I never go within the walls of Shanghai but with a shudder, and the taint of its contaminating atmosphere seems to hang about me long after I have left them." And after this statement, he declared that he would mention such unpleasant realities no more, having already shown, in amplitude, his cardinal esteem for the truth.

He was pessimistic about the results of missionary work in this country. He condemned the Chinese penal system. And to that nameless advocate of universal peace, who had cited China as a pacific nation, he declared with now ebullient disgust and wrath: "Welcome be the thunder storm which shall scatter and break up, though by the means of fire and blood, this terrible stagnation."

In concluding his remarks about this nation, moreover, he suffered no change in his feelings: "It is my deliberate opinion that the Chinese are, morally, the most debased people on the face of the earth. Forms of vice which in other countries are barely named are in China so common that they excite no comment among the natives. They constitute the surface-level, and below them are deeps on deeps of depravity so shocking and horrible that their character cannot even be hinted. There are some dark shadows in human nature which we naturally shrink from penetrating, and I made no attempt to collect information of this kind; but there was enough in the things which I could not avoid seeing and hearing—which are brought almost daily to the notice of every foreign resident—to inspire me with a powerful aversion to the Chinese race. Their touch is pollution, and, harsh as the opinion may seem, justice to our own race demands that they should not be allowed to settle on our soil."[11]

This surging distaste for the most peaceable of earth's inhabitants was arrested by Commodore Perry's arrival in May. Taylor had spent six weeks waiting for him. There was an interview from which he emerged a master's mate on Perry's flagship, "subject to all the regulations of the Navy Department, especially to that order promulgated for the benefit of the officers of the expedition, which obliged them to give up to the department every journal, note, sketch, or observation of any kind made during the cruise."[12] Special permission was given him, however, to write letters to the *Tribune*.

He enjoyed his new station. "Yes, George," he wrote Boker, "I give you liberty to laugh at me to your heart's content. I am nothing but a 'Master's mate' in the navy, privileged to wear an anchor on my cap and a blue coat with eighteen buttons; allowed to go up and down the gangways by the port ladders, to smoke cigars forward of the main shaft, to mess in the cockpit, to salute the quarter-deck, to take off my cap to the Commodore, and swear at the seamen. I appear at 'general quarters' with a cutlass belted at my side."[13]

The Commodore had four vessels in his squadron. He left one for a time at Shanghai, to protect American

11. *Ibid.*, p. 354.
12. *Ibid.*, p. 361.
13. Taylor-Scudder, *op. cit.*, I, 252 (8-11-53).

merchants there, and proceeded to Loo Choo, convinced that summary measures were necessary in dealing with the evasive natives. A small party was sent out to explore the island. "In order to avoid the cunning and deception of the authorities, no previous notice of our journey was given to them. We landed and marched directly into the interior, without so much as saying, 'by your leave.' " They were followed by spies, but were offered no violence. Usually, they found the villages almost deserted, and this meant that Taylor was left with only the scenery to admire. He admired it thoroughly. "The island is one of the most beautiful in the world, and contains a greater variety of scenery than I have ever beheld within the same extent of territory."

Perry proposed to interview the Regent at Shiu, the capital. He formed a party of 215, of whom thirty were musicians, and marched to the city. A conference followed, at the end of which the Regent was offered "any article on board any of the vessels." The Regent in turn served saki and a twelve course dinner, of which eight courses were soups. Twelve additional courses were in readiness, but the Americans excused themselves, after the Commodore had proposed a toast to the absent Queen Mother and Viceroy, adding: "Prosperity to the Loo-Chooans, and may they and the Americans always be friends."

Other trips were made to other islands, for the purpose of disposing the Japanese favorably toward American traders. Receptions were not always cordial. The squadron sailed to Saganii, where Japanese officials of importance were to be interviewed. An under-official first came out to meet the Americans, but he enjoyed no success. "He was told that the commander of the squadron was an officer of very high rank in the United States, and could only communicate with the first rank on shore." This message brought out the vice-governor, "a fiery little fellow, much exasperated at being kept waiting. He was told that we came as friends, upon a peaceable mission; that we should not go to Naugas-Aki, as he proposed, and that it was insulting to our President and his special minister to propose it. He was told, moreover, that the Japanese must not communicate with any other vessel than our flag-ship, and that no boats must approach us during the night. An attempt to surround us with a cordon of boats . . . . would lead to very serious consequences."[14] The Commodore's decided stand "produced an immediate impression upon the Japanese."

And so it happened that by brusqueness and arrogance and menacing gestures the natives were awed, and the emperor finally induced to send "one of the chief counsellors of the empire" to receive from Perry the President's message. To Taylor, this was cause for great rejoicing. "We had obtained in four days, without subjecting ourselves to a single observance of Japanese law, what the Russian embassy failed to accomplish in six months, after a degrading subservience to ridiculous demands. From what I know of the negotiations, I must say that they were admirably conducted. The Japanese officials were treated in such a

14. *India, China, and Japan*, p. 414.

polite and friendly manner as to win their good will, while not a single point to which we attached any importance was yielded."

Gifts were exchanged later. One native authority asked permission to examine a pistol. He had never seen one before. A steam whistle on the flagship astonished him. The spectacle of four men of war gliding out of the bay "keeping equidistant from each other to a hair's breadth, yet moving through the water at the rate of eight or nine knots, must have struck the Japanese as somewhat miraculous." America had amazed the unindustrial East, and Taylor was staggered with pride that he had had a part in it. But he no more perceived the implications of the gesture than would have a child, offering poison to a strange playmate. It was sweetness and light that America was bringing there, and a culture which, though material, was so, he thought, in a surface way only, in a way which deceived merely the blind or the perverse.

## 2

While Taylor was journeying in the Orient, his family had been busy in his interest at home. The Pusey farm was an eighty acre estate adjoining his father's property. It had lain uncultivated for two generations. "Two heaps of stones were all that marked the site of the house and barn; half a dozen ragged plum and peach trees hovered around the outskirts of the vanished garden, the melancholy survivors of all its bloom and fruitage; and a mixture of tall sedge grass, sumacs, and blackberry bushes covered the fields. The hawthorn hedges which lined the lane had disappeared, but some clumps of privet still held their ground and the wild grape and scarlet-berried celastrus clambered all over the tall sassafras and tulip trees."

A grove of oaks, more than one hundred feet high, hid this place from the road. "In another wood of chestnuts, beyond the field, the finest yellow violets were to be found; the azaleas blossomed in their season, and the ivory Indian-pipe sprang up under the beech trees. Sometimes [as children] we extended our rambles to the end of the farm, and looked down into the secluded dells beyond the ridge which it covered. Such glimpses were like the discovery of unknown lands. How far off the other people lived! How strange it must be to dwell continually down in that hollow, with no other house in sight. But when I build a house, I thought, I shall build it up on the ridge, with a high steeple, from the top of which I can see far and wide."[15]

His mother and father bought this land for him, as he directed. He would rename it Cedarcroft. It should adjoin his father's property, which had been owned by the Taylors for more than a century. He would buy forty acres more from his father, still another forty acres from an uncle. Yes, he would build a house on the ridge, a place which should stand out above all the other places of the town, and he would crown it with a square tower, and everyone would know about it and admire it. Here might all his kinsmen come and find welcome, and here Boker would come and Stoddard and Read and Whittier and Longfellow and all

15. *At Home and Abroad*, II, 3 ff.

the others. After months of journeying and constant writing, he would rest here and be a gentleman, and, when guests were absent, walk alone amid infinities of cool spring flowers and know the deliciousness of quiet nights and murmuring winds in immemorial forests. Here he would find, by slow degrees, fit end to a life that had hitherto seemed too crowded by far for his liking. And how would he pay for these lovely things? Why, with what he had saved already, and with his present royalties, and with what three new travel books and a volume of poems—all based upon the experiences of his past two years—would bring him. And if this were not adequate, then he would lecture about the world's ways to his countrymen—though only for a little while, because after this while it would no longer be needful.

# THE LYCEUM

## IX

TAYLOR left the naval service in September, 1853. He had done the letters Greeley desired about the Japanese expedition, and was thoroughly tired. On the slow voyage back to New York he wrote poetry and remembered the friends from whom he had been so long absent. He landed the twentieth of December. Before the year was out he wrote Boker, in delight, that he was "overwhelmed with invitations to lecture," and that he would "have to visit every town from Maine to Wisconsin, between now and April."[1] America had seized upon him in its own enthusiastic if reckless fashion and had dubbed him, in all intended kindness, "the great American traveler."

The reassuring item in this far from reassuring title was the fact that America was willing to pay its traveler-lecturers from fifty to more than two hundred dollars an appearance. Poetry could wait a little longer, its muse finding warmth in the comforting reflection that in a later season she would receive an allegiance as devoted as might possibly be wished. The goddess of verse had become, in brief, a lady of peculiar tolerance. She rarely scolded now. She was kind, no longer imperious. One could be faithful to her, as to Cynara, after his fashion.

1. Taylor-Scudder, *op. cit.*, I, 264.

{ 146 }

Soon he was busy touring the country, meeting every type of American, kissing babies, and being pointed out as "the man who had been to Africa." February 5, 1854, he wrote Boker that he had not a single evening vacant "before the middle of April," and that he was refusing invitations daily. In Baltimore, he added, he had addressed four thousand people, in a hall three hundred and fifty feet long. Hundreds had been turned away at Albany. Two weeks later he was telling Fields, "this lecturing is a great business.... Everywhere I have crushing houses."

His popularity continued into March, but not his enthusiasm. "Crammed houses" met him everywhere: "women carried out fainting, young ladies stretching their necks on all sides and crying in breathless whispers, 'There he is! that's him!' " But he added, in his letter to Stoddard, "believe me, this lecturing is a miserable business.... Oh the vanity and vexation of hearing the same remarks twenty times a day, and being obliged to answer questions that have become hideous by endless repetition. I wonder how I retain my patience under it all. Sometimes I snap them rather short off, but they think it's my way of talking, and are not offended. I find that traveling has entirely swamped and overwhelmed my poetical reputation, except with a few sensible people here and there."[2] This letter was mailed from Buffalo. Two weeks later he was writing his mother from the "wilds of Wisconsin," Milwaukee. The next month he was in St. Louis, "the Missourian wilds." A week later he wrote Fields from New Albany,

2. *Ibid.*, pp. 271-2.

Indiana. Still another week found him in Newark, Ohio, but "thank God, this western tour is nearly over." He had spoken on eighty different occasions. Soon he would be in New York for a short rest before visiting Boston and New Hampshire. "I am tired to death."

Taylor took to the Lyceum platform for a very simple reason: He needed the money. It is safe to say that, for all his interest in civilizing his countrymen, he would never once have consented to attempt the task in this particular fashion had the economic urge been absent. It is interesting, in view of his motives, therefore, to trace out in his letters the financial arrangements he made with those who engaged him.

His first really important season was that of 1854-55, during which he made 128 separate appearances.[3] His terms were $50 a lecture.[4] In May, 1856, he wrote a life-long friend, Martha Kimber, that "in two-and-a-half years I have accomplished 285 lectures, by traveling 40,000 miles."[5] He was apparently, throughout this period, charging the usual $50, for in the fall of 1858 he was still quoting this figure to interested inquirers.[6]

In 1859, however, he raised his terms to $60, but he was still making a "special rate" of $50 in some cases.[7] This new rate represented his "lowest terms" at the beginning of the year 1861,[8] which, he pointed

3. Huntington Mss. (14564). See *Unpublished Letters of Bayard Taylor* (Huntington Lib. Pub., J. R. Schultz, ed.).
4. Huntington Mss. (14544).
5. Huntington Mss. (14556).
6. Huntington Mss. (14570). To R. W. Christy 10-29-58.
7. See Huntington Mss. (14577). Letter of 11-28-59.
8. See Huntington Mss. (14585). Letter of 1-7-61.

out, was extremely modest, since he was "paying his own expenses." But as the war progressed, his fees mounted remarkably, if somewhat uncertainly. In December, 1864, he requested $150 for an address in Pittsburgh.[9] In April, 1865, he wrote that he was planning to limit the number of his engagements during the next winter "to 10 or 15 at one hundred dollars each."[10] Nor does he appear in later years ever to have gone below this figure. In 1869 he had "more invitations than I can accept," and $100 was still his lowest price.[11] It remained his price during the following decade.[12]

What was he saying to the Lyceum patrons of America, to the intellectually hungry thousands who were paying their two dollars for a year's course in culture? One cannot with certainty determine. But one can infer with fair conviction that he was saying in substance what is to be found in the fourteen surviving and hitherto neglected[13] lectures preserved in the town library at West Chester, Pennsylvania. The more important of these manuscripts constitute a curious index to Taylor's thinking.

Possibly the earliest lecture in point of date is, appropriately, "The Animal Man."[14] There has been too much emphasis on *spirit*, he boldly asserts, and not

9. See Huntington Mss. (14639). Letter of 12-1-64.
10. Huntington Mss. (14648). Letter of 4-28-65.
12. See Huntington Mss. (14796 and 14786). Letters of 11-4-74 and 2-5-76.
13. A brief summary of a few of these lectures was written by Robert Warnock for *American Literature*, May, 1933. This was the first notice of the manuscripts.
14. Feb. 4, 1855. Probably finished several years earlier.

enough on *body*. Catholics enjoin fasts. This is wrong; it leads to disease. "Who can tell how much political oppression, how much harsh and bitter theology, how much individual cynicism and mistrust, may have their origin in the scrofula of the monarch, the dyspepsia of the priest, or the disordered liver or lung of the layman?"

Moral and mental traits are almost uniformly revealed in the physical appearance of a race. The African negro is tall, but absolutely without grace or beauty. Correspondingly, he has no significant art. The bodies of the Chinese lack *harmony*. Moreover, "their crooked eyes are typical of their crooked moral vision." Young Arabs are physically almost perfect, he said: But he did not indicate the spiritual correspondency here; and recalling his sketch of Arab character already quoted, one is not surprised that the item was ignored. The thought of physical beauty lured him away from his thesis. He remembered the young girls he had met in the mountains of European Russia. "The women of Circassia are beyond doubt the most beautiful in the world." He had seen them all, from California eastward to Japan, and the palm of superlative went to a tribe whose geographical identity he was compelled to explain, for to his average audience the Circassians were unheard of.

The human race he concluded to have been smaller in earlier times than at present. Proof: He once tried in vain to squeeze upon his little finger a signet ring of Cheops, builder of the great pyramid. Also, he had examined the hilts of the swords of certain chieftains "of the race of Odin, found in Scandinavia," and had discovered that they were "much too small for any modern hand to grasp."

Oh, but for all their diminutiveness, men were vigorous and lusty in the past! Now we are hothouse plants. "Each year 2,000,000 teeth are extracted in London alone! Yet there are no signs of bad teeth in mummies or fossils." And further, there were no surgical instruments among the Egyptians. And even during the middle ages, men wore armor weighing 150 pounds. We are a degenerate people; it is apparent in our literature.

"No man of ordinary penetration can fail to detect, in the poems of Elizabeth Barrett Browning, or in the tales of Poe, the evidence of a diseased body. Byron, with all the shifting play of his wit, pathos, and passion, cannot wholly purify the pages of *Don Juan* from the smell of gin; and Mrs. Radcliffe, in the nightmare horrors of her *Mysteries of Udolpho*, betrays the suppers of raw beef in which she indulged. Contrast the dark and sinful fascination of *Lucretia*, written by the exhausted and dyspeptic Bulwer, with the ruddy and healthy tone of *The Caxtons*, written by the same Bulwer after his system had been restored by the water cure."

He passed on to a castigation of his age: "The characteristic of those books which now best suit the popular taste in this country is morbid emotion." "Gutter literature" has become fashionable, "lewd French novels," flagrantly reprehensible. "Give me the fresh, hearty, warm-blooded creations of Fielding and Smollett, with all their coarseness, rather than the refined and insidious immorality of modern French novelists."

Give him, indeed, the glorious, healthy Elizabethans, those "splendid animals" who were not "pale and anemic," who were not "long-haired dreamy youths," but "master spirits." Give him Shakespeare, Beaumont, and Fletcher. Give him the inspired, wise Greeks —their drama and their philosophy. Give him mountain air, the summer surf, a swift horse, a tumultuous river. Give him the great winds and storms and the long rains from heaven: "What—in the name of physiology—*what* sort of a race shall spring from the loins of those tallow-faced, narrow chested, knock-kneed, spindle shanked simpering sons of rich fathers whom we see every day." In "three generations" we shall have become simians.

His prescription, like his diagnosis, was simple, too simple indeed, when one remembers his own harassed way of living, to appear anything but ironic. His countrymen were deteriorating, racially, for one reason: "We do not know how to *rest*. The average American works fast, sleeps fast, dresses in the twinkling of an eye, runs to his meals, eats fast, and when he has run through with his stock of health, dies fast. Our public teachers cry out to us: Think! Think! or Work! Work! but never Play! Play! or Rest! Rest! We need fresh air and exercise, we need to "open the windows and let in the sunlight, even if the carpets do fade."

In "Man and Climate"[15] he is considerably more

15. Dated 11-9-60, incidentally, three years before Taine's *History of English Literature*.

sober. "Climate is beyond all doubt the most powerful of these external influences which give shape to the plastic nature of man." Certain races have always inhabited particular zones of climate. Indeed, there is no such thing as a cosmopolitan race, "one, that is, which can exist in any climate." He classifies all races, explaining their idiosyncrasies in terms of temperature. The African, for example, "is careless of the future because his existence is certain, the Esquimaux because it is a matter of chance. The former does not advance because he has not the stimulus of necessity, and the latter because he has too much of it. The African has nothing to do but live, while if the Esquimaux *is* living, he is accomplishing all that can be expected of him."

Two important conclusions follow from these facts. The first one, immensely flattering, is "that every important triumph which man has achieved since his creation belongs to the Caucasian race. Our mental and moral superiority is self evident." The second is in part a warning. "Permanent, self-supporting colonization in another climate is impossible. This knowledge should restrain our national ambition." We cannot with safety extend our territory below the eighteenth parallel, or below Cuba and Mexico. The English have tried this, in India, but find it expedient to import fresh blood there almost constantly. Republican government, he is convinced, simply cannot succeed in the tropics. Thus it follows that the seat of government of the United States should always be where it is now, in spite of "gassy politicians who prate of pent-up utopias and claim the whole unbounded continent."

"The American People" was perhaps the most vigorous of all his speeches. It was written in November, 1861, and is burdened with his loyalty to the Union cause.

But not at first. At first he talks wisely about social differences between America and Europe. He is qualified to make comparisons: "I have had the opportunity of becoming familiarly acquainted with all the civilized races of the earth; and I know no people so paradoxical, so difficult to be fully understood, as the Americans."

We differ from the inhabitants of Europe in particular on one point. "There one finds a strongly ribbed social system" independent of the distinctions of rank and wealth. "That is, there are certain understood usages and habits of society, which are so many silent laws for its government. They exist as part of that domestic order which the American traveler finds in the families of Germany and England. It enters into the education of children, and it shapes, in one way or another, every man's plan for the future. In society it gives the charm of ease and grace, by making each person master of his position; in public intercourse it promotes a courtesy—let me rather say a *humility*— in the manner of the people at large."

Sadly, he must report that this principle is not operative in the United States. "A man's cultivation, refinement of manners, and moral fitness for society is not, with us, the only test to which he must submit.

His degree of wealth is a very important consideration in some quarters, his family in others, his religious views in others, the stand which he takes on some moral or political question in others again; while in certain cities, the street on which he lives, and in certain communities, the very fact of his superior cultivation would be a disadvantage to him. "In Europe," to rephrase the idea, one finds "political despotism and social freedom; here, usually, it is political freedom and social despotism." In England, no amount of recovered fortune could restore in a social way a man known to have been dishonorably bankrupt. "With us, if a man has wealth, and the power which wealth gives, his dishonesty is gracefully veiled under the term of 'sharp practice' and does not disqualify him for social consideration." This was a vicious circumstance to Taylor, as it had been a decade before to Dickens; for "one of the noblest uses of society is to step in and punish those slippery forms of injustice, and peculation, and immorality which avoid the grasp of the law. Society thus deals with character, while the law deals with actions.

"I am emphatic upon this point because I perceive, among us, a social demoralization, which is the result of giving an over-due importance to wealth. We are tormented by a feverish emulation to keep pace with one another and, as our wealthy class represents neither the intellect nor the refinement of our people, success in the race exhibits itself in display, in extravagant habits, in an ambition to keep up appearances as the main business of life."

How does he account for this blatant false pride? Largely through the realization that a comfortable living is in America so easy to obtain that poverty is regarded as a reproach, as something indicative of a want of industry or energy.

Let us place character before wealth, he goes on, and believe again that the grand old name of gentleman is a richer possession than an illustrious coat of arms. "The treason of the degenerate Washingtons of our day is not gilded by the immortal patriotism of our country's father: it becomes a blot of blacker damnation. When you hear a man boasting that he belongs to an old family, remember that you, too, are descended from Adam and Eve. I have heard so constantly from citizens of a certain state that they were connected with the best families, that I longed—for the sake of change—to make the acquaintance of a few of the worse families."

Yes, the Virginians are intolerable people, with their assumption of grandeur, and leisure, and conviviality, and their contempt for progress. They have talked of the South as though it were better and more civilized than the North—these preposterous and arrogant slaveholders who have no large cities and who gamble outrageously on horses and who are often drunk. Let us look at this section of rebels, fairly.

"The white trash of the South [according to J. T. Adams these 'poor whites' comprised only five per cent of the white population before the Civil War] represents the most depraved class of whites I have ever seen. Idle, shiftless, filthy in their habits, aggressive, with no regard for the rights of others, these barbarians seem to have united all the vices of the negro with those of their own race, and they almost shake our faith in the progressive instinct of the Anglo-Saxon blood."

He continued his indictment: "Society there has been slowly drifting back toward the conditions of the feudal ages. The planters have gradually absorbed the wealth and political power, and the poorer classes, utterly neglected, unschooled, unencouraged, despised even by the chattles of the former—have become, not indeed serfs but savages. In the North, the superior dignity of *labor that is free, the beneficent system of education,* [16] and the absence of any recognized caste, have subdued the inequalities of society to a greater extent than the human race has yet known. The surest guarantee for the permanence of our system of government is afforded by this result."

The South must be broken, by force. "It has been reserved for *us* to hear the most monstrous treason of history encouraged, under the plea that the suppression of it would be 'coercing' a people! In a crisis, when our national existence is at stake.... we still hear the lament that the simplest measure of self preservation on the part of the government is a dangerous assumption of power.

"I have never believed in submission to outrage since I was attacked by highwaymen. I have never believed in 'moral suasion' since I read that the Savior *scourged* the money changers out of the temple."

16.  Present author's italics.

The doctrine of states' rights is merely a device whereby to escape obedience to the will of the majority.

"The idea of loyalty to a state is so childish that a man of ordinary intelligence should be ashamed to entertain it. I was conversing, last winter, with a Virginia secessionist—one of the first families, of course—who actually had the hardihood to say: 'I am a Virginian first and an American afterwards. Allegiance to my state is superior to my allegiance to the Federal government.' 'Very well,' said I, 'step outside the United States and see what good your Virginia loyalty will do you. Go to Europe with your governor's passport and see how far you will travel. Say you are a Virginian and people will ask, "What's that?" Hang out your state shield with its *sic semper tyrannis*—the meaning of which we shall make you understand some day—and you may hear the question: "Is that one of the new Polynesian kingdoms?" But say you are an *American*—point to the star of Virginia on the national flag—and no other explanation is necessary.'

"I must do the man the justice to say that he answered: 'Well, I never thought of it that way.'"

This was a hectic lecture. Taylor digressed for a time to pay his courtesies to corrupt politicians. Again, because of the overwhelming prosperity of the country, he declared, we have grown careless of the means people employ to get money. The further fact that federal and state salaries are inadequate encourages administrative dishonesty. Why not have an intelligent civil service, within which the holders of government positions are promoted according to merit? His plea for this improvement is convincing so long as he extols the increased efficiency that would result from its adoption. But the South, monstrous ogre, blinked at him again, and again, he paused to hurl his rhetorical thunderbolt: Political corruption is widespread for a good reason, "when throughout the South the standard [of political probity] has fallen so low that an oath has lost its sanctity, we must not suppose that even the sublime loyalty of the North has yet purified us from a share of the reproach."

But let us take heart and "sink all narrow interests, all state arrogance, all sectional jealousies, in the nobler sentiment of loyalty to the American union. . . . We shall not exchange the security of the past for the constant presence of a rival and hostile power. For God has united North and South in a common destiny, and the devil, with rebellion as his agent, shall not put them asunder!"

In the address "Ourselves and our Relations"[17] he repeats a good deal of what was more comprehensively stated in the above discussion. Pleading for a stronger central government, he cites instances abroad of price fixing, condemns our identifying culture with religious orthodoxy or financial success, and deplores the tendency in rural sections to "resent the least departure from accepted ways and habits of life." In this regard the average small community exercises so narrow and tyrannical an influence "that whoever desires a little

17. Written toward the close of the war, 1864, and probably revised several years later.

social freedom is driven to seek it—or rather the nearest approach to it—in our larger cities."

He condemns the electoral college. It thwarts majority rule and, hence, is not democratic in spirit. He pleads again for a civil service. He is frightened by the spectacle of immigration. After five years' residence here an immigrant can vote, and in so doing neutralize the will "of our wisest and most experienced native." The immigrant is a temptation to our politicians; he is easily drilled. Consider our criminals: seventy-five per cent of them are foreign born! We should remember that "in a republic every unintelligent ballot is dangerous." It is the positive duty of every citizen to vote. Severe punishment should be meted out to those who persistently fail to do so. Education is our only hope.

The great danger this republic faces is that of decentralization—not its opposite. "Local pride—state pride, if you choose—is a natural but contracted sentiment. Yet our politicians, our authors, [probably in their regional fiction] have all been guilty of exalting it above the grander, *national* pride which should bind and blend all narrower affection.... I have been a citizen of three states, and have found that my allegiance is as easily transferred as my residence. So far from the national government encroaching on the rights of the states, I think it has allowed them the exercise of functions which properly belong to itself. As only the nation can levy war, so the militia system, which is designed to furnish it with resources, should be entirely in the nation's hands..... A state should be obliged to guarantee not only a republican government to its citizens, but the education without which that form of government has no certain permanence."

The South declared that the right to secede was not denied by the Constitution. Taylor answered that no government granting that right can survive. Secession was *assumed* to be a crime. The right of suicide, for that matter, is not denied in the Bible. He who helps to build a nation upon the basis of the secession principle "is either a dishonest man or a hopeless fool." The history of all confederacies—from the Greek to the German confederacies of our own day—has been one of inevitable failure." And, of course, if the mere fact of survival is to be the only criterion of greatness, he is right, though not a few tightly-knit empires have failed, unaccountably, as well. "Do those who advocate confederacies know what they mean? Better than such a miserable abortion—which has no national name or sentiment, enjoys no respect abroad and inspires no faith at home, cheats the present of half its harvest and sows no seeds for the future—better than this would be the absolutism of Russia!"

"Life in Europe and America"[18] contains much of Taylor's criticism of the Gilded Age. To the reformers who were beginning to agitate against the use of alcohol he mentioned the European custom of taxing the stimulant and of saying, in effect, "the citizen may do as he pleases; but if he does drink he shall be furnished the genuine article." He commends again the practice, in Germany, of fixing the price of necessities

18. About 1865, later revised.

like "bread, meat, and beer." And he talked, with considerable foresight, against the Whig philosophy of governmental protection of business, a philosophy which his friend Greeley had long advocated in the *Tribune*.

The interests of business, the Whigs had reasoned, through their eloquent spokesman, Henry Clay, are the interests of society; it is therefore the duty of the state to help its citizens to make money. "Whiggery is the expression in politics of the acquisitive instinct, and it assumes as the greatest good the shaping of public policy to promote private interests."[19] Now the fly in this sweet ointment did not escape Taylor's notice. He saw that the ideal of paternalism in the common interest had a way of degenerating, in practice, into legalized favoritism. "Lesser interests are sacrificed to greater interests, Whiggery comes finally to serve the lords of the earth without whose good will the wheels of business will not turn. To him that hath shall be given."[20]

Protecting a business, Taylor declared, "makes that business able to cheat and oppress and corrupt the public." Was the true aim of our government apparent "when an individual three years ago chose to stop traffic between New York and the West at Albany, or when three or four individuals recently gambled with the value of gold and disturbed the business interests of forty millions of people? It is perhaps owing to this

19. V. L. Parrington, *The Beginning of Critical Realism in America*, p. 21.
20. *Ibid.*, p. 21-2.

regard for the individual that, with us, corporations are far more irresponsible and tyrannical than in any other civilized country. Our politicians, of whatever party, cry out against corporations, and yet we see them controlling entire states, electing their own legislatures and members of Congress, demoralizing voters, and exercising other dangerous privileges in defiance of public interest. We are silent under impositions which would raise a popular tempest in many countries of Europe."

Materialistic personal ambitions he also deplored. "One of our prevailing national characteristics might be called *Discontent*. The more splendid and far reaching our aims, the more haste we make to realize them, seeking short cuts and accepting all kinds of risks and hazards. The present requirements of society—a fine house, handsome furniture, and a pew in a fashionable church—are not very difficult to fulfill. Those who distance their competitors and reach what is called *the top*, encourage the others to struggle after them. These in turn stimulate others farther behind until, from top to bottom, we find the whole people engaged in a struggle to keep up appearances." In Europe, this condition is anomalous. Ambition there "is sober, and aims at realizations which are not quite so far and splendid." The result is a greater stability, a peace unknown to more aspiring societies.

Finally, he deplored the rise of the cities. Throughout the republic one was able to trace "a natural ambition for further advantages, more flattering successes than small communities can offer. In a great many cases, the true remedy would be, not in deserting those communities, but in improving them. Too many of our farmers' sons become dyspeptic clerks or indifferent lawyers, or shiftless adventurers, through a mistaken estimate of their own powers. They do not see that it is more prudent to stand at the head of a simple universal profession than at the tail of any other." A city, moreover, is an expensive place in which to live. For that reason "it imposes a tax upon matrimony and thus encourages vice. There is not in the world—and probably never has been—a city where one must pay so much and get so little in return as in New York. We already behold there, and in our other cities, those extremes of reckless luxury and still more reckless poverty which we once supposed were peculiar to Europe." The home as an institution cannot long stand against the disintegrating fury of such an environment.

## 2

Certain other of Taylor's opinions will be indicated later. But we have seen already perhaps his most important social and political convictions. In the way of positive improvements, he endorsed the civil service, an educated citizenry capable of intelligent voting, and most emphatically, a strong central government possessed of approximately dictatorial powers over corporations and commonwealths alike. Negatively, he decried wealth as a measure of one's social prominence, the exploitation of the public by big business, the philosophy of acquisitiveness, the rise of the city, the waning influence of the home, and the southern way of life.

During the six years preceeding the war, Taylor was one of the most popular lecturers in the country, and the reason for this popularity is not far to seek. Much that he said was profoundly sensible, even prophetic. It was also important and needed saying. His delivery, moreover, was direct and forceful; he had a fine sense of humor, and his courage in expressing his views was above question. The fact cannot be emphasized too strongly that Taylor was entirely sincere in his political convictions; had they differed from those then current among northern audiences he would probably not have modified them in the least degree. It happened, however, that these convictions coincided with the vast majority of those to whom he spoke, which means simply that he was a true child of his age.

Yet it is only reasonable to add that one may be a child of his age without being, at the same time, either balanced or entirely trustworthy. And in the interest of preserving a degree of balance regarding some of the topics Taylor discussed, it would therefore perhaps be only fair to mention briefly the southern side of that picture which he painted with so much eloquence and force. To begin with, it should be set down at once that, in spite of his sweeping declaration that "the white trash of the South represents the most depraved class of whites I have ever seen," Taylor had actually visited only as far South as St. Louis and Washington, that the Mississippians he knew were those (in no sense typical of the state) whom he met on the boat which took him to California, and that he had never seen the states of Alabama, Georgia, Florida, the Carolinas, and Tennessee, except to pass through a few of them on the train, and partly at night, en route to New York from Mobile. Taylor didn't know the South.

It should be mentioned, again, that in his defense of "free labor and a beneficent system of education" he appears to have been blind to a good deal that, appreciated, would have considerably sobered his enthusiasm. There is little point in dwelling here upon statistics, but it is well known that in 1860 higher education in the South was in a much more flourishing state than in the North.[21] It is also well known that the reason elementary education was not as universal as elsewhere in the country is traceable to a belief—by no means refuted yet—that it is unwise to educate members of the lower classes beyond the station they will probably occupy as adults. In his tragic inability to identify himself with his race, the emancipated intellectual negro of today presents a case which seems to indicate, at any rate, that the point of view of the one section possessed as much validity as that of the other.

On the question of "free labor" also, it appears that to determine how sound Taylor's argument was involves, first of all, a definition of terms. "The slave," as James Truslow Adams has noted,[22] "was indeed a

21.  See W. E. Dodd, *The Cotton Kingdom* (*Chronicles of America Series*). Also Allen Tate, *Jefferson Davis*, pp. 37-8.
22.  "The Dilemma of Edmund Ruffin," *Va. Quarterly Review* (April, 1934), pp. 312-26

chattel, but in exchange for liberty he obtained security. From birth to death, in sickness and in health, he was guaranteed subsistence—including food, clothing, and shelter—medical attention, and the other necessities of life. He or she need not fear the loss of a job, the arrival of another child, or a bad crop. Whatever happened, the slave had a first lien, so to say, on the industry, indeed almost on the whole social system, of which he formed a part. It was of the very nature of that system that the profits of industry had to be such, and distributed in such a way, as to ensure security during life and at least a minimum of life's needs to every laborer contributing to the total result."[23]

When one is faced with the further consideration that in a state of "freedom" pregnant women were harnessed to coal carts, that six year old children were worked fifteen hours a day in ill-ventilated factories and mines, that one mill owner in Holyoke, Massachusetts, found his laborers able to "produce 3000 yards more of cloth a week if he worked them without breakfast,"[24] that another manager in Fall River frankly admitted regarding his employees "just as I regard my machinery," and added that "so long as they can do my work for what I choose to pay them, I keep them, getting out of them all I can. What they do or how they fare outside my walls I don't know, nor do I consider it my business to know.... When my machines get old and useless I reject them and get new, and these people are part of my machinery".....

23. *Ibid.*, p. 325.     24. *Ibid.*, p. 324.

When, in short, one finds such attitudes and practices to have been typical [25] in a society of "free labor" one is led to suspect the phrase of a deceptive emptiness all but criminal in its implications.

That the phrase deceived Taylor is plain. Indeed, by identifying himself with the passions of the fifties and sixties, he seems in his thinking to have been led into a basic intellectual contradiction. For that South which he despised was naturally, as a result of its way of life, more studious of manners and leisure than the North, was less acquisitive, was less prone to endorse futile hurry and speed and to mistake these things for progress, represented an established order such as he had come to admire in Europe, opposed by the very nature of its institutions the rampant rise of the cities, centered its interests in home life—exemplified, in short, practically all the virtues of civilization and decency which he was given to commending.

But there were two other characteristics of the South which blinded Taylor to these virtues. He held, as we have seen, to the sentimental conviction that there can be but one kind of slavery—the slavery of physical ownership. And the South openly practiced that kind, deaf to the hysterical protest of Garrison and other Abolitionists. He held also to the Hamiltonian conception of government, that of a government controlled by the rich and powerful. And the South was unregenerate here. There were, of course, corollary griev-

25. "Although the statement [just quoted] was brutal in its frankness the truth it expressed was the cornerstone of the *laissez-faire* philosophy with regard to the relation of the individual worker to industry and society." *Idem.*

{ 168 }

ances against the section: The war—brought on, he believed, by Southern stubbornness—had hurt the publishing business and the lyceum business, and he looked to these activities for his income. Besides, the rebels had killed his brother Fred at Gettysburg. The South, in brief, could not possibly be virtuous. He hated the South.

And this was unfortunate. For it happened, as a result of his hatred, that the one region in America which practiced the virtues he extolled, the one region which despised the vices he despised, he was able neither to tolerate nor understand. There was nothing real, nothing tangible, with which his point of view might be identified. He was driven, because of his dilemma, to commend the forces of unification, which were the forces of industrialism and predatory wealth; and in so doing he became in an unconscious way an advocate of all the brutality and corruption and spiritual depravity which he deplored. Universal education, he thought, would prevent this villainy. But a later and more chastened wisdom is beginning to imply that his ideal of universal education cannot arrest in mankind the impulse of selfishness, cannot commend nobility in any sweeter way to his contemplation, is indeed usually wasted upon that wretched creature—predestined, it appears to some, to perversity and evil.[26]

26. This chapter, in substance, was published in the *American Review* (April, 1934).

# POETRY

## X

AS we have seen, Taylor began his lecturing in January, 1854. As we have seen further, he was tired of it by March, but finished the season, making something like one hundred appearances. The following summer he went home, too exhausted, he complained, to do anything except to lead "an animal life in the open air and flourish like a green bay tree": Yet he added, in this note to Stoddard, that his hands were blistered from "trimming out and civilizing a favorite pine grove," that the birds knew him already, and that he had "learned to imitate the partridge and rain dove." "I have not written a line," he concluded, "and could not if I would." He scarcely considered as activity at all the preparation for the press of his *Journey to Central Africa, The Land of the Saracens,* and *Poems of the Orient,* all three of which were published before November. He was also working at his *India, China, and Japan,* and, desultorily, upon a revised edition of *Views Afoot.* Aside from these interests, and the business of putting together a few lectures, and the writing of almost innumerable letters to friends, he was, as he said, comparatively idle!

But with the coming of the autumnal equinox he was baited again into activity. There were many more dollars to be harvested in the once fallow fields which the lyceum speakers had fertilized. And so he set out again, grimly acknowledging that it was a cursed world which demanded prostitution of its children, but realizing, shrewdly, that since prostitution was demanded, it became his first duty as one of the damned to sell himself dear, to have all the details arranged by an agent who would leave him nothing to do except to "talk and take in the money."

He went to Auburn, New York, to Montreal, to Ogdensburg, up the St. Lawrence ("It was so cold that the pitcher in my stateroom held a lump of ice instead of water"); to Utica, Boston, Cincinnati, Columbus, Chicago, Detroit. He gave, in all, another one hundred and thirty lectures. He was pestered by strange females. They seemed—a few of them—to follow him about from place to place, thin waspish, scant-haired, weakeyed women, whose advances he did not greatly encourage. Curious men questioned him about his occupation. One, from Iowa, "wanted to know whether I was in the dry goods business. I told him no, I was in the hardware line; and we had a long talk about hatchets, files, shovels, locks, and pickaxes. . . . . I am disgusted with this way of lecturing and shall never adopt it again."[1]

If he was disgusted anew with lecturing, he was highly concerned with his *Poems of the Orient*. Fifteen hundred copies were sold within six weeks of publication. This volume deserves some notice, because in it,

1. To Mr. and Mrs. R. H. Stoddard, 11-9-54. Taylor-Scudder, *op. cit.*, I, 293-4.

Taylor's critics have said, he came nearer than any poet since Byron to expressing the true spirit of the East. What was that spirit, whose elusive essence he is said to have woven so ably into his stanzas? One may well inquire.

It was, to begin with, a very rare and etherealized something, a quality distinguished mostly by accelerated heart beats and breathlessness. Some of the titles in his volume are revealing. There is, for instance, "A Pæan to the Dawn," "The Temptation of Hassan Ben Kahled," "El Kahil," "Amran's Wooing," "The Garden of Irem," "The Wisdom of Ali," "Bedouin Song," "Nubia," "The Birth of the Prophet," "Hassan to his Mare" (Hassan prefers a horse to a woman because he knows that the equine is more faithful), "An Arab to the Palm," and "To a Persian Boy." In other words, Taylor seeks his local color largely through the use of names submitted as typical of the region about which he writes. But what of the inhabitants of this region? The question is valid, because in the "Proem Dedicatory," to Stoddard, he announces that he has, of late, been trying "to learn the native tongue of earth"; that while his friend is content to dwell "in Fancy's tropic clime," he has "pitched his tent upon the naked sands," has come to be more pleased "with one living rose" than with "all the God's ambrosia"; that his deepest joy and concern now lie "in the warm red blood that beats in hearts of men."

Let us consider Ben Kahled's temptation. First there are delectable foods, which recall the luxurious sensuousness of "The Eve of St. Agnes":

*There came a tramp of swarty slaves who bore*
*Ewers and pitchers all of silver ore,*
*Wherein we washed our hands; then tables placed*
*And brought us meats of every sumptuous taste*
*That makes the blood rich—pheasants stuffed with*
*    spice;*
*Young lambs, whose entrails were of cloves and rice;*
*Ducks bursting with pistachio nuts, and fish*
*That in a bed of parsley swam. Each dish,*
*Cooked with such art, seemed better than the last*
*And our indulgence in the rich repast*
*Brought on the darkness ere we missed the day.*[2]

Later, Hassan is induced to drink, and afterwards a damsel comes to him, singing and playing upon a lute. He describes his predicament himself:

*    As she sang, her glance*
*Dwelt on my face; her beauty, like a lance,*
*Transfixed my heart. I melted into sighs,*
*Slain by the arrows of her beauteous eyes.*
*"Why is her bosom made" (I cried) "a snare?*
*Why does a single ringlet of her hair*
*Hold my heart captive?" "Would you know?" she*
*    said;*
*"It is that you are mad with love, and chains*
*Were made for madmen." Then she raised her head*
*With answering love, that led to other strains,*
*Until the lute, which shared with her the smart,*
*Rocked as in storm upon her beating heart.*
*Thus to its wires she made impassioned cries:*

2. *Poetical Works*, p. 57.

*"I swear it by the brightness of his eyes,*
*I swear it by the darkness of his hair;*
*By the warm bloom his limbs and bosom wear;*
*By the fresh pearls his rosy lips enclose;*
*By the calm majesty of his repose;*
*By smiles I coveted, and frowns I feared,*
*And by the shooting myrtles of his beard—*
*I swear it, that from him the morning drew*
*Its freshness, and the moon her silvery hue,*
*The sun his brightness, and the stars their fire,*
*And musk and camphor all their odorous breath:*
*And if he answer not my love's desire,*
*Day will be as night to me, and Life be Death!"*

*Scarce had she ceased, when overcome, I fell*
*Upon her bosom, where the lute no more*
*That night was cradled; song was silenced well*
*With kisses, each one sweeter than before,*
*Until their fiery dew so long was quaffed,*
*I drank delirium in the infectious draught.*
*The guests departed, but the sounds they made*
*I heard not; in the fountain-haunted shade*
*The lamps burned out; the moon rode far above,*
*But the trees chased her from our nest of love.*
*Dizzy with passion, in mine ears the blood*
*Tingled and hummed in a tumultuous flood,*
*Until from deep to deep I seemed to fall,*
*Like him, who from El Sirat's hairdrawn wall*
*Plunged to endless gulfs.*

The poet, who listened in raptures to this confession, certifies bravely when it is completed that Hassan was very fortunate and need deplore no longer his vanished virtue.

This sort of thing is honestly typical. In a "Song" Taylor speaks of drowning his manhood in the black waves of a lady's hair.[3] In "Amran's Wooing":

> *Passion sobs on Sorrow's breast,*
> *And mighty longings, tender fears*
> *Steep the strong heart in fire and tears."*

Later the pulse of love runs through his boyish senses and makes him a man. Elsewhere, the "Sheik's divan" beckons him. A lady has suitors, numerous "as leaves upon the tamarind tree." Still later, the eloping maid rushed to him "trembling, and panting, and oppressed," and "threw herself upon his breast."

> *By Allah! like a bath of flame*
> *The seething blood tumultuous came*
> *From life's hot center as I drew*
> *Her mouth to mine: our spirits grew*
> *Together in one long, long kiss—*
> *One swooning, speechless pulse of bliss*
> *That throbbing from the heart's core met*
> *In the united lips. Oh, yet*
> *The eternal sweetness of that draught*
> *Renews the thirst with which I quaffed*
> *Love's virgin vintage; starry fire*
> *Lept from the twilight of desire,*
> *And in the golden dawn of dreams*
> *The space grew warm with radiant beams*

3. *Ibid.*, p. 62.

Which from that kiss streamed o'er a sea
Of rapture, in whose bosom we
Sank down, and sank eternally.[4]

Facsimile from an original manuscript

Bedoun Song.

From the Desert I come to thee,
On a stallion shod with fire,
And the winds are left behind
In the speed of my desire.
Under thy window I stand,
And the midnight hears my cry.
I love thee, I love but thee,
With a love that never shall die,
Till the sun grows cold,
And the stars are old,
And the leaves of the Judgment Book
unfold!

Look from thy window, and see
My passion and my pain;
I lie on the sands below,
And I faint in thy disdain:
Let the night-winds touch thy brow
With the heat of my burning sigh,
And melt thee to hear the vow
Of a love that never shall die,
Till the sun grows cold,
And the stars are old,
And the leaves of the Judgment Book
unfold!

4. *Ibid.*, p. 66.

*My steps are nightly driven*
    *By the fever in my breast,*
*To hear from thy lattice breathed*
    *The word that shall give me rest.*
*Open the door of thy heart,*
    *And open thy chamber door,*
*And my kisses shall teach thy lips*
    *The love that shall fade nevermore,*
        *Till the sun grows cold,*
        *And the stars are old,*
        *And the leaves of the Judgment*
            *Book unfold!*

Oct. 29, 1853.

Then, of course, there is the "Bedouin Song," in which (as may be seen from the manuscript) the lover comes out of the desert on a stallion shod with fire, faints below his lady's window in her disdain; yet proclaims in italicized hyperbole that his love shall not die

> *Till the sun grows cold*
> *And the stars are old*
> *And the leaves of the judgment book unfold.*[5]

In all charity, one is fairly well obliged to term this work little more than a pedestrian debauchment of Shelley's "Indian Serenade." But on the other hand, it has not been forgotten. Indeed, it has been set to stirring music, and the college glee clubs of the country have made it a favorite program number. Whatever distinction this fact implies—and it at least implies

5. *Ibid.*, p. 69.

acceptance—ought to be recorded faithfully. It is Taylor's most popular poem.

"The Birth of the Prophet" gives another footnote to his imitativeness. This time he uses the octameter line of Tennyson's "Locksley Hall," employing, however, three lines to a stanza. But further illustration of his work is needless. He concludes the volume by declaring in "L'Envoi," that he found

> *Among those Children of the Sun,*
> *The cipher of my nature—the release*
> *Of baffled powers, which else had never won*
> *That free fulfillment, whose reward is peace.*[6]

Certainly, he did find release of a sort. Lovers actually have mistresses in these poems; there are flaming consummations, pagan abandonments, rapturous immoralities which declare that, for once, the pall of New England did not weigh upon his imagination. Lowell, indeed, after reading the volume, realized as much and wrote him in haste a kindly but somewhat pontifical warning:

"Beware of becoming too deeply enamored of the sensuous in poetry. It is natural that the pendulum of us Yankees should swing very far away from our Puritan and Quaker extreme—only we must remember that Bacchus was the God of severe tragedy also. What I mean is that you must not trust too far to your own purity, because few of your readers will be able to match it."[7]

6. *Ibid.,* p. 81.
7. Taylor-Scudder, *op. cit.,* I, 295-6 (12-4-54).

These works fairly well proclaim their own criticism. Obviously, Taylor is concerned with little except the passion of men for women or horses. This passion is quite too electrical and furious to endure. It is perhaps comparable to the few ecstatic moments a sensitive soul experiences when, according to Poe, he reads for the first time a poem of approximately one hundred lines in length. It constitutes an æsthetic debauch. There is nothing sane or balanced or temperate in the East, as Taylor conceives it. Always, moreover, this feverish emotionalism is pictured in its romantic or nascent state—in other words, before fulfillment. This is the typical romantic approach, the approach which reasons, in effect, that the greatest delights are the delights of anticipation and suggestion, and which adds that these represent the only authentic subject matter of art. Accordingly, sleep, in his verse, usually draws its portals at the instant of consummation; the after-glow— often fairly dull, as rumor saith—is left to the reader's thwarted conjecturing.

Just what his defenders mean when they tell us that Taylor is the true poet of the East it is difficult to understand. One suspects that the East, aside from a surface exoticism, is quite as prosaic and sober as the West. Taylor's own travel books confirm this suspicion. He is, rather, the poet who expresses for adolescence its blurred notion of what any people are like who live in a more torrid climate than its own. He is the poet of sensation, merely, drunk with the red sweet wine of Keats. To term the result sentimental and derivative would be superfluous. To add that, in spite of its being sentimental and derivative, it was vigorous enough to send off Stoddard and Aldrich and many other less favored versifiers into vacuous ramblings through star-lit Ispahans is to comment, in a note of heaviest melancholy, upon the starved nature of the genteel poetic imagination in Taylor's America.

2

He lectured on into the spring of 1855, throttling his disgust. While in Cincinnati, in February, a publisher had induced him to agree to compile a *Cyclopædia of Modern Travel*—"a piece of hack work to be sure, but one which I could do with some spirit." Moreover, "it would bring me in a very handsome sum."[8] Comforting news from Putnam in March indicated that his royalties—apparently on *Africa and Saracens*—had mounted to $2,650 by the first of the year. "Henceforth, I shall get a good income from my books alone. I want to purchase two more shares of the *Tribune* in July, if possible. I feel now perfectly relieved of all further anxiety about money matters, which is a great satisfaction." He added, in this note to his mother that the *Cyclopædia* "will yield me at least five thousand dollars in the course of two years."

In July he was tempted in another way. Commodore Perry "proposed that I should apply for the appointment of United States Commissioner to Japan." Through the recommendations of Irving, Bryant, the historian Bancroft, and Seward—all acquaintances—

8. To Boker. 2-24-55. Taylor-Scudder, *op cit.*, I. 298.

he would be almost certain to get the place. What does it pay? was his first question. It paid $5,000 yearly, while yearly expenses there would be only about $2,000. A government ship would take him over. Mrs. Taylor disliked, naturally, the idea of her son going away for another two years into the heart of barbarous Japan. "But what can I do, Mother? Look at the matter with my own eyes, not with yours. . . . I am in the world at the most active and ambitious part of a man's life, with an opportunity of achieving things worthy to be remembered. I must travel again somewhere, soon. I was born for it, and it is the best thing for me."

But a long silence from Perry and the government blunted this early enthusiasm. By the end of July he gave up all hope of the place. It went to Mr. Townsend Harris. It was the first time, but not the last, that the ways of politics proved beyond his predicting or comprehension.

He labored on through July upon the *Cyclopædia*. In August he went to Newfoundland, with a fairly large party, to report for the *Tribune* an attempt to lay a cable between that island and the mainland. It was a timely change for him. "I have been working and sweating for the past six weeks like a Congo nigger." Ticknor and Fields had urged the publication of his collected poems, and this had increased his labors. In addition, of course, he was preparing *India, China, and Japan* for Putnam.

A glimpse of Newfoundland tempted him again with the idea of traveling in the North. This temptation—to be off at any rate *somewhere*—was augmented by a letter from Bufleb, his companion during the trip into Africa. Back in Gotha, in Germany, Bufleb had bought "a piece of property adjoining my estate, a garden with a small modest house." It was a present to Taylor, to be his home "when he keeps his promise next year and visits us."[9] Against the force of this pleasant announcement and prospect, he found awaiting him on his return from Newfoundland "fifty invitations to lecture." "I could easily make five thousand dollars again this winter if I were willing to undertake it."

Well, he was willing. By December he had "fairly commenced" his campaign, with seventy-four engagements ahead. The "book on Japan" had sold 10,000 copies. "There is a prospect that the states of Ohio and Indiana will order copies of all my works for the common schools, making two thousand copies of each." Opulence, almost too much to be borne, seemed imminent now. Fame, too, kept pace. The artist Hicks was doing his oriental portrait. "I shall get him to put Achmet [his Egyptian dragoman] into the picture." Thackeray was in New York, and Taylor gave him a breakfast at Delmonico's, inviting Boker, Stoddard, Glass, an English artist, and other friends. "We had a glorious time: the breakfast lasted five hours. . . . . Thackeray says he will try and come with me to Kennett for a day or two next April. When I go to London next summer, he promises to introduce me into the literary society of England."[10]

9. *Ibid.*, p. 307 (7-27-55).
10. *Ibid.*, p. 309 (to his mother, 12-8-55).

He went on into the middle-west in the dead of winter—giving lecture after lecture. The cold was severe. News of unusual dividends from his *Tribune* stock sustained him at first, but not for long. By the middle of February his health was definitely shattered. He was feverish, could not sleep, and morphine gave him no rest. Nature, for a time at least, stopped his doing what Prudence and the memory of his art had long complained against without effect. His physician advised him to cancel all engagements for the season. He compromised by resting three weeks. He lost almost a thousand dollars net, but wrote his mother, resignedly, "I would much rather lose the money than my health." March 15 he informed her that during the past six months, dividends on his *Tribune* stock and his book royalties had amounted to $5,400. He would need it for his trip abroad.

What must he have thought, at probing intervals, of the unending mad cycle into whose vortex he now seemed drifting inevitably? He would travel through a country, he would return to America, he would publish a book on the subject, he would lecture about it until interest waned. Then he would set out once more, to begin for another time the relentless fixed sequence. Perhaps such intervals never disturbed him. The gathering years found him, perhaps, knowing only the perennial enthusiasm of departure, the perennial weariness of the last days of a journey, the perennial drudgery of book preparation, the perennial disgust with lecturing—knowing all these things, but knowing them merely as they came, greeting each one with an undisciplined rapture or with a no more disciplined disappointment—seeing life, as it were, in terms of countless unrelated episodes, from which no wisdom was recoverable, except, perhaps, the wisdom of a blind acceptance.

He finished the lecture season and found more work —much more than he had anticipated—yet to be done on the *Cyclopædia*. "I have compressed ninety volumes into one, and made I think a most interesting and salable work, for which I hope to receive thousands of dollars." It was to be a "record of adventure, exploration, and discovery for the past fifty years, comprising narratives of the most distinguished travelers since the beginning of the century." Taylor had worked up the material largely from his own travel library, which contained by this date more than seven hundred rare editions.

He had dedicated his *Rhymes of Travel* to Boker. He had persuaded Ticknor and Fields to publish, in two volumes, Boker's *Plays and Poems*. Their friendship was in 1856 more intimate than ever, and they wrote of it unabashed, in a way that the now pleasantly defunctive Freudians of the 1920's would have found delectable indeed: "I have loved women, dearly and tenderly, but I never loved anything human as I love you. It is a joy and a pride to my heart to know that this feeling is fully returned." But this was not all. They sustained each other in difficult times, they criticized, often to some purpose, they reminded each other of their earlier ambitions in poetry. Boker added, in the above letter even, a tolerant but direct complaint: "I suppose that your muse sits shivering in a corner while this infernal *Encyclopædia of Travel* is afoot! Well, Well! At the end of your labor you will have earned a heap of money, and put together one of those 'valuable books' which no gentleman's library should be without. But it is a funny thing to salute you in the character of a man of science, as one who has added to the practical knowledge of the world a thousand and one 'facts, sir, facts! Damn facts!' "[11]

A man of science and a compiler of facts! Boker was right. The rôle was not appropriate; Taylor's appearance belied it. Let us look at him again, this time through Stedman's eyes: "It needed not Hick's picture of the bronzed traveler, in his turban and Asiatic costume, smoking, cross-legged, upon a roof-top of Damascus, to show us how much of a Syrian he was. We saw it in the down-drooping eyelids which made his profile like Tennyson's, in his aquiline nose, with the expressive tremor of the nostrils as he spoke, in his thinly tufted chin, his close curling hair, his love of spices, coffee, colors, and perfumes."[12]

Taylor sailed for Liverpool in July, 1856. With him were two sisters, his youngest brother, and a sailor, John Braisted, who was to serve him as valet on the northern trip. The literary echoes which reached him from America the following months were less pleasant than he might have wished. To begin with, there was the *Cyclopædia*. Its sale was wretchedly small. The publishers blamed an exciting presidential campaign

11. Boker to Taylor, 6-11-56. *Cornell Univ. Mss.*
12. Quoted by N. K. Foerster, "Later Poets," *C.H.A.L.*, III, 39-40.

and public fear of a financial crisis. But to an author who was planning, with his royalties, to build a stately home near Kennett, this announcement brought scant comfort.

Yet the works of his friend Boker had been well received. A second edition was called for within thirty days. Other friends—Stoddard and Read—were also being published. Stoddard fared badly at the hands of the critics, and Boker wrote Taylor about the fact in language which, thanks to the early editors of these gentlemen, we can scarcely imagine them using:

"Dick's book is out,[13] and he and I are engaged in cursing the critics. Those who treat him with insufficient consideration we curse bitterly, and those who treat him with injustice we curse more bitterly, and those who do not notice him at all we curse most bitterly. Our correspondence is as full of 'damns' as a New England river, and the most complimentary terms we employ even toward the most favorable of critics is to call him a 'lousy son of a bitch!' I know that will meet with your approval."[14]

The sour reception which Read's volume met with was a source of considerable satisfaction to Boker. Read had been for several years in England, painting and writing. He had met Tennyson and Coventry Patmore, among others, and had assumed a condescending attitude toward his early friends which they were very far from relishing. Boker announced his deflation: "His last volume, *Sylvia and other Poems,* is a dead failure.

13. *Songs of Summer.*
14. Boker to Taylor, 1-24-57. *Cornell Univ. Mss.*

Speaking only as Read's friend, I must say that I think he needs his humbling lesson, and that its good results will be visible in his later works. He was laboring under the Wordsworthian error that all was gold which fell from him."[15] What had probably served, more than anything else, to irritate Boker was Read's casual announcement, earlier in the year, that he was likely to publish soon a volume with the title *Sweepings from my Portfolio*. This was quite too much. "I'll be damned if I will any more read the sweepings of his portfolios," Boker declared, "than I would feast upon the little man's dung."[16]

But at any rate, Read had published. The trinity of mediocrity—as one wit had dubbed Taylor, Stoddard, and Boker—had also published, not once but often.[17] Henceforth, no literary circle in the land could term itself modern and leave their names unmentioned. And no anthology of verse, henceforth, could face the public without examples of their work. To say that they were conscious, imitative artists, writing always in the warmth of literary models; to say, further, that they reflected with no adequacy whatever the stormy life about them, the promptings of a unique and fresh insight, is to venture a critical estimate which time alone has been able to clarify. Upon them this estimate had as yet cast no shadow. They regarded themselves as definitely significant: that reviewer who dis-

15. *Ibid.*, 6-21-57.
16. *Ibid.*, 1-24-57.
17. In the sixties this group was made up of Aldrich, Taylor, and Stedman. See Taylor to Aldrich, 10-2-66. *Cornell Univ. Mss.*

agreed was a lousy son of a bitch. And doubtless, as the world wagged then, they were significant indeed. For excepting that uncouth creature Whitman, what other poet in America was doing *anything* in the middle fifties very much better than this loving trinity could do it?

# SCANDINAVIA

## XI

WHEN Taylor reached London, Thackeray kept his promise. "I found him jovial and as tender hearted as ever. His daughters came to see the girls, took them out driving a whole afternoon, and we all dined together in the evening. The dinner came on the first." Most of the writers for *Punch* were there. "It was a capital dinner, in Thackeray's own house." Later he breakfasted with Barry Cornwall and Browning. "Dear old Barry! I loved him from the beginning. He is reputed silent, but he opened his heart to me like an uncle. He showed me all his Mss., lots of unpublished poems, and talked out of the abundance of his golden nature." Born in 1790, here was the last of the fluent Cockneys, who had written any number of delightful little songs about the sea, and who remembered an almost inexhaustible store of personal anecdotes concerning Shelley, Keats, Coleridge, Lamb, and the other great men of the early years of the century.

Browning was equally cordial. "He wanted me to call on his wife, and I did so, and a jolly hour's talk I had with the two. She is about publishing a poem of eleven thousand lines [*Aurora Leigh*], something entirely new in design, and she feels a little nervous about it." Taylor soothed her on this point. "I told her she should not worry, for if it was good it would surely be appreciated sometime or other, and if not, the sooner it was damned the better. . . . Browning is much pleased with the American success of his last volume [*Men and Women*]. He assaulted me with 'From the desert I come to thee, on a stallion shod with fire,' etc., which he knows by heart and says is the finest thing of the kind he ever read."[1]

He went on to Germany, to visit Bufleb and to take possession of the house his friend had bought for him. "It is one of the most charming little places I ever saw. . . . It is furnished in the antique style with high-backed red velvet chairs, Brussels rugs, sofas, mirrors, flower-stands, matches and cigars on the table, tea and sugar in the cupboard, and beer in the cellar. . . . A flight of stone steps, with statues at the foot, leads to a broad terrace, in the middle of which is a fountain, always playing. The basin is deep, and I have three big fish which come to be fed."[2]

His fame was spreading in Germany. The poet Rückert had read his works, the Frau Professor Jacobi had translated some of his poems, Auerbach the novelist, Gutzkow the playwright, Julius Hammer the poet, "welcomed me as a friend and brother author." There were trips to Jena and Heidelberg, long walks through the Thüringian forest, a hurried excursion to Switzerland and Italy. Indeed, all that he saw proved so enjoyable that, for once, he neglected his regular letters to the *Tribune;* and it was only when he seemed much

1. To Mr. and Mrs. R. H. Stoddard, 8-4-56. Taylor-Scudder, *op. cit.*, I, 322.
2. *Ibid.*, p. 323. To his mother, 8-20-56.

too richly immersed in the soothing indolence of his holiday that Duty's voice again grew plain and drove him to the fulfillment of his "destiny"—a visit to the far cold North.

December 1, 1856, the visit had fairly started. Already, with the temperature at 16°, the air was brisk. With Braisted, he walked the deck of the vessel, which was taking them to Sweden, "enjoying the keen wind and clear faint sunshine of the north."

At Dalaro, a small port, they learned that "Stockholm was closed with ice." They were forced to disembark and to take a sled for the city. Before they reached it, the thermometer registered 2° below zero. This delighted him; it seemed a thrilling augury of lashing winds and of the ice to come. His yearning to know all climates, his long quest for the bitter sensation of cold, was soon to be satisfied, amply.

They must stop at the capital for maps and equipment. How disappointing it was, once there, to find a dense fog settling over the city and the mercury climbing—how stupidly like home! "My blood stagnated, my spirits descended as the mercury rose, and I grew all impatience to have zero and a beaten snow track again."[3]

Maps were hard to get: the only one available for Lapland was dated 1803. Information was equally scant. He could find no one who had made the trip in winter, "or who could tell me what to expect, or what to do." But this did not daunt him! He bought provisions, shot and slugs, "four bottles of cognac for cases

<hr/>

3. *Northern Travel*, p. 24.

of extremity," sword, butcher knife, screw driver, and other necessities, "all contained in a box about eighteen inches square." Furs of every sort they already possessed. Taylor had also been taking "double lessons" in Swedish. After a week he felt capable of traveling without an interpreter.

Riding through Norrland in a sleigh was exciting. They were a good way north of Stockholm now. It was 22° below. "My nose occasionally required friction, and my beard and moustache became a solid mass of ice, frozen together so that I could scarcely open my mouth, and firmly fastened to my fur collar."[4] In twelve hours they had traveled forty-nine miles. "Yet we feel no inconvenience from the temperature."

The people of this land awakened his admiration: They "are noble specimens of the physical man—tall, broad-shouldered, large limbed, ruddy, and powerful; and they are mated with women who, I venture to say, do not even suspect the existence of a nervous system. The natural consequences of such health are: morality and honesty—to say nothing of the quantities of rosy and robust children which bless every household. If health and virtue cannot secure happiness, nothing can, and these Norrlanders appear to be a thoroughly happy and contented race."[5]

Christmas day it was 36° below. Still they pushed on.

"My beard, moustache, cap, and fur collar were soon one undivided lump of ice. Our eyelashes became snow white and heavy with frost, and it required constant motion to keep them from freezing together. . . .

4.  *Ibid.*, p. 45          5.  *Ibid.*, p. 46.

Our eyebrows and hair were as hoary as those of an octogenarian, and our cheeks a mixture of crimson and orange, so that we were scarcely recognizable by each other. Everyone we met had snow white locks, no matter how youthful the face, and whatever was the color of our horses at starting, we always drove milk white steeds at the close of the post. The irritation of our nostrils occasioned the greatest inconvenience, and as the handkerchiefs froze instantly, it soon became a matter of pain and difficulty to use them. You might as well attempt to blow your nose with a poplar chip. We could not bare our hands a minute, without feeling an iron grasp of cold which seemed to squeeze the flesh like a vice and turn the very blood to ice. . . . I had rarely been in higher spirits."[6]

Again he praised the people of the North. No milk-sops they, but clear-eyed, "straight and strong as the fir saplings in their forests":

"Under the serenity of those blue eyes and smooth, fair faces burns the old Berserker rage, not easily kindled but terrible as the lightning when once loosed. Men like these we should have in the new territories of America; there would be no vacillation then on the question of slavery! 'I would like to take all the young men of Sundsvall,' says Braisted, 'put them into Kansas, tell them her history, and then let them act for themselves.' 'The cold in clime are the cold in blood,' sings Byron, but they are cold only through superior self-control and freedom from perverted passions. . . . It is exhilarating to see such people—whose

6. *Ibid.*, p. 52.

digestion is sound, whose nerves are tough as whipcord, whose blood runs in a strong, full stream, whose impulses are perfectly natural, who are good without knowing it, and who are happy without trying to be so. Where shall we find such among our restless communities at home?"[7]

Now it was 40° below. "When the thermometer was brought in, the mercury was frozen, and on unmuffling I found the end of my nose seared as if with a hot iron." Strange lights dotted the heavens phantastically, advancing, retreating, merging in wondrous splendor, "and shedding a pale unearthly radiance over the wastes of snow." At an inn they met a stranger, who suspected them of a secret political mission. Taylor proceeded to bewilder the gentleman by speaking to him, alternately, in English, French, German, Spanish, Italian, Arabic, and Hindustanee. When they parted, he stood for some time shaking Taylor's hand dumbly and saying, over and over: "You are a very seldom man."

Yet another time he was constrained to pause in admiration of the characters of these people. In this instance it was a servant girl who aroused his praise. She was cook, chambermaid, hostler; "she made our fires in the morning darkness, and brought us our early coffee while we yet lay in bed." Outdoors and indoors she worked, from long before dawn until midnight. Her salary was the equivalent of eight dollars a year, and board.

"The thought has often recurred to me—which is

7. *Ibid.*, p. 54.

the most truly pure and virginal nature, the fastidious American girl, who blushes at the sight of a pair of boots outside a gentleman's bedroom door, and who requires that certain unoffending parts of the body and articles of clothing should be designated by delicately circumlocutious terms, or the simple-minded Swedish women, who come into our bedrooms with coffee, and make our fires while we get up and dress, coming and going during all the various stages of the toilet, with the frankest unconsciousness of impropriety? This is modesty in its healthy and natural development, not in those morbid forms which suggest an imagination ever on the alert for prurient images. Nothing has confirmed my impression of the virtue of the northern Swedes more than this fact, and I have rarely felt more respect for woman or more faith in the inherent purity of her nature."[8]

They traveled on into Finland—as usual, by hiring horses and postillions who drove them from one village to the next. Soon they were "beyond the daylight." The moon did not set at all, "but wheeled around the sky, sinking within eight degrees of the horizon at noon day." The thermometer dipped to 44° below and their progress was no longer pleasant. Braisted's feet were all but frozen, Taylor's hands were numb, "the country was a wilderness of mournful and dismal scenery," their horses "were ready to drop at every step." Food was scarce; there was a famine this year in the country. After seventeen hours of travel, they got nothing but hot milk, and after sleeping for the

8. *Ibid.*, p. 74.

night they got nothing but coffee. Taylor was bored.

Later, in Lapland, he took a bath. A virgin servant girl, as bathing master, did "the usual scrubbing and shampooing. This is the general practice..... and is but another example of the unembarrassed habits of the people in this part of the world." Afterwards, he stood for some moments in the open air—it was only zero now—and was delightfully refreshed. "The Finns frequently go out and roll in the snow during the progress of the bath."

Now he was using reindeer instead of horses, and the beasts often proved fractious. Once Taylor's animal seemed especially to enjoy overturning his sleigh and sousing him with snow. He was furious, but all his kicks and shakings and cuffings seemed administered to no purpose. Long Issac, a native, passed him at the height of his rage and muttered gravely: "The deer will go well enough, if you know how to drive him." "Long Issac may go to hell," was Taylor's inviting reply.

He talked with a village pastor, who had frequently preached in a temperature of 35° below. "At such times," said he, "the very words seemed to freeze as they issued from my lips, and fall upon the heads of my hearers like showers of snow." Taylor had wondered about religion there. "Our souls are controlled to such a degree by.... our bodies that I should doubt whether any true devotional spirit could exist at such a time. Might not even religion itself be frozen?" The pastor agreed. All the better impulses in man disappeared as the mercury fell, and in those still intervals of ultimate frigidity human nature, too, assumed the image of despair and death.

Lapland was not attractive to Taylor:

"The Lapps as a race were as disappointing as the Swedes had been commendable: I had already seen enough of them to undeceive me in regard to previously formed opinions respecting them, and to take away the desire for a more intimate acquaintance. . . . I could distinguish little, if any, trace of the Mongolian blood in them. They. . . . resemble the Esquimaux (to whom they have been compared) in nothing but their rude filthy manner of life. . . . . They are a race of northern gipsies, and it is the restless blood of this class, rather than any want of natural capacity, which retards their civilization. Although the whole race has been converted to Christianity and education is universal among them—no Lapp being permitted to marry until he can read—they have but in too many respects substituted one form of superstition for another. The spread of temperance among them, however, has produced excellent results, and in point of morality they are fully up to the prevailing standards in Sweden and Norway."[9]

What Taylor especially deplored was their loss of a former picturesqueness. The wizards had departed; twilight had fallen on their older pagan divinities. They were "frightfully pious and commonplace." Instead of chanting to the spirits of the winds and clouds, "they have become furious ranters who frequently claim to be possessed by the Holy Ghost. Christianity

9. *Ibid.*, p. 136.

was—of course—good for their souls, but as a race, fearful anomaly, it had rendered them stupid and uninteresting.

He turned southward again, "with a feeling of relief." "Our faces had already begun to look pale and faded from three weeks of alternate darkness and twilight. ... Every day now would bring us further over the steep northern shoulder of the earth, and nearer to that great heart of life in the south, where her blood pulsates with eternal warmth." His first sight of the sun was eminently welcome. He had had only a foretaste of an arctic winter, but his desire for the experience of cold was surfeited and, in a final sense, quiescent.

He complained about the missionaries. They had scattered "the seeds of spiritual disease among this ignorant and impressionable race." He complained about the reindeer, their inadequacies for work, their unwillingness to be tamed, the bitterness of their milk. He noted the odd way in which they were prepared for draft duty. "The male deer. ... are always castrated, which operation the old Lapp women perform by slowly chewing the glands between their teeth until they are reduced to a pulp, without wounding the hide."[10] He complained that many other customs of these people could not be mentioned in his book "on account of that moral prudery so prevalent in our day."

Characteristics not socially questionable he dwelt on with considerable thoroughness. The Finns seemed

10. *Ibid.*, p. 145.

unusually chaste. Illegitimate births were rare "and are looked upon as a lasting shame by both parties." Marriage, however, removed the stigma. Bundling had been discontinued. One particular moral observance disturbed Taylor greatly. "While both sexes freely mingle in the bath, in a state of nature, while the women unhesitatingly scrub, rub, and dry their husbands, brothers, or male friends, while the salutation for both sexes is an embrace with the right arm, a kiss is considered grossly immodest and improper." But no conclusion about the nature of taboos and morality suggested itself. Here, as in his other travel books, Taylor remained essentially the reporter.

Back in Stockholm, he wrote often about the manners of the people. "The Swedes pride themselves on being the politest people in Europe." They dress admirably. King Oscar is a delightful fellow, widely read and a brilliant conversationalist. But there are so many bastards in the city! "Very nearly half the *registered* births are illegitimate, to say nothing of the illegitimate children born in wedlock."[11] Not one servant girl or shop girl in ten is chaste. "The number of broken-down young men, and blear-eyed, hoary sinners is astonishing." Old men in restaurants "place their hands unblushingly upon the bosom of young waitresses." Everyone, it seemed, drank outrageously. These statements, printed first in the *Tribune,* were challenged by certain editors in Sweden, but Taylor verified them by reference to government statistics

11. *Ibid.,* p. 218.

and declared afterwards that he saw "no reason" to change his first impression.

He went later to Norway, but was pleased with little except its scenery. The people there were entirely too prejudiced. One could mention nothing, for example, which did not compliment the people or the country. This attitude reminded Taylor of a certain backward section in America. "Let a Norwegian travel in the Southern states, and dare to say a word in objection to slavery!" Or in the Northern states, with equal extravagance he might have added, and dare say a word in defense of it.

For a moment, before he left this country, he was moved to pity its inhabitants, as one who had known a warm summer moonlight might pity any creature to whom that blessing had been denied. Surely, he said, they deserve to enter heaven at death, having dwelt while alive in earth's equivalent to hell. Nature, in fact, had made their fate almost sinless: they had no neighbors to injure, there was nowhere anything to steal, and murder was rare because the usual incentives of hate and revenge were absent. The mere problem of living involved so difficult a struggle that the leisure for sense indulgence never obtruded. But how is it endurable at all, Braisted—this living without friends and society, this loneliness beside the everlasting ice? Alas, they know no other world, Braisted answered, "and their ignorance keeps them from being miserable. They do no more thinking than is necessary to make nets and boats, catch fish and cook them, and build their log houses. Nature provides for their mar-

rying and for the bringing up of their children, and
the pastor, whom they see once in a long time, gives
them their religion ready made."[12] "Then, God keep
them ignorant," said Taylor, prayerfully dismissing a
mood that was rare to him.

2

We have now sketched, if inadequately, the contents
of six of Taylor's travel books. He wrote five more,
but these seem to differ in no very remarkable way
from those already considered. Briefly, they recount
further travels in Greece and Russia, a trip to Colorado, another to Egypt and Ireland, and the miscellaneous briefer visits written of in *By Ways of Europe*
and in *At Home and Abroad*. This latter work appeared in two series.[13] *Views Afoot*, his first, was published in 1846; *Egypt and Iceland*, his last, in 1874.
Four years later he died.

What of the value of these volumes? That they
brought him a wide and genuine popularity we have
already seen. They brought him, as well, the more
tangible reward of money. They substantiated his
work as a lecturer. Without them he would have remained an obscure editor, an unrecognized poet, little more than one of the five dollar a week men with
whom the cities were overflowing. Why has oblivion
claimed, with seeming finality, the hard-wrested product of those vigorous years? Why is he forgotten

12. *Ibid.*, p. 312.
13. See bibliography for dates of publication.

now, except for a few scattered verses and a translation?

To answer these questions requires, first, some attention to the nature of our more enduring travel books. Henry Fielding wrote such a book when he did his *Voyage to Lisbon*. He also wrote a preface, in which he set forth several wise precepts to guide future authors of this kind of work. These precepts deserve notice even now.

Preëminently, the traveler should be a man of good sense, with a nice ability to discriminate beween the useful and adventitious:

"When I say the conversation of travelers is usually so welcome, I must be understood to mean that only of such as have had good sense enough to apply their peregrinations to a proper use, so as to acquire from them a real and valuable knowledge of men and things, both of which are best known by comparison. If the customs and manners of men were everywhere the same, there would be no office so dull as that of a traveler, for the difference of hills, valleys, rivers. . . . would scarce afford him a pleasure worthy of his labour."

In addition to avoiding undue emphasis upon topography, the good traveler, in Fielding's judgment, should be able to overlook a great deal of what he sees. Here, again, the selective process must apply. "Nature is not, any more than a great genius, always admirable in her productions, and therefore the traveler, who may be called her commentator, should not expect to find everywhere subjects worthy of his notice." Perhaps Fielding's entire philosophy of travel is in essence present in a single statement: "I shall lay down only one general rule, which I believe to be of universal truth between relator and hearer, as it is between author and reader: that is, that the latter will never forgive any observation of the former which doth not convey some knowledge that they are sensible they could not possibly have attained of themselves."

Mr. Henry Seidel Canby adds the conviction that important travel books have been concerned "with the study of the influence of the earth's surfaces upon life." The best of such studies "will have facts enough and adventure enough, if it happened, and anecdotes, if they are relevant, and romance, if romance there was; but it will be written for none of these things. It will be an achievement, because good travel should be an achievement; it will be an exhibition of the art of geography." Geography he defines, simply, as "the study of the influence of earth's surface upon life."[14]

These views seem convincing enough. Summarized, I suppose they declare, in effect, that the traveler's primary interest should center around his effort to understand the people whom he visits; that his work is in spirit informational and serious. He is essentially a teacher, an exegete, as opposed to an enthusiast; his approach to his subject should be intellectual, not emotional; his appreciations must be identified with the predicates of criticism; he is, in fact, the social

14. "Traveling Intelligently in America," *Essays of Today* (Century Co. 1928), p. 168.

critic who has mastered the faculty of comparing foreign institutions and customs with his own.

Taylor, of course, was guided by no such ambitious program. He freely confessed that his purpose was, rather, "artistic, pictorial—if possible, panoramic."[15] He went abroad, he often said, to complete his education. College was beyond his means, and, at any rate, offered no certain escape from the environment whose inadequacies he had perceived even in youth. Yet one of his early biographers is authority for the contention that this earlier conception suffered a sea change, "matured";[16] that after his return from Japan he realized that his experiences were significant in a sweeping, impersonal way; that he was able to offer to a culturally famished America something of which it appeared to stand in imminent need; that he could broaden it, and perhaps in a small way civilize it. A brief appraisal is in order.

To begin with, it should be freely confessed that Taylor did bring a certain color to his countrymen, probably a certain exoticism. He continued, in a sense, the more thoughtful achievement of Irving and Long-fellow. Willis, too, as we have suggested, had preceded him as a colorist and apostle of the picturesque, and had written in an even more sprightly way of the surface brilliance and charm of Europe. But Taylor's work was more comprehensive than that of this forerunner, his accomplishment fuller and more influential. Though he did nothing essentially new, as a

15.  Preface to *Northern Travel*, p. 1.
16.  Taylor-Scudder, *op. cit.*, I, 326.

traveler he was talked about more, read more, and was better known.

But as we have mentioned, he remained almost uniformly a reporter. The business of selection and rejection and of revision did not bother him. He inserted trivial and important with equal emphasis. Realizing that Greeley and his public would pay for what he did, he looked upon the problem of organization as irrelevant. It was so much simpler to write in diary fashion, since the world seemed interested in his every movement. After all, he was not looking for immortality in these works. The thought, indeed, was repugnant to him. His poetry—in all confidence he believed it—would bring *that*. He was thus no artist here, but rather a workman, to whom even grammatical orthodoxy was no great matter.[17] And throughout these volumes one may trace a certain carelessness which weakens, to the point of obliterating, what otherwise might amount to a genuine admiration for the facility, if not the distinguished polish, of his style.

There is, admittedly, evidence of the sort of thing Fielding commended: There are shrewd appraisals of the Arab and Chinese character, especially shrewd appraisals of the character of the Swedes and Lapps, but these gleaming intervals appear sadly buried beneath other too lengthy accounts of his daily insignificant activities. There is social criticism even; but it in turn is offered in an incidental sort of way, is labored and far from complete.

17. See Boker's letter on his grammar in *Africa* (9-28-54). *Cornell Univ. Mss.*

Naturally, his trouble is incident upon his haste. Always in his books of travel one senses his desire to be moving, to keep going, a conviction that an exalted virtue is resident in activity itself. He early formed the habit of making sketches of the sights which intrigued him. This habit may indicate a great deal. The sketch, the panorama meant, to Taylor, very much more than the still life or the studied portrait. He had unusual powers of observation and retentiveness, but how rarely he allowed these powers to fix themselves long upon the contemplation of a single really important trait! Movement is his deity; variety replaces thoroughness. The result is, most often, confusion and disappointment. He saved his more solid conclusions for his lectures.

Of the dozen works there are nevertheless three which hardly deserve the complete neglect into which they have fallen. *Views Afoot* remains a curiosity, and is yet far from devoid of the freshness that attracted readers throughout his life. *At Home and Abroad* is still interesting because of the unusually intimate nature of its revelations; and finally *Northern Travel* retains a modicum of significance as the record of an out-of-the-way and fairly courageous adventure, and as the one of his travel books most rich in social criticism. To acknowledge this much in favor of their immortality is to acknowledge perhaps more than Bayard Taylor ever hoped would be forthcoming from the impersonal, crabbed, and withal rather petulant spokesmen for posterity.

# WAR

## XII

BEFORE Taylor left Stockholm, in May, 1857, he had learned to do some very queer things. Realizing that his last few years had been almost entirely lacking in regular physical exercise, he went in for the Ling-Branting system of "anatomical gymnastics." Specifically, his desire was "to increase the girth of my chest." But to its advocates there were all sorts of astonishing possibilities in this kind of training, and after two months Taylor agreed with them. Besides having acquired the remarkable ability "to climb a smooth pole thirty feet high and run up a rope with my hands"[1] he had reached the conviction that the exercises were "a remedial agent in all cases of congenital weakness or deformity, as well as in those diseases which arise from a deranged circulation." Branting insisted that his method would also cure "consumption, malignant fevers, and venereal afflictions," At any rate, Taylor thought it should be introduced "into every civilized country as an indispensable branch of the education of youth."[2] Had it not swelled his own chest an inch and a half beyond its former proportions, and banded his sagging muscles with iron?

The savage, swift vigor with which these exercises

1. To his mother, 4-21-57. Taylor-Scudder, *op. cit.,* I, 331.
2. *Northern Travel,* p. 206.

awakened fell heir soon afterwards to a sweet sublimation. He returned to Gotha and became engaged to
"Marie Hansen, daughter of Hansen the distinguished
astronomer, and niece of Mrs. Bufleb." After a pleasant interlude he went over to England, visited Thackeray again, met Tennyson and spent two days with
him. Later, Read introduced him to Leigh Hunt. "I expect to see Dickens before I leave. I met last Sunday
with Layard, the discoverer of Ninevah, and Kinglake,
the author of *Eothen*."

Of all this distinguished company, Tennyson
seemed to please him most. "Take my word for it,
Boker, he is a noble fellow, every inch of him. He is
as tall as I am, with a head which Read capitally calls
that of a dilapidated Jove, long, black hair, splendid
dark eyes, and a full mustache and beard. The por-
traits don't look a bit like him; they are handsomer,
perhaps, but haven't half the splendid character of his
face. We smoked many a pipe together and talked of
poetry, religion, politics, and geology.... He had read
my oriental poems and liked them. He spoke particularly of their richness of imagery and conscientious
finish. I need not tell you that his verdict is a valuable
one to me.... His wife is one of the best women I
ever met with, and his two little boys, Hallam and
Lionel, are real cherubs of children."[3]

With Bufleb he went on into Norway, to "round
out" his impression of Scandinavia by a sight of that
land in summer. In the fall *Northern Travel* was pub-

3.  Taylor-Scudder, *op. cit.*, I, 334.

lished simultaneously in London and New York and, translated, in Germany. October 27 he married.

It was a fortunate match. Marie Hansen was the daughter of Peter Andreas Hansen, a native of Schleswig-Holstein, who for a number of years had served as director of the Ducal Observatory at Gotha. He was almost entirely self-educated: he learned French and Latin independently and, says Mrs. Taylor, "wrote treatises in both languages."[4] For his most important work, *The Tables of the Moon*, the English government had awarded him £100. Little is known of Mrs. Hansen, except that she was descended "from a long line of huntsmen."

Still there were those who did not view Taylor's marriage favorably. He confessed to Grace Greenwood Lippincott that he had "been amazed by the letters of unknown women, who reproach me for having proven false to their ideal of constancy." But he had a ready answer for such busybodies! "If I have been false" to their ideal of constancy "I am still true to my own, and there will be no reproach in that other world where I am better known than in this."[5] "Marie is a noble woman," he continued, "a true and tender wife."

Of course, Boker wrote him rapturously as soon as the news reached America: He mustn't "settle down" in this matrimonial business. "So far as worldly prospects go, 'settling down' is eminently proper, but never let it invade the heart.... Let me confess, by way of

4. Marie Hansen Taylor, *On Two Continents*, pp. 4-8.
5. April 3, 1858. From Athens. *Unpublished Letters of Bayard Taylor (Huntington Library Publications).* J. R. Schultz, ed.

illustration. I have been married for fourteen years, yet my feelings toward my wife are as fresh as on the day I first told her I loved her. She is now lying before me, fast asleep, in all the unromantic negligence of night cap and wrapper, her brilliant eyes are shut, her pretty mouth wide open, and all her features lapsed into the meaningless quietude of heavy slumber. And yet I cannot turn toward that silly little bundle of flesh and linen and think how I love it without my eyes overrunning with tears, my heart filling with indescribable emotions, and a wild desire possessing me to throw myself upon her bosom, and drink up her sweet breath, and kiss her sweet lips, not with the old kiss of satiety but with the long, long, frenzied kiss of love.... She is always new to me, always repaying my study of her by fresh revelations of beauty.... Do not call my pleasures sensual; they are not so, or they would have faded, or at least lost their intensity."[6]

This tender announcement was blurred by another that was far from salutary. There was a shortage of money in America; "literature and lecturing were both at a standstill." The effect of this news was to induce Taylor to forego a projected trip into Russia for the purpose of gathering "fresh material for another volume of travels." But Greece beckoned none-the-less— warm, mellow, and unexploited. He would take his bride there and spend the winter. It would not be expensive; he could continue to write for Greeley. They went to Greece.

Winter passed, a balmy idyll. He wrote no poems

6. Boker to Taylor 1117-57. *Cornell Univ. Mss.*

("I need American air when I write poetry"), but he thought of writing a great many. He made "excursions" into the interior and to neighboring islands. He sketched plans of the house he would soon be building at home. He thought long about art and beauty before the crumbling Parthenon. He learned of the language what it was practical to know. When spring came, his wife was with child.

They returned to Gotha. In late summer the child was born; it was a boy. "I am a father. Do you hear— *a father....* I look at the little thing with a sort of childish delight and wonder, and continually ask myself: Is this helpless being really sprung from my loins? I see my own brown eyes in its face, my hair on its head.... and wonder how much of my soul goes with these features."[7] As soon as it was possible, he sailed with his family for America. By November they were in Kennett Square. Mary, sleeping at nearby Longwood, had merged in his imagination with the beauty of riotous fall. He had taken his new bride to visit her grave and had felt somehow, as they walked toward home, her blessing on all he had done.

## 2

Now that he was married again, and a father, and the owner of a fine piece of land, he could think of delaying no longer with the house. But he had recently bought the stereotype plates of all his prose works, leasing them to Putnam, as his agent. Washington Irving had made a similar arrangement with the same

7. Taylor-Scudder, *op. cit.,* I, 341-2. To Stoddard.

publisher. This purchase seemed quite shrewd, but it had cost $5,000. The result was that insufficient money remained with which to complete his building program. Yet the thought of a home less pretentious than he had planned was intolerable. Again he must take to the lecture platform.

With the Stoddards he rented a place in Brooklyn, left his wife and son, and started out still another time to enlighten his interested countrymen. The questions which these countrymen propounded cried woefully of their need of him! Where do you go tomorrow? Where did you lecture last? What's your real opinion of the human race? Is the marriage custom false or true? Sprinkling or immersion, which do you prefer? What might be your birthplace? Don't you suffer awful from the heat and cold? So you are now a German citizen, I'm told? Where's your lady staying? What's your baby's name? Do you think you'll ever be a settled man?

> *Aint you now the greatest*
> *Traveler alive?*
> *What's the land where turnips*
> *Seem the best to thrive?*[8]

So the queries went, and in patience he smiled "the fixed smile of the seasick," answered them, and pocketed his fee. "He entered," says his wife, "with a certain athletic joy upon the task of making literature, not a stick or a crutch, but a horse on which he proposed to

8. "Recreations of a Rainy Day," a poem to Stoddard. *Ibid.*, I, 345-8.

ride hard into prosperity."[9] And doubtless as he finished each address, he saw Cedarcroft in his mind's eye wheeling out, further and further, from the incoherence of paper plans to the tangibility of brick and mortar. All of life's good things are to be wrested from life only through inconvenience and suffering. So he had been taught in childhood and, in many ways a child still, so still he believed.

This business kept up until the summer of 1859. He then moved his family back to Kennett, and work on the house started. Taylor superintended all activities. He was also writing travel sketches for the New York *Mercury*, revising his letters about Greece for the volume, *Travels in Greece and Russia*, revising also his *Cyclopædia of Modern Travel*. Money was needed now as never before. "It is really a Napoleonic business to build a house." And time was needed too—time to repair the damned hydraulic ram that somehow, for all the gold it cost him, simply wouldn't work properly. And so, with rare courage, he struggled through the summer against these insistent demons, Time and Money. But at the close of the summer Money won out, and demanded that he leave his house to other hands and go to California in its service.

Five thousand dollars, so a literary society promised, awaited his taking in that gutted land. He could lecture for three months, and since travel there was easy now, he could bring his wife with him. He went in September. At his first appearance he had one thousand customers, and his future prospects seemed bright.

9. *Ibid.*, p. 348.

Everywhere were signs that man had brought Nature's immemorial wilderness to order. "There are splendid roads, villages, lines of stages, and fenced and cultivated farms." Perhaps Taylor was among the earliest literary contributors to the California legend: "The fruits and vegetables are the finest in the world. Apples are raised weighing three pounds apiece, pears four pounds, beets fifty pounds, and pumpkins two hundred and sixty pounds. We have seen bunches of grapes two and a half feet long and eighteen inches wide."[10]

But this was written before he went into the hinterlands. In these parts Nature and human nature still proved unregenerate. "I travel fifty miles a day in torrid heat and infernal dust, and lecture in the evening to a lot of miners who go out every fifteen minutes to take a drink, and then come back again.... I have traveled seventy-five miles today in killing dust, and must to bed, as I go sixty tomorrow and lecture there afterwards."[11]

This confession came from Sacramento. Placerville proved an even worse stop. He was compelled to do his own advertising. "I am disgusted with the process of getting up lectures myself in the mining towns. It is a terribly shabby, nasty business and humiliates me immensely." At one village, with his wife, driver, and guide, he was taken for the leader of a quartet club and invited to stop and give a concert. The final disappointment came when he realized that, for all his heroic exertions, he would earn little more than half

10. *Ibid.*, p. 351. To his father, 9-4-59.
11. *Idem*. To Stoddard, 10-3-59.

of what had been promised him. He returned to New York in November and was revived by the knowledge that his book on Greece had sold seven thousand copies. Again he toured the East and Middle West, lecturing desperately. And by March he was able to announce to Boker that his $15,000 house was paid for, that his married life was happy, his friends faithful, his struggle with the world almost over (nor had it soured him while it lasted), that he had adopted a cheerful philosophy "which bears me lightly over all unpleasant experiences," and that there stretched before him "six months for poetry." He moved into the house near the end of May, bringing all his family with him. After buying furniture for it he had one hundred dollars left.[12]

People were curious about Bayard Taylor's house, and he had a way of catering in print to curiosities of almost any variety whatever. In the second series of his *At Home and Abroad* papers he wrote the history of Cedarcroft, from the beginning. The result indicates a genuine and commendable interest in landscaping and architecture. His place, he decided early, "must be large and stately, simple in its forms, without much ornament—in fact, expressive of strength and permanence. The old halls and manor houses of England are the best models for such a structure, but a lighter and more cheerful aspect is required by our southern summer and brighter sky. There must be large windows and spacious verandas for shade and air in summer, steel roofs to shed the rain and winter

12. To Stoddard, 5-10-60. *Ibid.,* I, 357.

snow, and thick walls to keep out our two extremes of heat and cold. Furthermore there must be a tower, large enough for use as well as ornament, yet not so tall as to belittle the main building."

All this sounds eminently sensible, with the exception perhaps of the tower. The tower doesn't seem to belong. With the house occupying the highest point of land in the neighborhood, it is gratuitous. He needed no lookout; he was no weather prophet. It was probably built to satisfy his childhood desire "to see far and wide," was probably indicative of the expansiveness of his nature, of his directionless, ebullient unresting curiosity, was in a sense a symbol of himself and therefore valid. Certainly, the house itself betrays no "little eddies of eclecticism,"[13] no rage for the mansard roof and for the German gothic blended with Queen Anne domesticity; is guiltless, largely, of the dispersed fashions of the Gilded Age.

He had the rooms finished admirably. For this business, he declared, "there is nothing equal to the native wood, simply oiled to develop the beauty of the grain. Even the commonest pine, treated in this way, has a lustre beside which dreary white paint, so common even in the best houses, looks dull and dead. Nothing gives a house such a cold, uncomfortable air as white paint and white plaster. This color is fit only for the tropics."

But let that reader interested in building a house for himself bear one primary fact in mind. When Taylor wrote this statement his soul spoke out: "Get all

13. Lewis Mumford, *Sticks and Stones*, p. 105 (N. Y., 1924).

216

the estimates from the various mechanics, add them together, and increase the sum by fifty per cent, as the probable cost of your undertaking." And don't be certain even then; you had still better allow for further lamentable contingencies.

The subject of landscaping received as much attention as that of architecture. This art, he wrote in another series of papers,[14] "should aim to develop and make attractive, not to conceal or change the individuality of scenery.... In the way of cultivation, contrast, and careful finish not a great deal can be done in this country without ample means; but there are two things which cost very little, and upon which the first effect of home scenery depends—to spare and to relieve."

He was especially insistent about the first of these principles. "Not a single oak shall be destroyed," he wrote his mother when first engaged in buying the property. He cut away only a few stunted cedars from his future lawn. Then he cleared this space of bushes and briars, plowed and fertilized it for two years before sowing his grass seed. There was an orchard on the place, and even here his respect for his cedars outdid all practical arguments against them. He allowed them to stand, he said, "for a triple reason —they are beautiful, they protect the tender varieties of trees, they help to feed birds through the winter." There were pines and oaks in plenty upon the place, furnishing "very delightful contrasts of form and color." He set out deliberately to increase these contrasts

14. For *Hearth and Home*, ed. by Donald G. Mitchell (1869).

by planting "a purple beech or two to show against the oaks; a birch in front of the darker mass of cedar," magnolias to add richness, cypress "for its tender vernal green." There were black walnut and locust trees near one corner of the house, two others, chestnut, in another direction. Though partly dead, he banked them with fresh soil and so preserved them. The general result of this sensitive planning was that the lawn remains to this day one of the most beautiful and restful in the East.

3

Taylor settled down to write poetry. He did perhaps his best short piece, "The Quaker Widow," and sent it to *Harpers*. "Songs," declares his wife, "flew from his mind like birds set free from a cage." Within a month he had practically completed another volume, *The Poet's Journal*.

But if songs flew in marvelous fashion from his mind, money, in ways no whit less marvelous, winged itself free from the tyranny of his pockets. He had begun borrowing from Boker the year before. He kept on borrowing, and repaying, and borrowing again.[15] The house, it developed finally, had cost $5,000 more than he had planned, and though he had paid the builders he was indebted to his friends. But he had to entertain, and on a grand scale. The Stoddards came, and the Buflebs from Germany, and the Bokers, and Fields, and many others. He looked anxiously to the

15. See Cornell Mss., Boker to Taylor, 7-12-59, 12-23-59, 5-4-60, 3-14-61.

fall, when the lecture season would once more be flourishing. He wrote hasty articles for the *Independent* and the *Atlantic*. He borrowed in advance from his publishers. He praised Freytag's *Pictures of Life In Germany*, and proposed that Fields engage him to translate it. Still he was pressed, sorely pressed.

And when fall came the lecture business did not flourish. Lincoln had been elected, the South was definitely moving toward secession, money was scarce and the people unwilling to trade it for culture. Those few invitations which did come in he accepted eagerly. His talk, now, was was all about union and freedom, and against the spurious claims of the slaveholders. Not everywhere were his audiences sympathetic. His friend George W. Curtis had been mobbed in Philadelphia for making a strong plea for war. Taylor lectured soon afterwards in Brooklyn, roundly upheld Curtis, and roundly condemned the audience which had silenced him. This brought forth strident hisses from his own hearers. He was compelled to shorten his speech, but, by God, his dander was up now! He went to Philadelphia and delivered his speech again— this time with half a dozen policemen on the platform beside him. President Buchanan—now gratefully near retirement—had called for a day of fasting and devotion; he would pray the South into humility.

Taylor flayed the president. He also wrote a vigorous ballad, "Prayer Meeting in a Storm," and sent it to the *Tribune*. It recounts the fate of the good ship Constitution, about to be dashed to pieces in a storm while its captain stands by in pious meditation. But waves wash the rapt captain overboard—as sullen waves of indignation were washing Buchanan out of the White House—and with God's right hand and the will of true sailors the ship, he predicts, will be saved.[16]

When war was declared, in April, Kennett Square was wild with excitement: "Everything here is upside down. We live almost in a state of siege, with rumors of war flying about us. Everybody is arming. There are reckless secessionists only twelve miles to the south of us. The women are at work night and day, making clothes for the volunteers. Brother Fred has raised sixty riflemen and in a few days will go to the front. All the young Quakers have enlisted. We are so near the border that if those damnable traitors in Maryland aren't checked within a few days we may have to meet them here. There are no factions in the neighborhood anymore; we are all brothers, drawn together by a common danger. My county will furnish one thousand men, and dangerous men to meet. I had planned to go to Europe, but that must be postponed. I must sell one of my *Tribune* shares. I need the $5,000. One thousand must go to the purchase of Fred's commission, more to the payment of his pressing debts. Give this letter to Putnam and tell him to send me *immediately* one hundred dollars, or fifty dollars, or twenty-five dollars, or any sum he can spare. I must

16. It is interesting to note that these stirring times called out his first serious and prolonged thinking on American Life: He began his novel, *Hannah Thurston.*

buy firearms. I will write again soon. God and Liberty!"[17]

He wrote again two days later: "An armed band of traitors has been within forty miles of us. We are preparing to defend our homes. We have night patrols, mine being armed with African swords and spears, in default of better weapons. Yesterday I was out scouting. Every night I make patriotic addresses. Today I am going into Delaware to stir them up. The women here are heroes. Old Quaker women see their sons go without a tear. Money is poured out like water. Our plowshares are beaten into swords."

The next month he changed his plans and went to Germany, taking with him, his wife, his son, and his mother. Why he went is not entirely plain, except that there had been some talk in the family about a vacation. One might suspect, however, that he went because, as always, he needed fresh experiences to write about; because, lacking generally a meditative mind, he realized that only added sensations could furnish him with ideas for the articles which it was now imperative to turn out. At all events, he wrote a good deal, once there—letters for the *Tribune,* one essay for *Harpers,* ten more for the *Independent.* By the middle of September he was again at Cedarcroft.

They were living simply now. It was harvest time, and what necessities they were compelled to buy were abundant and therefore cheap. He was doing an article for the *Atlantic* on Hebel, "the German Burns." An-

17. See letter to Stoddard, 4-21-61. Taylor-Scudder, *op. cit.,* I, 375-6.

other, "A German Shooting Match," was soon to appear in the *Cornhill Magazine*. Yet these successes were not enough. "I must write something else for money—no matter what; for the invitations to lecture don't come in, and without them I am lost." Putnam was bringing out a new edition of his works, the Caxton, trying to revive the waning interest of his public. "I hope he does something with it! These war times are hard on authors; the sword of Mars chops in two the strings of Apollo's lyre." [18]

But for all the war's raging he was puzzled about the Lyceum depression. He wrote anxiously to Curtis. Was he, too, suffering an eclipse? Has the whole institution "suspended," or is America simply tired of Bayard Taylor's brand of inspiration? "I must know what calculations to make. Nevertheless I do not despair of lecturing in Richmond before I die."

Curtis admitted that "the business" was in a bad way; he was receiving only half the usual number of offers. Taylor got far less than that proportion; and since this was inadequate, he resumed his activities with the *Tribune*, this time as head war correspondent. He was now pretty heavily involved. He had paid off Fred's debts, but there were more which his father had amassed. Another brother, Howard, had turned out a complete rascal and had "gone to smash," as Taylor expressed it, leaving still further obligations.[19] He was trying to mortgage Cedarcroft for $8,000; it would be a good investment for Boker. But Boker's money was

18. To Mrs. Stoddard, 10-14-61. *Ibid.*, 380-1
19. Taylor to Boker, 3-14-61. *Cornell Univ. Mss.*

tied up. He was compelled to borrow from strangers.

He spent the winter in Washington or at the front, leaving when opportunities came for hurried lecture engagements. General McClellan infuriated him. "He is a perfect imbecile. I rode from Centreville to Manassas with his staff, and watched him carefully. I don't believe he has a single plan of any kind in his head. Of all colossal humbugs in history, he is the worst. I was hauled up before the Senate Committee yesterday to testify as to what I saw."[20]

And now, when he was disgusted with McClellan, and harassed by debt, and very, very tired, the inconstant swift winds of fratricidal war brought in his way what seemed a rare blessing. Mr. Simon Cameron, the new minister to Russia, called to offer him the position of secretary, with the promise that his own stay there would be short and that Taylor should remain as *chargé d'affaires*. This latter place paid $6,000 a year. "I was surprised," he wrote the Stoddards, "undecided, and inclined not to accept. I consulted with Forney, with Sumner, with Vice-President Hamlin, and others, all of whom said: 'Go, this is only the first step. Cameron will not stay long and you will be his successor.'.... The vice-president came afterwards, saying: 'I earnestly request you to go, and will almost insure you the succession.'" He went with Cameron to see President Lincoln. "I said to him (Lincoln): My only reason for accepting is the chargéship, after Mr. Cameron's departure.' He smiled, nodded his head, and said 'all right.'" He must sell another *Tribune* share,

20. *Ibid.*, 3-14-61.

to meet initial expenses, but then, in time surely, he would have the Minister's place, with a salary of $12,000 a year. This would give him "unbounded facilities for exploring Central Asia under Russian protection—the great ambition of my life.... If I have not good friends in Washington to assist me, we are a race of hypocrites." June 15 he was in St. Petersburg.

4

"Since I am again in Europe," he wrote his mother, "I don't want the war to end too soon." But his remark was impersonal. "The longer it lasts, the more certain is the doom of slavery. And if the war is over without slavery being utterly crushed, we shall have a second war in ten years. Being farther off, I can see all sides clearly, and I say that slavery must fall, or all this struggle has been thrown away."[21]

"Damn England forever!" he was exclaiming in a letter to Boker soon afterwards. "You have no idea of the concentrated venom of the English. They are actually furious because the Union is not divided."[22] He had had his first taste of insidious diplomacy, and he simply could not stomach it diplomatically. In September he was "sick" over news of the Second Manassas. More cheerful reports came the following month: he was happy, while the English were sick. He was also busy with a novel, *Hannah Thurston*, and with occasional articles and poems about Russia.

But he was beginning to realize that his coming to this country had involved a considerable risk: "In a

21. *Ibid.*, 6-19-62. Taylor-Scudder, *op. cit.*, I, 388.
22. *Cornell Univ. Mss.*, 7-2-62.

word, George, I must make a desperate struggle for the sake of a splendid one. I have made the right beginning here, and if I succeed will be able, in the course of years to produce my greatest literary work. If I fail, I shall have spent money to no purpose, and will be lucky if I have funds enough to bring me home."[23]

Cameron, as he had promised, left soon after his arrival, and Taylor was placed in charge of the mission. A "crisis" in Americo-Russian diplomacy seemed imminent. The French and English were proposing that Russia join them in intervening in the struggle, possibly to the extent of recognizing the Confederacy. Taylor hastened to the Russian Prince Gortchakoff. He pointed out the vastly superior resources of the North. He mentioned the new iron clad vessels which would soon blockade every southern port. He informed the prince that 300,000 men had been added to the Union army "within the last two months." "The prince assured me, in reply, that the action of Russia would be governed, as heretofore, by the most friendly feeling toward the United States."[24]

But Taylor's solicitude for his country's interest did not stop with this conversation. He prepared an elaborate paper for the prince, setting forth "the present national debt of the United States; the estimated annual revenue under the new laws; the additions made to the active force of our armies during the last three months; the number of iron clad vessels in process of construction; and the important movements already commenced in the West and on the sea-coast. . . . This

23.  To Boker, 9-28-62. *Ibid.*
24.  To Sec't. Seward, 11-12-62. Taylor-Scudder, *op. cit.*, 395-6.

statement was forwarded. . . . as a simple exposition of facts, which would clearly show that an armistice at this time could only be of advantage to the rebellious states, and that no proposition of the kind could be entertained by the Federal government."[25]

Seward could not fully condone this last well-meant gesture. It seemed to posit the assumption that the European powers were justified in doubting the ultimate success of the North. The whole matter of proposed intervention was to be ignored by representatives of the United States. Taylor was instructed to inform the prince "that the government would not have instructed you to write the paper,"[26] nor would it have approved, had it been informed beforehand.

He worked on through the winter. He was ill for a time, then Mrs. Taylor was ill, then his second child, a girl, was ill. He intercepted papers on the subject of slavery for J. P. Benjamin, the Confederate secretary of state, then in Russia. In general, his conduct was admirable and efficient. He made many friends. But rumors he received about certain vile machinations in Washington convinced him finally that the office of minister was to go to another—to Cassius M. Clay, who had held it before Cameron.

He was bitter. "If I had succeeded in bringing ridicule on the legation, if my dispatches were written in shocking English and without the least evidence of prudence or judgment, I might have some chance. But as every dispatch from home expresses complete sat-

25. *Ibid.*, 11-28-62. I, 398.
26. W. H. Seward to Taylor, 12-23-62. *Ibid.*, I, 400.

isfaction with my proceeding, I am sure that I shall fail. I am serious."[27]

He was even more serious the following week in a letter to another friend, E. C. Stedman. Though he has carried his country's interests "through the most critical period of our relations with Russia that has occurred in the last fifty years," he has not the least expectation of being appointed. "On the other hand, a man who (*entre nous*) made the legation a laughing stock, whose incredible vanity and astonishing blunders are still the talk of St. Petersburg, and whose dispatches disgrace the state department that allows them to be printed, will probably be allowed to come back to his ballet girls (his reason for coming) by our soft-hearted Abraham. Let the government send a man here who will not be laughed at—who has one grain of prudence and one drachma of common sense, with a few moral scruples—and I shall gladly give up all my pretentions and go home. From my private correspondence I know that Lincoln says Clay is not fit for the place 'but he is an elephant on my hands, and I guess I shall have to give it to him!' "[28]

Boker, wise in the ways of politics, tried to restore Taylor to sanity. "Clay's claims were on the party, your claims in that direction were slight; and all personal or literary claims go to the wall when they are opposed by strict party claims—Cameron is vexed, but Cameron is nobody just now, in a political

27. To J. T. Fields, 2-18-63. *Ibid*, I, 408.
28. *Cornell Univ. Mss.*

⊷{ 227 }⊱

sense."[29] But trailing this brief lecture came a new rumor that excited him again. Lincoln and Seward, it was intimated, "feel that I have been treated rather shabbily. . . . and propose a special piece of work for me." He cannot tell his mother even. It will take six months. No one outside the family must hear about it. "It is altogether more distinguished and important than the Russian mission." Silence and secrecy, mother.

Well, mother was silent and secretive, but so was the state department. Taylor waited in patience, until patience had long ceased to be a virtue. In September he came home. He called on Seward and requested an explanation. The secretary was evasive. He called on the President and repeated his request. Lincoln stared at him in amazement. "Hell," he said finally, "I thought you were in Persia."

29. *Ibid.*, 3-16-63.

# FICTON

## XIII

It was autumn, 1863, and Bayard Taylor was thirty-eight years old. He had written six volumes of verse, nine books of travel, some five hundred newspaper and magazine articles, and more personal letters than anybody could very well count. Further, he had edited a two volume cyclopædia, delivered a thousand lectures, built a fine house, married a second time, and was the father of two children. Still further, he had nearly finished a long poem, *The Picture of St. John*, and was beginning a much longer translation, Goethe's *Faust*. One might imagine that he was also beginning to feel tired, was beginning to sense an overwhelming futility with regard to the whole exacting business of literature, was beginning to look wistfully toward retirement and long days of peace. But such was not the case. He was looking, rather, in a new direction, was impatient to conquer still another rich field. He was ready to publish his first novel, *Hannah Thurston*.

It came out in November. Kennett Square is the scene of the story, thinly disguised as Ptolemy, New York. Into this town, which teems with reformers, comes Mr. Maxwell Woodbury, who has wandered, like Taylor, all over the world. He is personally attractive, also like Taylor, broad, suave, shallow, but civilized. He goes to several reformers' meetings. There are

Hunkers, Barnburners, Abolitionists—no Quakers!—Grahamites, Spiritualists, Prohibitionists, and Woman's Rights advocates, all snarling at one another, narrow, and despicable. Naturally, Mr. Woodbury is vexed.

But he is also attracted, strangely yet strongly, by Hannah Thurston, who is fighting for the freedom of her sex, who scorns cheap compliments, and who desires, pre-eminently, to dissect male torsos at a proposed female medical college. This is too much for Mr. Woodbury: he enters into a period of Pride and Prejudice. Hannah reciprocates. In time a platonic friend of the hero comes over from India and talks to Hannah, persuading her finally that too much serious campaigning for anything is bad. Hannah's pride and prejudice declines, and so does Woodbury's in turn. He pays court to her, writes a letter, Mr. Darcy fashion, explaining his motives and his past: he was once betrothed, but later rejected when his family's fortunes declined; he once felt a violent attachment for a married woman but—as we have seen—he kissed her only in farewell and holy repentence. Hannah forgives. Vows are plighted before her dying mother, and they marry soon afterwards. Woodbury later makes a speech in his wife's place in which he advocates the Victorian compromise; and as the story ends we learn that a child is born to Hannah—a child who will remind her always that, like Tennyson's Princess, her true place is in the home.

The similarities of this work with Jane Austen's novel and with Tennyson's poem seem too frequent

*Bayard Taylor in Northern Costume*

and obvious to be purely accidental. Taylor also adopts Fielding's manner of introducing chapters with a series of *which* clauses: "Chapter XV, which Comes near Being Tragic; Chapter XVIII, which Solves the Preceding One; Chapter XXIII, which contains both Love and Death," and so on. But the story suffers chiefly, one feels, because of a general lack of humor. Its groups of reformers inspire little except disgust. Detachment on the part of the author would probably have dictated the comic approach to his material; but in sober fact, Taylor had seen in his own neighborhood too much of the kind of narrowness he describes to feel amused by it, except sporadically. In his letters one finds frequent allusions to this narrowness; it really may to a considerable extent explain his early desire to get away to a New England school, to Europe, to New York. There was prejudice against a man's living by writing—witness the Agnew's opposition to his first marriage. There was violent prejudice against alcohol; there was violent prejudice against religious liberalism. And there was, in turn, a disposition to favor many of the perverted *isms* which accompany such prejudices—Spiritualism, Hunkerism, Phrenology, and Perfectionism. Largely as result of his travels, Kennett Square had become to him a narrow and unpleasant town, yet endeared to him in spite of this fact because of unnumbered memories of home.

In four months the book sold 15,000 copies. But not because of the review it received in the *Atlantic!* Who wrote this review it does not appear. It does appear, however, that the writer knew his Dr. Johnson well and thought well of the doctor's philosophy of the novel.[1]

To begin with: according to the *Atlantic*,[2] Taylor's subtitle, "A Story of American Life," is misleading, since no single town contains as many divergent types as he presents. His characters are conventional; there is nothing new in his sewing circles, in the small talk of the women, in his refined hero and noble heroine. But these complaints are incidental. A far graver fault is apparent in Taylor's implied criticism of foreign missions, "the most Christ-like movement," insists the reviewer, "ever originated by man." Taylor had said that in India there was hope for missions but that we must work there from the top down, starting, that is, with the Brahmin class. Religion doesn't attempt such an approach, the reviewer replied: Christ started from the bottom and worked upward.

To continue: Taylor is too complacent on the subject of drunkenness. Drunkenness "destroys hopes, desolates hearths, breaks hearts." No move against it, even a misdirected movement, should ever be discredited. The author in his novel, rather, should openly admit the evils of drink.

To conclude: Taylor should not satirize revivals. He pictures a sect, after a competitor had ended a successful meeting, staging one of its own in order to win back the new converts. Here, specifically, is the

1. Compare what follows with *The Rambler*, No. 4. "On the Modern Novel."
2. The reviewer was probably Howells. See Portia Baker, "Walt Whitman, and the Atlantic Monthly," *American Literature*, VI (Nov. 1934), 286.

danger of such writing: "Young feet, already wavering downward, will not be strengthened to pause, to steady themselves, but will rather be lured by the author's words," probably, into the devious ways of sin.

As an afterthought, this reviewer did concede that Taylor had done a creditably different kind of thing in portraying his heroine as strong-minded, austere in her faith, past her first youth, and given to public speaking." In brief, Taylor combines these traits with the conventional traits of purity and refinement. This, he concludes, is Taylor's distinctive contribution as a novelist.

But in other quarters, there was much cause for rejoicing about the novel. "Great is my triumph!" he wrote Martha Kimber, "I have now the opinions of J. G. and Elizabeth Whittier, Hawthorne, Lowell, Bryant, Harriet Prescott, and Mary Earle about *Hannah Th.* —all favorable. The sale is unabated. Conway writes from England that it has made a 'hit' there, and that he finds the book in every house he enters. Women readers are amazed at my knowledge of the female heart and nature! So after making all allowances which my own excessive modesty requires, I consider the book a success."[3]

The approval of the above-named critics was what really mattered. He replied to the *Atlantic* reviewer and to others who charged him with caricature by saying that he knew flourishing specimens of every type

3. *Unpublished Letters of Bayard Taylor* (Huntington Library Publications), J. R. Schultz, ed.

satirized. The book was published in London, and New York, as we have seen, and was translated and published in Germany and Russia. This, at the moment, was what really mattered. He worked away at his second novel.

The story of *John Godfrey's Fortunes* is told in the first person. It begins in John's sixteenth year. His father dies and his mother sends him away to boarding school. There he finds a cousin, Penrose, a cynical young man with a prim sister and a father who has taken the family cook for a second wife. John's mother dies. He goes then to Aunt and Uncle Woolley, to work in Woolley's General Store. Here he begins an interest in literature: he buys the poems of Milton, Collins, and Gray, and subscribes to the *Saturday Evening Post*. He is happy, is writing for the *Post* as "Selim," and has journeyed to Philadelphia to meet the editor; but this period of his life is ended when his uncle learns that he is a Lutheran and that he will not abandon that sect.

John teaches school in another town. His poetry is now appearing in the *Post*. He acknowledges his identity to Amanda, and they are soon in love. Then John goes to New York, to find work as a writer. He becomes a condenser of news and a general hack at six dollars a week. He meets certain Bohemians. He meets Swansford, a poet and musician who comes to his rooms on week-ends, to talk about poetry and other concerns of the spirit. He attends Mrs. Yorkton's literary soirées and hears a vast deal of shallow discourse on the subject of art. He meets Mr. Brandage, an arch poseur, who writes very little but talks exceedingly about the creative process and about literary people. John is living carelessly now because Amanda has jilted him, as the false Blumen jilted Teufelsdröckh, and he is trying hard to recover from a mood of ultimate tartarean despair.

He meets an heiress, Miss Haworth, whom her foster brother desires to marry, for the usual reasons. Godfrey seems about to outride this competition when the lady abruptly dismisses him. Later, it develops that the rival has told Miss Haworth that Godfrey kept a mistress. The truth was that he had rescued a poor girl, Jane Berry, from the most hideous of all fates; yet his attitude toward her had remained purely fraternal. But before this news reaches the heiress, Swansford dies and John loses himself again in the society of the despicable Bohemians. Jane, however, tells Miss Haworth the truth, Uncle Woolley leaves John a legacy, and he weds the heiress. His fortunes are now made, his wife having brought him $80,000. Their child, a son, they name John Swansford Godfrey.

There is much fairly good satire in this novel. Taylor especially enjoys the literary lady, Mrs. Yorkton. Here she is describing a visit of the muses:

"I feel the approach of Inspiration in every nerve; my husband often tells me he knows beforehand when I am going to write, my eyes shine so. Then I go upstairs to my *study*, which is next to my bedroom. It always comes on about three o'clock in the afternoon, when the wind blows from the south. I change my dress and put on a long white gown, which I wear at no other time, take off my stays, and let my hair down my back. Then I prance up and down the room as if I was possessed, and as lines come to me I dash them on the blackboard, one after another, and chant them in a loud voice. Sometimes I cover all four of the boards—both sides—before the inspiration leaves me. The frail body is overcome by the excitement of the soul, and at night my husband finds me lying on the floor in the middle of the room, panting—panting."[4]

Godfrey was alarmed at this description. Inspiration seemed about to ravish her in his very presence. But no: her hair was not down; she had not removed her stays. "I should think it must be very exhausting," he remarked.

" 'Killing!' she exclaimed with energy. 'I am obliged to take restoratives and stimulants after one of these visits. It wouldn't be safe for me to have a penknife in the room—or a pair of scissors—or a sharp paper cutter—while the frenzy is on me. I might injure myself before I knew it. But it would be a sweet, a fitting death. If it ever comes, Mr. Godfrey, you must write my 'Thanatopsis.' "[5]

Brandage added a little later that he didn't dare compose verses any more: he had ruptured a blood vessel in Paris, "caused by writing a poem on hearing a nightingale singing in the Rue Notre Dame de Lorette."

Elsewhere in the book there is a considerable account of the Bohemians, who meet at a beer cellar,

4. Household Edition (1888), p. 275.
5. *Ibid.*, p. 276.

"The Cave," plan magazines which are uniformly short lived, talk aimlessly, work very little, and fleece their acquaintances of whatever money extravagant promises and flattery can induce them to part with. The author's contempt for this group is hardly concealed. In still another place there is an excellent account of a revival meeting. Taylor's ability as a reporter doubtless assisted him here. There is also a pleasantly readable sketch of schoolboy pranks, played on the teacher. All four of his novels, it might be added, are fairly rich in local color.

One attitude which utterly disgusted Taylor was that of the critic who attempted to find autobiography in his works. Ticknor and Fields had announced *The Poet's Journal* as a confessional. He never quite got over it. "Why, oh why *did* you issue such an advertisement.... the newspapers are beginning to speak of my "Life Story," which is dreadful."[6] He dedicated *Hannah* to Putnam and complained in his letter "against the popular superstition that an author must necessarily represent himself in one form or another. I am neither, 'dear Putnam,' Mr. Woodbury, Mr. Waldo, nor Seth Wattles.... The intelligent reader will require no further explanation." But when he dedicated *John Godfrey* he assumed, shrewdly, that not all his readers were intelligent, and returned to the subject again: "Those who imagine that they recognized the author in Maxwell Woodbury, will not fail to recognize him in John Godfrey, although there is no resemblance between the two characters."

6. To Fields, 12-16-62. Taylor-Scudder, *op. cit.*, I, 404.

So it went. Smyth, one of Taylor's biographers, found "memories of FitzJames O'Brien in Mr. Brandage,"[7] and "at least one whimsy of Estelle Ann Lewis" in the portrait of Mrs. Yorkton. He might easily have gone on to find that Swanford was two-fifths Stoddard and that "The Cave" was two-fifths Pfaffs Beer Cellar. It is always pointed out that the highwayman in the *Story of Kennett* was a portrait of Fitzpatrick, an *actual* highwayman, that the hostler Dougerty was his *actual* accomplice, that the character Martha Dean was *really* Ruth Baldin, the character Deb Smith was *really* well-known in the town, that the house of Gilbert Potter, the hero of the *Story of Kennett, really* stood "two miles south of Kennett," that the characters Joe and Jake Fairthorn were *really* Taylor's father and uncle, and so on. Writers on Taylor to the present day are continuing this kind of thing. But what does such criticism matter, except to indicate the already amply indicated fact that Taylor's imagination was limited, largely, to obvious combinations of his experience? In his fiction, as in his other prose, he remained fundamentally the reporter.

Taylor wrote *John Godfrey's Fortu*nes in five months, and amid numerous interruptions. He finished it in August, 1864, published it the following November, simultaneously in New York and London. In March, 1866 his third novel was brought out. It was *The Story of Kennett*.

This is a historical novel, the action taking place in 1796. There are grave uncertainties about the identity

7. *Bayard Taylor*, p. 165.

of Gilbert Potter's father. His mother, Mary, will not allay them. Gilbert is a young man, trying to pay off the mortgage on his farm. He is also a young man deeply in love with Martha Dean, daughter of the town physician. But Doctor Dean thinks his Martha could do much better were she to marry Alfred Barton who, though in his forties, is the son of a hard old miser and the likely heir to his fortune.

The highwayman Sandy Flash is busy in the neighborhood. He is excellent with disguises and has already robbed Alfred Barton. Later, he robs Gilbert, when Gilbert is on his way to discharge the debt on his land. Posses seek him. News of this last villainy is too much for Deb Smith, a rough, queer woman whom Gilbert has often befriended. Deb is secretly married to Sandy, but she demands that Gilbert's money be returned. Sandy refuses, beats Deb, and Deb gives him over to the constable, in spite of the curse with which he threatens her.

Later old Barton dies, and the mystery of Gilbert's parentage is disclosed. The old man was in love with Gilbert's mother, but his son Alfred loved her also and ran off with her to Philadelphia. There they were married, Alfred extracting a promise from her to keep the fact suppressed until after his father's death. This often-looked-for event was twenty-six years happening, and when it did happen, and the will was read, it was found that $20,000 had been left to Mary. Alfred got only the farm. Gilbert and Martha married soon afterwards. Deb was found horribly dead, doubtless from Sandy's curse.

The plot of this novel is not its redeeming feature. Much more attractive are the characters of Old Barton, Deb Smith, and Sandy Flash, the pranks of the Fairborn boys, the accounts of huskings, barn raisings, and fox hunts, and the really moving, if half naïve, description of the "betrothal scene" between Gilbert and Martha.[8] There is a freshness about the story, a picturesque simplicity, a freedom from weak satire, which makes it still fairly readable—certainly the *most* readable of his four long works of fiction. In the summer of 1933 it was given in Kennett as a pageant and was extremely well liked.

*Joseph and his Friend* was not published until 1870. Its hero is an orphan, also working to pay off the mortgage on his farm. He meets Julia Blessing, a city visitor, and falls in love with her. He visits her family and is pressed into marriage. The family is poor, the head of it a visionary Beriah Sellers, with no small degree of Seller's eloquence and breeziness.[9] Joseph takes Julia back to the farm, where she immediately sets about running him into debt and injuring his reputation with their conservative neighbors. She also persuades him to invest in certain oil stocks her father is selling. His initial investment is by no means his last, and soon he finds his prospects heavily involved. His friend, Philip Held, provides his only comfort amid gathering domestic difficulties. Finally, Joseph confesses his hatred of Julia to a girl of the village. Julia overhears, rushes inside, takes arsenic, and dies.

8. Household Edition (1887), pp. 125-8.
9. *The Gilded Age*, of course, was not published until 1873.

Joseph is tried, and for a time the evidence seems all against him. It is believed that he poisoned his wife. But Philip, in time, handily brings to light a confirmation of the fact that Julia took arsenic in small doses to improve her complexion—unknown to Joseph, her real age was past thirty—and later a salesman recognizes her picture as that of a woman he saw buy the drug. Difficulties clear up, the oil stock isn't entirely worthless, the farm is saved, and though Joseph appears about to marry again as the story concludes, Philip realizes that nothing can ever displace their friendship entirely.

Bismarck read the novel and told Taylor afterwards that he allowed the villain, Mr. Blessing, to escape too lightly.[10] Joseph had merely advised his father-in-law to give up his promotion schemes and enter politics, which afforded perhaps a "higher area" for his talents. The distinguished German might have complained, further (though he did not), against the depressing drabness of his remaining characters, of a tendency on the author's part to stop and moralize heavily about the way young men should be brought up, and about other ordinary matters concerning which moralizing is usually a waste of patience and effort.

He might even have taken, had he been inclined, a more sweeping perspective of Taylor's entire work as a novelist, might have talked—after talk was pleasantly too late to be of any vulgar use—concerning his more general virtues and defects. Had he done all this he would doubtless have praised him for writing about

10. A. H. Smyth, *op. cit.*, p. 177.

what he knew, rather than about what he had tried to imagine. He would doubtless have acknowledged that there were, at least in one of the stories, some interesting and unusual characters. But justice would have constrained him to add that there were elsewhere many more decidedly wooden characters, that Taylor had almost uniformly failed to endow his work with a genuine significance, that he was quite often tedious in his narration, weak in his prose style, in the main deficient in humor, quarrelsome, only lamely satirical, unselective, and given unduly to conventional situations and to insipid heroes.

And withal he might have concluded—this Man of Iron—by saying that fundamentally there is a lack of intensity and vigor in this phase of his work, that it is in essence bloodless, passionless, and strangely thin in spite of its prolixity. And had he said this—not meaning to be harsh, not meaning to be bitter—Taylor himself might have taken comfort in the thought that he had concluded the same thing himself, years before, intuitively, when he wrote a rare and beautiful sentence in his second novel: "I have touched neither the deeps nor the heights: I have only looked down into the one and up towards the other, in lesser vibrations on either side of that noteless middle line which most men travel from birth to death."[11]

11. *John Godfrey's Fortunes*, p. 320.

# MONEY

## XIV

NOW, in the middle 1860's, he is a thriving country gentleman, writing his first long poem, planting, and entertaining constantly. "I have three hundred and sixty-three fruit trees to take care of, and any quantity of onions, beets, parsnips, and celery" to set out.... "Good-by! There are signs of the sky clearing, and I must air my hot beds." A fortnight later he heard that Stedman was ill. He must come to Cedarcroft to convalesce. The family is too busy to notice him much. "You will get neither wine nor much whiskey (Woe! Woe! the whiskey's low!). But come and be one of the household." Aldrich must visit him too—this relatively new friend who is creating such a stir in Boston. Labor is scarce and Taylor is working hard; he weighs only 190 now, but Cedarcroft is beautiful this May, Grant will soon be victorious, "and we rejoice."

The next year he was busier and more contented than ever. "The *Tribune* declared a dividend of $500 a share, besides laying by a surplus of $60,000. This gives me $2,500 [he owned five shares]."[2] Putnam had sent him another five hundred dollars as his quarterly copyright earnings. The *Atlantic* had sent $350 more for a story, an essay, and a poem. "The thorn"

1. To Fields, 4-25-64. Taylor-Scudder, *op. cit.*, II, 420.
2. To Stedham, 7-19-65. *Ibid.*, p. 438.

was pulled out of his breast. He was writing much better verse.

In fact, he decided, he was completing the second stage of his development as a poet, was entering into his third stage, a far grander consummation of his genius, perhaps the last he would ever know.[3] "Do you feel these transitions in your own work, George? You see, I have inherited from my Quaker ancestors a tendency to ripen, in an intellectual way, very slowly. I realize now that in 1855 I was ten years behind other writers of my physical age. But I am catching up with them.[4]

"You shall judge for yourself about all this when you read *The Picture of St. John*. It is a sustained achievement. I have thought of it for fifteen years. I even began work on it long ago, but stopped because I realized that more maturity was required to do the subject. This poem is exclusively my own. It will probably not be liked by the general public, but damn the general public. I am writing this time to establish myself alongside the truly illustrious names in American literature. I am working to become one with Bryant and Longfellow, with Lowell and Whittier. They shall appraise it."

And now, in October, 1866, the work upon which his faith had builded so grandly came out. He waited with the breathlessness of a child for the sovereign judgment (mighty to damn, but O mightier still to praise!) soon to thunder from the priesthood in New

3. To Boker, 8-21-65. *Ibid.*, p. 441.
4. See letters to Mrs. Stoddard, 10-5-62. *Ibid.*, I, 393-4, to Longfellow, 12-30-66; II, 465. They expressed this conviction often.

England. That judgment came—not thunderous, not awful, but sweet and kind, like the golden cool mists that transfigured his verdant lawn in late summer. "I congratulate you on having produced the best of your longer poems," wrote Bryant, "and that is no small praise." Longfellow's acknowledgment was apparently no more reserved, for when Taylor answered it, he said: "When you praise the poem for the very qualities I aimed to reach, you confirmed the hopes of my life." Lowell declared that "no American poem except the *Golden Legend* can match it in finish and sustained power." Holmes was pleased, and Whittier "marveled" at "its exquisite beauty and finish."[5] Taylor was, past all measuring, delighted. He had at length, he confessed, "won admission into that small company of American poets who have some chance of life."

The poem is in narrative form, running to some 3200 lines: St. John, the hero, is at first a youth in Renaissance Italy. He sees Veronese, Georgione, and Titian at work.[6] He is a student himself, torn between love for the celestial in art and love for the physical in his models. This latter force soon overwhelms him. He explores passion's delicious maze and finds his own pictures improved. He leaves Venice, and becomes a more adolescent Childe Harold, ravished more readily than Byron's hero by Architecture and the

5. See *Ibid.*, II, 466-8, *passim*.
6. Taylor's chronology is sadly awry here. The dates of these painters are: Titian, 1488-1576; Veronese, 1528-1588; Georgione, 1478-1510. Obviously his hero could not, as a youth, have seen Veronese and Georgione "painting the dames." Yet see stanza 24, *Poems*, p. 184.

creations of the "Saints of Art." His spirit kneels "unquestioning to their authority."

A lady, during his travels, threw a wreath to him as he passed her window. He painted her face from a dream. Her father saw the picture and engaged him to do the original. She is Clelia, about to wed a typical middle-aged count, Colonna.

How could this artist, once before her, content himself with painting merely "the mouth he burned to kiss"—a mouth so near him that "the airy wave her voice set free smote warm against my cheek"—so near, indeed,

*"I heard*
*The folds that hid her bosom, as they stirred*
*Above the heartbeat measuring now for me*
*Life's only music."*

He speaks to her at length. Now they are meeting in her garden by moonlight, now pledging an ageless pledge. And now she is pleading with her father Pandolfo to free her from her engagement to a wanton prince, pleading that, unwed, she may have one room in his lonely palace. Pandolfo refuses, goes to Rome, and she elopes with St. John.

They go to a chapel and wed themselves, "in lack of earth's ordinary rite." They go to a cold, rude home. Always it seems bleak there; his neighbors have been crushed to savagery by labor; they do not inspire him. When summer comes, a child, Angelo, is born. They live in this place for some years, until Clelia's death. The father and son then travel throughout Italy.

St. John is painting again. He is famous, one of the great artists, but he is saddened by the awareness that his son is growing to entertain only materialistic ambitions: he wants a "marble house," horse and hound, a golden sword, and the privilege of ruling men. And while his father meditates upon the implications of these desires, and is working upon an ambitious portrait of Angelo, the boy is kidnapped by his own grandfather.

Later, Angelo is killed accidentally when his father attempts to rescue him. Inevitably, art becomes "a Devilhood" to St. John. He does a picture of Evil. But this mood is interrupted; the child, in memory, haunts him again. Again he works at the picture, and when rebellion assails him once more, he hears in answer the voice which bewildered Job of old, and afterwards he is advised that sorrow is God's agency for making the artist in man ascendent. The poem ends with St. John reconciled and busy:

> *Not clamoring for over-human bliss*
> *Yet now no more unhappy—not elate*
> *As one exalted o'er the level state*
> *Of these ungifted lives, yet strong in this,*
> *That I the sharpest stab and sweetest kiss*
> *Have tasted, suffered—I can stand and wait,*
> *Serene in knowledge, in obedience free,*
> *The only master of my destiny.*

It is a very smooth, a very polished, thematically a very ordinary work. It is never brilliant, nor is it ever glaringly dull. Its language uniformly fails to approximate the inevitability of great verse. Its plot is not developed without considerable diffuseness, without frequent yieldings to the temptation to describe such things as the towns and cathedrals of Italy (Taylor never mastered, in prose or poetry, the impulse to be pictorial), but aside from these complaints the narrative itself is well sustained.

Yet one cannot but feel that the author brings no distinctive addition to the sadly overworked story of the artist who loses his love, plunges into despair, but finds a more enduring consolation later. It is true that Taylor does not allow this final consoling force to be another woman, as Poe did occasionally in his fiction, but substantially here are the same wounds, the same charms, the same ardors—in brief, the entire fixed series of conventions—which the romantic school has employed for decades. Except in the matter of length, the higher stage in his development Taylor spoke of is imperceptible. The cardinal fact about *The Picture* now is that it is dead to us. One suspects that it was born in disease, that a fragile prettiness (not Beauty, but Beauty's shadow, rather), devoid of content, cannot sustain through later generations a thing so unsubstantial as poetry.

## 2

Now Taylor must go abroad again for a well-earned rest! "My blood is thick and sluggish; I sleep badly, for the first time in my life, and have a general sense of discomfort, though I can't put my finger on one ailing spot."

One suspects that the elusive ailing spot was un-discoverable because merged with the stuff of his blood, that the idea of leisure had become incomprehensible to him. Travel was now a fever; denied, it raged in him and gave him no rest. A strange anomaly was here: he must rush about the planet aimlessly until exhausted. He lived by destroying himself. Cedarcroft was now finished, Cedarcroft was lovely, but no, we must all go to Germany. "Marie's mother complains of ill health." Any excuse would serve. Let me translate Mugge's Norwegian romance for you. I need a thousand dollars.[7] He hurried through Colorado, describing its wonders for the *Tribune*, organizing his descriptions later into book form, lecturing, raising money. In February, 1867, he sailed with his wife and daughter.

Taylor left enjoying the good will of every important American author who knew him, with perhaps a single exception. That exception was Stoddard. It is unpleasant to revive unpleasantness, but probably it is needful to point out that all was not entirely harmonious within the seeming inviolate world wherein Boker, Stedman, Taylor, Stoddard, and Aldrich stood out, like so many continents, to one another. Being in reality mortals, and not continents, they were often complaining, any two of them, about the villainies of a third. And it usually happened that this third was "Poor Dick," or simply "Stoddard," or "that idiot Stoddard," or "that damned morbid Stoddard," ac-

7. See letter to Stedman, 5-21-66. Taylor-Scudder, *op. cit.*, II, 459.

cording, of course, to the measure of his insolence at the moment and to the humanity of him who had been offended.

Stoddard's life had not been enviable. His forebears had lived in Hingham, Massachusetts, since 1638, but his father had died when he was very young, leaving his mother in poverty. A small boy, rheumatic, he was taken to Boston and sent only occasionally to school. His early recollections of his mother were of her washing and doing general "slop work" for sailors. The first poem he remembered reading was Willis' "The Widow and her Son."

His mother married again, and they went to New York. He attended a private school for five years. Then, at 15, he was put to work as a shop boy, at one dollar a week. A year or so later he learned the blacksmith's trade, later the trade of iron moulding. At the end of three years his salary was $3.25 a week. Here he worked until 1853, when he was made inspector of customs at the Port of New York. His salary was three dollars a day, and he was married. But he fared no better until 1870, when he was discharged abruptly. And then for a time he fared even worse.

Obviously, Stoddard couldn't afford to travel. He couldn't even run up to Boston occasionally, assuming he desired to. But one suspects that he didn't. He admits that he was diffident. He was also abnormally sensitive, not brilliant, not jovial, as Taylor was, but more exacting, more critical, sterner, at times stubborn and sullen, at times even morbid, envious of a friend's success. Besides, he felt that his wife was writing "the best blank verse in America." He knew that her novels about New England, *The Morgensons, Temple House,* and *Two Men,* were splendid things. Yet she received little popular recognition. This embittered him. Hawthorne and Lowell praised her work, but that didn't help. "She was not cursed with mediocrity," he wrote in old age, "but had the misfortune to be original." He was still bitter, perhaps justly.

As a critic, he believed—unlike Taylor and Longfellow and most of their literary acquaintances—that the fact of friendship should not be permitted to influence one's estimate of a friend's work. Here was the shoal on which, to his contemporaries, Stoddard was constantly floundering. It was inexcusable, they thought. After all, what is criticism anyhow but a cabalistic ritual your well-wishers exercise in print in order to cajole ordinary buyers into purchasing your book? The sole excuse for public comment is this kind of subtle advertising. For God's sake, if you can't praise, be silent! See what an ass Poe made of himself, through forgetting this one simple convention.

Well, Stoddard forgot it too, not once but often. Like Poe (who had charged *him* with plagiarism, shouting down his denial with "You lie, damn you! get out of here or I'll throw you out!"), Stoddard charged his friends with it—Taylor[8] and Aldrich[9] especially.

One of Lowell's volumes of verse, *Under the Willows* (1868), served as an occasion for bringing these critical differences to the surface. When the volume came

8. Taylor to Aldrich, 3-16-66. *Cornell Univ. Mss.*
9. Aldrich to Taylor, 11-29-77. *Cornell Univ. Mss.*

out, Stedman reviewed it very favorably for the *Post* and sent a clipping of his review to Taylor. "I read it," Taylor wrote, "with the greatest satisfaction. You have found the right track. I have always believed in Lowell. . . . and my present conviction is that he stands at the head of our literature. . . . nothing delights me so much as a criticism which is at once analytic, penetrating, and sympathic—which is the character of this of yours. . . . Dick [Stoddard] has sent me his *Albion* notice, with which I don't agree. While there is truth in his charge of ruggedness and occasional want of finish, he does not do justice to the splendid qualities of Lowell's genius. The article has a depreciatory air, which I am sorry to notice. Lowell has not had his due of recognition—and perhaps cannot have from the mass—and we, who know what he is, ought therefore to be all the more free and unstinted in our appreciation."[10]

"We ought to be all the more free and unstinted in our appreciation." Here was the whole story epitomized. Stoddard felt, doggedly (this is not a defense of his critical theories) that dishonesty in criticism was never excusable, not even for the best of reasons. Taylor tried to change his mind, but got only the following paragraph in answer:

"To answer your strictures on my notice of Lowell: in one word, the difference between you and me is, that you think a man should not be criticized much, at any rate not to his disadvantage, *after* he has made

10. Taylor to Stedman, 12-4-68. *Unpublished Letters of Bayard Taylor* (Huntington Library, Pub., J. R. Schultz, ed.).

a certain reputation, while I hold the exact contrary. The reputation of no artist is saved, in my eyes, when he writes badly. Lowell is a damned bad artist, and I said so frankly. I should have said the same of you, under the circumstances, and you would have liked it not at all."[11]

Stoddard talked more broadly, and more damagingly, about his fellow poets in his *Recollections*. T. B. Read gave him a text: "That Read was a poet there can be no doubt, but his poetry was a gift, not an art, and he failed in accomplishing what was clearly within his limitations through his inaptitude for reflection, investigation, and study. . . . Predominance of the fanciful over the imaginative was the poetic vice of the period here, and Read reveled in it, carried away by the example of its master, Longfellow, who was never so much himself as when he was indulging in a profusion of similes." Now Taylor would have sanctioned this judgment of Read, and Boker would have sanctioned it, as we have seen. But neither Taylor nor Boker would have entertained the idea of writing it out for the public. That was heresy.

What was so incredible about it all was the fact that Lowell had warned Stoddard against criticizing the Olympians years before—in 1850. Stoddard had managed to get to Boston that year, and he had also managed to summon courage enough to call on Lowell. He was kindly received. And who are your favorite poets, Mr. Stoddard? The timid lad liked Keats and Milton. Do you know Pope and Thompson? Vaguely.

11.  Stoddard to Taylor, 12-8-68. *Cornell Univ. Mss.*

That is unfortunate, Mr. Stoddard; you must learn to appreciate the historical position of *The Seasons*. Stoddard's frankness made him blurt out the opinion that "the Eighteenth Century writers had no idea what poetry was." And how would *you* define poetry then? The young man liked Milton's definition: "simple, sensuous, and passionate." He then moved nearer home, much nearer. He objected to comparisons in poetry. There is too much of this in Longfellow; for example, to call stars "the forget me nots of the angels" is to be very kind to the angels but very unkind to astronomy. Then, too, there is the "Beleagured City." It is filled with murky allegory. And there is an inexcusable predilection in Longfellow to moralize. It is ruining our young poets.

Oh, but my dear young man! You must remember that poets do what they can, and we have to take things for what they are! But even this ultimate utterance failed to demolish the fervent iron moulder. What Lowell had said was true, he admitted, "but when we have taken a poet for what he is, we have a right to judge him for what he is not." They parted. "Read Dante and Goethe," said Lowell, all radiant complaisance, in farewell.[12]

He read Dante and Goethe, all right, but they failed somehow to mellow his judgment of Longfellow. In a medley of prose and verse, published in 1882, Stoddard complained of the same shortcomings, and this time it was Whittier who was saddened: "I sometimes

12. *Recollections*, p. 212. Except where otherwise indicated the present discussion of Stoddard is based on this book, *passim*.

take exceptions to thy critical estimate of some of dear Longfellow's poems,' he wrote, "which may not be the equal of others, but which I like too well to find any fault with."[13] To the end, like Matthew and Waldo, the gentle Quaker stood guardian of the faith.

There was one other respect in which Stoddard appears to have differed from Taylor and most of his friends. He despised affectation. Once, shortly after Taylor's return from Japan, he came to Stoddard's home "in high glee, with a flask of wine which he had obtained on board a Greek vessel. He said that Homer had drunk of it, and when it was opened and we had tasted it, I wondered at the taste, not to say the courage, of Homer; for the 'Homeric beverage,' as he named it, was execrable. He stood up for it as long as he could, and tried to persuade himself that he liked it, but we laughed him out of his supposed liking and made him confess it was horrid stuff. He had his little enthusiasms, which he insisted on my sharing with him, though I fought against them strenuously. I tried once to smoke a Nargileh in his room, but I could not do it. Neither could he, when he set about it seriously."[14]

Again, it would be Taylor's pretensions in philology which irritated his friend. Taylor, he wrote, "was in the habit of making pilgrimages to Cambridge. He preferred Lowell, I think, to all the Gamaliels at whose feet he sat during these reverential visits, and he exploited for my benefit certain acquisitions that he

13. *Ibid.*, p. 294.
14. R. H. Stoddard, "Reminiscences of Bayard Taylor," *Atlantic Monthly*, 43 (1879), 242 ff.

made on those occasions, mostly in old English philology, wherein he was a novice."[15]

These incidents are in one sense slight enough, but in another they appear to indicate between the two men a rather fundamental difference in character, a difference which might, on the occasion of some incidental dispute, mount to outrageous proportions. At any rate, they were often in sad disagreement.

In May, 1860, Taylor had advised Boker not to lend money to Stoddard. The fellow is shiftless. It took me six months to get back a short term loan of five hundred dollars.[16] In April, 1865, they had an open dispute, and Stoddard was avoiding him. "When I do see him he abuses me. I remain passive. I shall let him go this winter, if he does not voluntarily make amends."[17] This unhappiness ran on into September; Taylor continuing to regret it. Boker consoled him. "I cannot understand this nursing a wrath [on Stoddard's part]. It is not my nature to sympathize with a man who turns a frowning face against the smiles of his friends, or refuses the hand that is extended him in reconciliation.... Let him go, my dear Bayard. His friendship is not worth the sigh that you shall send after it."[18] Christmas, 1865, it seemed that they would be cordial again: "Lizzie [Mrs. Stoddard] is as amiable as the born devil in her will permit. Dick is the same old simple hearted fellow."[19] In March they

15. *Recollections*, p. 102.
16. *Cornell Mss.*, 5-28-60.
17. *Ibid.*, Taylor to Stedman, 4-8-65.
18. *Ibid.*, 9-28-65.
19. *Ibid.*, Taylor to Boker, 12-27-65.

were once more estranged: "The utter indifference of the Stoddards toward myself this winter has cured me of any deeper feeling towards them. . . . The fact is, they've been over petted, over indulged by the rest of us."[20]

Taylor wrote Aldrich with more frankness. Lizzie, he said, "is hopelessly diseased, mentally and morally, and Dick, absorbed, dreamy, unpractical as he is, does not—in fact *cannot*—see her condition, but succumbs to her influence."[21] Lizzie had also offended Graham, the publisher.

In the spring of 1871 there was still another coolness. The Stoddards heard that the Taylors were going to Boston and planned to accompany them. Would Aldrich please write the Taylors a note, saying that he had planned lavish entertainment for them, a note which they could show the Stoddards and so get rid of them?[22] Fall brought a fresh dispute, "but really, George, we cannot feel any permanent anger against such a 'monstrous fool' as Lizzie. She told me yesterday that she had written you for some whiskey!"[23]

In this last case Stoddard had cause to quarrel. He had written Taylor in August, suggesting that a number of imitations and nonsense verses which they had done some years before with Fitz-James O'Brien be collected and printed "as the work of a new poet. I seriously think the wild stuff we have written would pass for serious art, if put before the public as such, and I would like to see the fools fall into the trap. What

20. *Ibid.*, 3-16-66.   21. *Ibid.*, Taylor to Aldrich, 3-16-66.
22. *Ibid.*, 3-20-71.   23. *Ibid.*, 12-8-71.

say you?"[24] Taylor probably got from this note the idea of publishing his own parodies in the *Atlantic*. They appeared there, in series, under the title "Diversions of the Echo Club." Stoddard complained, naturally, that his own poems were thus rendered worthless, since novelty was their major asset. He thought that Taylor should have informed him of his intention.

**3**

In March, 1867, Taylor reached England. He called on "dear old Barry Cornwall." He met Matthew Arnold. "He is a man to like, if not love, at first sight. . . . After Thackeray, I think I could soon come to like him better than any other Englishman. . . . I went to Browning, who had sent me a pleasant note of invitation. . . . He had *St. John* on the table." That evening he met Dante Gabriel Rossetti. At a breakfast the next morning came the historian, Froude, and the Duke of Argile ("Do you know,' he said to me, 'that *you* are the cause of Tennyson's visit to Norway? After he read your book he could not rest until he went there himself!' ") He also met Byron's grandson, Lord Wentworth, and the Bishop of Oxford. "I might have floated a month or so (with money and inclination) on the top wave of London society, but after the poets it would have been a descent. One thing, however, does pleasantly tickle my vanity: I am weak enough to feel it, yet frank enough to confess it. I have made myself a footing in England, in the last four or five years." My books are selling remarkably

24. *Ibid.*, 8-26-71.

here, and "from the authors I have the kindest and most cheering words." Thackeray's daughter Anne, "one of the dearest and best girls in the world, says she knows *Hannah Thurston* by heart!"

This letter to Stedman was one of the most interesting Taylor ever wrote. He visited Tennyson at Farringford (Remember, all this is private, my friend—things that I can't publish but wish to note as I go along) "The Laureate was delightfully free and confidential. I would write you much of what he said, but it was so inwrought with high philosophy and broad views of life that a fragment here and there would not fairly represent him. After dinner we left the ladies, retired to his study at the top of the house, lit pipes, and talked of poetry. He asked me if I could read his 'Boadicea.' I thought I could, I told him. Read it and let me see! he exclaimed. I would rather hear you read it! I answered. He did so, chanting the lumbering lines with great unction. I spoke of the idyl of Guinevere as being perhaps his finest poem. I told him I could not read it aloud without my voice breaking down at certain passages. 'Why I can read it and keep my voice!' he exclaimed triumphantly. I doubted this, and he agreed to try, after we went down to our wives.

"We first had drinks of thirty year old sherry, two glasses apiece. It was incomparable wine, meant, said Tennyson, 'to be drunk by Cleopatra, or Katherine of Russia.' Then he said to me, 'tonight you shall help me drink one of the few bottles of my Waterloo —1815.' Later, the bottle was brought and we all four had a glass. Then Tennyson began reading 'Guinevere.' His reading is a strange monotonous chant with unexpected falling inflections which I can't describe but which I can imitate perfectly. I became very much excited as he went on. Finally, when Arthur forgives his queen, Tennyson's voice fairly broke. I found tears on my cheeks. Marie and Mrs. Tennyson were crying, one on either side of me. He made an effort and went on to the end, closing grandly.

" 'How can you say,' I asked, 'that you have no surety of permanent fame? This poem will only die with the language in which it is written.' Mrs. Tennyson started from her couch. 'It is true!' she exclaimed. 'I have told Alfred the same thing.' "[25]

Though this was probably his most interesting letter, it proved also to be his most troublesome. It was terribly troublesome! For all his warning to Stedman, that friend could not resist passing such a juicy bit of gossip about among his choice acquaintances. And a certain lady—now "a thousand times damned," if God listeneth to prayer—allowed a certain reporter to copy the part about Tennyson. It was published in due time as a "lively piece of literary gossip." And in due time Tennyson read it. He was naturally abashed and disgusted, and in indirect fashion he conveyed the state of his feelings to Taylor. It was the first time Taylor had heard of the publication.

He was hopping mad! Oh God, Stedman! Stedman explained that he had all confidence in the lady, elaborated the old story of betrayal. He wrote Tennyson

25. Taylor-Scudder, *op. cit.*, 3-11-67, II, 471-5.

an apology. Taylor wrote a most abject apology. Fields wrote to supplement Taylor's apology. Still the Laureate grumbled.

Two years afterwards, Taylor was still wretched about the matter. "The practice of writing personal accounts of the lives of authors and artists is, as you know, an utter abomination to me. I talked upon this very subject with Mr. Tennyson when I was at Farringford, and he cannot suspect me of having knowingly allowed my account of my visit to be published, without the inference that I must be one of the meanest hypocrites in the world. I should be wanting in even vulgar tact (to measure the thing by the lowest standard)in doing an act which would justly shut the doors, not only of Farringford but of every English gentleman's house against me."

Tell me, Fields, "should I not publish a brief statement of the whole thing over my name? Would such a note be copied in England and help to set me right? Really the outrage of that damned, a thousand times damned woman, may affect my intercourse with all English authors. It is mortifying enough that Tennyson suspects me of making a paragraph out of him. He ought to know me better, even in two days."[26]

After the proper letters were written, Stedman was ready to brush the incident from his conscience. He advised Taylor to do the same thing. "If 'that Tennyson' be a reasonable man, he must be entirely satisfied with your explanation.... I talked the matter over with Fields, and he thought, with me, that nothing

26. *Cornell Univ. Mss.*, 2-26-69.

more could or should be done. He will go over there in April, and perhaps you should write him also, asking him to assist in fixing it up."[27]

Taylor remained in Europe until September, 1868. He wrote his usual letters for the *Tribune*, and he wrote a series of papers for the *Atlantic*—later collected as *By-Ways of Europe*. Another experience before his return was frightening. In Venice, in November, 1867, he had been stricken with a fever; and for weeks it seemed that he might die there—there in the same house, in Casa-Guidi, where Mrs. Browning had died six years before. He recovered slowly. He arose chastened. For the first time in his life he had confronted, intimately, the awful fact of his own death— that far-too-hateful compulsion, that ineluctable reality with which all his endeavor, when the next decade ended, was to merge in mysterious ultimate oneness.

27. *Cornell Univ. Mss.,* 3-11-69. Taylor was not the first American writer to abuse the hospitality of English hosts by published accounts of visits with them. Obviously, in his case, the publication was accidental. But Willis deliberately offended and was roundly condemned by Lockhart (Beer, *op. cit.*) and Mrs. Sigourney was even more guilty in her detailed account of Southey's insanity (Haight, *op. cit.*, p. 67).

# FAUST

## XV

THROUGHOUT the years 1869 and 1870 Taylor's major concern was with *Faust*. He was translating the poem *in the original meters*, an achievement before unheard of. His ambition was no less than to produce *"the* English *Faust,"* and he addressed himself to it with a thoroughness and an industry remarkable even for him. A labor of love, he called it; and it was a labor for which he was qualified, all things considered, more ably perhaps than was any other translator of the century in America.

But there was no virtue, to this many-sided man, in blinding oneself to what went on in the world, even when one's narrow private interest could be termed of supreme importance. And so, as always, he was busy with matters not related in the least to Goethe—with occasional articles for the *Atlantic*, with an extended preface to what he desperately hoped to be his last travel book, *By-Ways of Europe*, with acquiring more land, with lectures, with his last novel, and with many, many letters to friends, old and new.

One of these new friends was Paul Hamilton Hayne, a Southerner who had lost his home when Sherman marched to the sea, and who was now living in a log hovel near Augusta, writing the poems and reviews by which he had resolved to live or starve. Taylor and Boker seemed to him, without doubt, enthroned among the nation's great. With Boker he had written the essay "American Sonnets and Sonneteers," which appeared in Hunt's and Lee's *Book of the Sonnet*.[1] He had exchanged opinions with him on Swinburne, and had learned that to the Philadelphian, as to Taylor, this new English poet was "absolutely foul," that he had probably never entertained "a wholesome thought in his life," and that he had doubtless received all his perverted ideas about passion "from a secret vice of his own and from the struggles of copulating cats." One of Swinburne's favorite writers, Boker added, was "the Marquis du Sad, the author of the very vilest book that ever was written [*Justine*]. An imp of Hell, who had practiced Onanism from all eternity, could not have conceived of such a thing as that book is from beginning to end."[2]

In March, 1869, Taylor wrote Hayne out of gratitude for a kindly notice of his poems. "I place little value upon what is called 'popularity,' since it is generally based on the more obvious qualities of poetry .... I almost think that the real excellence of a poem is in inverse ratio to its popularity."

Hayne was grieved because all his books had been burned during the war. Taylor will send him copies of his own poems. "If I had been with Sherman's army, I would have tried hard to save your library and Simms's[3] also. I am so near the (former) border

1. See J. B. Hubbell, "Some Unpublished Letters," *American Literature*, V (1933), 147.
2. *Ibid.*, 149, 4-15-67.
3. William Gilmore Simms.

that while I was in Russia during the war, my parents, just before the battle of Gettysburg, buried all my manuscripts. If my place had been sixty miles farther westward, my books would have gone too. But I trust we shall all outlive the scars of these late terrible years."[4]

He was even, once, to give Hayne some heartfelt advice; and had Taylor lived he might have wondered why the Southerner did not take it. "Believe me, my dear Hayne, that I fully understand and sympathize with your isolation. Son of the South as you are, I must tell you that the South is no place for a born poet. It will be fifty or one hundred years before literature can take root in your soil. The very feelings and interests which make you *most* Southern are just those which impede the growth of true art among you. Don't be offended!—God knows, I write this in sorrow. And I don't mean you, personally, but your public: this you will take for granted. The *readers* are here in the North."[5]

What Hayne thought of this paragraph is not known. It would imply that a poet, like Burns for example, should have left his country because it was poor, should perhaps have gone up to London, or at least to Edinburgh, where the *readers* were. But Hayne chose to remain in the South, and one feels that whatever is enduring in his poetry is, somehow, a consequence of that choice.

4. Taylor-Scudder, 3-6-69, *op. cit.*, II, 510.
5. *Unpublished Letters of Bayard Taylor* (Huntington Library Publication), J. R. Schultz, ed.

Letters of a more spicy nature Taylor was writing and receiving from Stedman, now that the Tennyson episode was settled. What do you think of Mrs. Stowe's new book, *Lady Byron Vindicated?* Do you really suppose those scandalous things she says about Byron can be true—that amazing section about his half sister, for example?

Stedman was philosophic. "For my part," he declared, "I think Lady Byron a jealous virtuous prude, terribly thrown off her basis by Byron's Bohemianism, which she could never comprehend. I think Mrs. Stowe a gossipping green old granny. I don't believe that Byron cuddled his sister, but I think his genius would have justified such an operation—if anything would. Probably there is no doubt that Lady Byron suspected him of it—in fact the Count Johannes, in this morning's *Herald,* says that Byron defended himself, to Stanhope, for this very accusation. On the whole, let us hope that Byron was guilty; it will add another most dramatic page to the History of Incest. And yet Byron's attachment to his sister has always seemed to me the purest and whitest portion of his life."[6]

2

But these letters, though delightful and stimulating, proved during this period to be bright interludes only, interludes which served but to blanket in denser shadow the teeming disappointments that were wearing away his strength. Oh the senseless whirlwind of this world, which scatters our plans and destroys us!

6. *Cornell Mss.,* 9-1-69.

Mother, I must be rid of this house. I am tired of working so hard to keep up a place which gives me no return. During my last trip to Europe it cost me five thousand dollars in maintenance. It was a mistake to purchase that additional land from McFarland: I have been unable to sell any of my own. I am burdened; the many losses of this year come heavy upon me, and my health suffers. Since Cedarcroft was built I have had but two years of tolerable freedom from care. If only I could have known what changes were to come in this land, if only I could have known how vicious my neighbors would be, I would not have built at all. My pleasure in the place is spoiled by the drain upon me. It is wrong to live in this way, sacrificing the prime of life to a hollow sentiment. "Few men of my age have gone through so much, or done harder work; and it is time that this continual wear and tear must come to an end."[7]

What sharpened his grief in particular? Certainly, to an extent, his neighbors. One, a power in local politics, thought that a road should be cut through Taylor's land, and for a time this "improvement" seemed inevitable. He was now unpopular with the Quakers of the town; he did not belong to their Society; he entertained visitors who drank whiskey; he himself drank whiskey; he seemed rich and therefore, in their eyes, evil; he openly scorned their prejudices; he had said, in effect, that their most zealous reformers were asinine.

But it was all saddening to him—so despicable,

7.  To his mother, 10-6-70. Taylor-Scudder, *op. cit.*, II, 536.

mean, and vulgar! He wanted friends everywhere, wholesome, intelligent friends, who were not jealous of another's successes, who, rather, helped one another along, who believed that another's happiness made for happiness in themselves. Why couldn't sane men live in harmony? Why must ignorance and vindictiveness blight the ineffable flower of brotherhood?—oh God, why cannot love conquer hate?

His neighbors, sad circumstance, proved that love did not conquer hate, however readily it should. Finally, he went before them in meetings.[8] He pleaded with them. He talked to them about art and beauty. He talked to them about mortality. There was a place for reform, he said, but it should not blind the reformer. A man is vaster than any single institution which can pretend to remake him. Let us be kind to one another, generous, tolerant. They remained unregenerate, as before.

At length he despaired. Education was powerless in Kennett Square. He would leave the town to the devils who had damned it.

In April, 1870, he delivered six lectures on German literature at Cornell University. This was about the only profitable speaking he did that year. The members of a literary society in San Francisco invited him to the state for another tour: he could give twenty-five addresses, at least, in the small towns; he could deliver half a dozen more in their own city. It would be quite profitable, they could assure him.

Now Taylor had learned, only a few years before,

8. *Ibid.,* II, 515.

that a Californian's assurance took color from his sun-
sets and had a way, in practice, of not fulfilling itself
at all. But he was desperate! Besides, after two months
of labor, he could rest again—delicious thought! He
started out with Mrs. Taylor. On the new transcontinental railroad it was now only a seven days trip!

Six weeks later he was home again, disgusted. "I
have been hideously deceived. The population in California is the deadest I ever saw. Nobody, now, seems
to read a book, or go to a lecture, except a small class
in San Francisco."[9] He had not earned a cent. He had
lost five hundred dollars. "I shall lecture no more."

The reasons for this waning interest in the Lyceum
appear fairly evident. The 1840's have been often mentioned as a decade characterized especially by endless
political and social and moral discussions. To a people
newly awakened to the fact of their imminent exalted
destiny ideas were interesting, arguments of greatest
moment, since upon the issues of argument the future
of a republic hung trembling. What course America
would take in its development had by no means been
settled; anything seemed possible, and lacking a criticism, the product of an established order, anything
was listened to—and anybody—indeed, many bodies
to whom a strictly reasonable and efficient Deity might
well have denied voices altogether.

Would the frontier win out in its struggle for political dominance? Would the South be able to maintain its strength? Would slavery? What of the rising
importance of New England and the slavery of a dif-

9. *Ibid.*, To Fields, 10-25-70., II, 529.

ferent kind, more subtle, which was developing there, insidiously but swiftly? What of the women, who are clamoring for equality? How shall we settle the temperance question? And is it true that the phrenologist, by feeling the bumps of one's head, can predict with blind certainty the way a man will live, and what he will do? Can true Shakers talk with angels? Can Perfectionists? And will education save us all? Will Graham flour save us? Or will the world end next year before we can eat enough Graham flour, as that dismal but terrifying Mr. William Miller declared it would? Gentlemen of the platform, tell us!

Then gold in California, mountains after mountains of it, clear river beds that dazzled your eyes with it, and the transcontinental railroad, and the South prostrate and vanquished. And then the giants of industry, terrific monsters, stalking the land, staking it, branding and gutting it by bribing the government which controlled it. Money was master, and the black-bearded general who shattered Henry Adams' faith in evolution sat enthroned in the White House, squat and contented. America's future was irretrievably mapped out; and so suddenly had the miracle happened that Taylor was left in blank bewilderment, helpless, knowing only that money meant power, and that he himself was woefully plagued because of his torturing lack of it.

There was simply no further point in speaking, or in listening to speeches. The slavery question was settled. The world hadn't ended. The Union was saved. Diet didn't matter. And that moralist who decried political shoddiness, or even business shoddiness, was aware of knowing winks and nudges, even titters and snorts, from the average dandyish but lusty audience he tricked into a cynical toleration of his message.

### 3

Yet he would do one more thing for this apostate age. He would fling against its adamantine materialism the greatest work of the greatest German poet. He would give it *Faust*. He would confront the force of chaos and darkness with the greater force of civilization. Part I of the drama came out in December, 1870, Part II the following March. The translation deserves to be classified with Longfellow's *Dante*, Bryant's *Homer*, Norton's *Via Nouva*, and Cranch's *Virgil*.

These works are significant. They represent, perhaps, the culmination of a movement a century and a half old, as old as William Byrd, a movement which has grown out of the deeply spiritual conviction that the old world, for all its many villainous incrustations, held something which no civilized person could do without, held a food as necessary to his sustenance as bread and drink, offered a perspective without which there can be no maturity. They represent, to put it differently, a quest for completeness, for philosophy, for the abundant life.

Irving, as we have noted, was among the first to undertake a general indoctrination of his people. He saw Europe in terms of happy peasants, cheerful, eccentric landlords; in terms of ruined grandeur, flooded by wistful moonlight and steeped in still-echoed romance. Willis saw it at times as a glittering bazaar, at other times as the home of brilliant conversation and manners and elegant dress. To Longfellow it was a place of strange sculpture, of legends, of Gothic towers and quaint towns and prayer. To Lowell it meant literature and art.

These are but a few of many who did, in their own peculiar ways, what Taylor had been doing now for a quarter of a century. They worked against odds, as all men work who would enrich the cultural heritage of a race; they did not work with financial indifference, but they brought, to those who would have it, the one thing for which America was famished then—perhaps is famished still.

Taylor had a theory of translation. He believed that the translator's personality, his "tastes and habits of thought," should never obtrude in the finished work. He believed that a nearly equal knowledge of both languages was essential. He believed that only a poet could translate a poet—in fact only a poet should attempt to. He believed that if the language admits of it ("as English does of German") the metrical form of the original work should be preserved, line for line —when possible, foot for foot.[10]

He was most emphatic on this question of form. Indeed, as a writer of verse, form had always been a consideration of cardinal importance to him. He never had very much to say, as a poet; his content, as we have seen, was usually derived and conventional; he was no thinker; but this does not mean that he was

10. See preface to Part I. Oxford (World's Classics), 1932. See also Juliana Haskell, *Bayard Taylor's Translation of Goethe's Faust* (Columbia, 1908), pp. 19-21.

no artist. And so he declares, with no mean insight: "Poetry is not simply a fashion of expression: it is the true form of expression absolutely required by a certain class of ideas. Poetry indeed may be distinguished from prose by a single circumstance: it is the utterance of whatever in man cannot be uttered in any other rhythmical form. It is useless to say that the naked meaning is independent of the form: on the contrary the form contributes essentially to the fullness of the meaning. In poetry which endures through its own inherent vitality, there is no forced union of these two elements. They are as intimately blended, and with the same mysterious beauty, as the sexes in the ancient Hermaphroditus. To attempt to represent poetry in prose, is very much like attempting to translate music into speech."[11]

This is all very fine—excellent criticism—but when Taylor rides his theory so hard as to allow himself to match iambics and trochaics and anapests with his master he seems nigh to producing a *tour de force*. For form is not wholly a matter of poetic feet: it may be wrought inextricably into the conceptual phase of the work in question; it may depend upon the mental sequences of the artist himself; it may be simply a manifestation of the mind of the artist in words—in words which, because of the most primary racial difference, can never pretend to communicate with completeness to a foreigner the author's own reading of life.

In other words, Taylor seems to have been led to

11.  Preface to Part I, xxxvii-xxxviii.

believe that (assuming entire success with the ordinary issues involved) through an imitation of Goethe's metrics he could surmount the one insuperable difficulty of all translation: he could give to English readers precisely what Goethe had given to German readers. Of course, had he succeeded perfectly, the major problem of all communication would have remained as baffling as before: the fact would have persisted, sadly, that no artist can with exactitude convey his vision to another person, even to another artist, because the intellectual and emotional associations of no two human beings are identical. But this last awareness is rooted in pessimism, and Taylor was anything but a pessimist. He therefore allowed it to give him no pause, no discouragement. He saw one problem, the metrical problem, and concluded that, were he to conquer it, the dense mystery would unfold itself. I do not say that he made his translation the worse thereby. He merely assigned himself an infinite deal of mostly unnecessary labor. Yet, as a result, he made of his edition something of a literary curiosity. And indeed, in so far as form *is* rooted in metrics, he communicated it to his readers.

What persuaded him to attempt a reproduction of the original meters he indicated plainly in his Preface. "It is true that the metrical foot into which the German language most naturally falls is the *trochaic,* while in English it is the *iambic;* it is true that German is rich, involved, and tolerant of new combinations, while English is simple, direct, and rather shy of compounds; but precisely these differences are so modified in the German of *Faust* that there is a mutual approach to the two languages. In *Faust* the iambic measure predominates; the style is compact; the many licenses which the author allows himself are all directed towards a shorter mode of construction. On the other hand, *English meter compels the use of inversions*,[12] admits many verbal liberties prohibited by prose, and so inclines towards various flexible features of its sister-tongue that many lines of *Faust* may be repeated in English without the slightest change of meaning, measure, or rhyme..... I am satisfied that the difference between a translation of *Faust* in prose or meter is chiefly one of labor—and of that [kind of] labor which is successful in proportion as it is joyously performed."[13]

One other point deserves notice. Taylor apparently overestimated the number of inversions one finds in English poetry. As a matter of fact (if one may indulge once more in the luxury of generalization) long before Wordsworth spoke of the business of poetry being to imitate the language of everyday life, our important poets had largely observed that principle, so long as it related to sentence construction. Even in the case of those who wrote usually in the couplet—Waller, Dryden, Pope, Goldsmith, and Crabbe, for example— inversions are comparatively rare, so rare that an attentive reader is at once arrested by them. The pertinence of this truth, with respect to Taylor's translation, is that there seem to be an overabundance of inversions in it. They mar the sense of naturalness in

12.  Biographer's italics.      13.  Preface, Part I, xliii-xliv.

the work and give it, often, a foreign flavor. These inversions are present, of course, because for all of Taylor's ingenuity, he could not avoid them, when they impressed him as unnatural, without failing to reproduce Goethe's metrics. He thus many times lost something which was much more fundamental than his gain.

It was the first time Part II had been translated by an American; it was probably the first time an American had even appreciated, fully, the artistic values of Part II.[14] Critics in England, from Lamb and Coleridge to Goethe's defender, George H. Lewes, had been notably blind to the merits of the section (Lamb, indeed, in a letter to Ainsworth, referred to *Faust* as "a disagreeable canting tale of seduction"). In spirit, said Lewes, Part II is "of mediocre interest, very far inferior to the *First Part* and both in conception and execution an elaborate mistake."[15]

Taylor disagreed. He spoke in his Introduction of the "higher intellectual character" of Part II; he termed it "the conception of Goethe's prime"; he praised "its grand design, its wealth of illustration, and the almost inexhaustible variety and beauty of its rhythmical forms."[16]

This was enthusiasm, but it was also something more. It was critical insight, and it led Taylor to the realization that though Part II was involved, at times

14. See letter of C. T. Brooks (first American translator of Part I) to Taylor, 3-3-71. Taylor-Scudder, *op. cit.*, II, 554.
15. See Oxford edition, 1932. Introduction by Marshall Montgomery, p. vi.
16. *Ibid.*, Taylor's Introduction, p. xlix.

turgid even, though it was not a classical performance in the sense of a performance whose outline was clear and rather obvious, it did not become necessarily, on that account, a bad performance. Taylor, that is to say, sensed the fact that the origins of Goethe's artistic inspiration were not altogether Grecian, just as the origins of his philosophy were not altogether Grecian. He may not have known—doubtless he did not know—that the philosophy, or rather the theology, of *Faust* was grounded in Lebnitz' idea that happiness for mortals—who, because God is immortal, can never know this state completely—consists "in a continual progress, of delights and new perfections"; he may not have known, again, that Goethe's concern with the question of man's imperfection and man's perfectibility had been the cardinal interest of the Angelic Doctor and of other important medieval minds.[17] He may not have known either of these things academically, but the fact of his ignorance appears mainly irrelevant. He compared Part II to "a great mosaic, which looked at near at hand shows us the mixture of precious marbles, common pebbles, of glass, jasper, and lapis-lazuli; but, seen in the proper perspective, exhibits only the Titanic struggle of Man, surrounded with shapes of Beauty and Darkness, towards a victorious immortality."[18] He spoke elsewhere of "the suggestiveness"—*i.e.* the romanticism—of this part of the work, of the way its substance "overflows its bounds on all sides," of its "circles within circles," of

17. See Montgomery's Introduction, pp. xiii-xv.
18. Taylor's Introduction, Part II, p. xlix.

its elusiveness. He was unwilling to declare, in brief, that because a Gothic cathedral is without the chaste lines of the Parthenon of Phidias it is therefore value-less as architecture.

There was an English edition and a German edition. Taylor's friends liked the translation greatly, his enemies not so well. Fields gave him a dinner, inviting almost every American author of importance. Longfellow, Lowell, Holmes, Howells, and Aldrich came. Emerson and Whittier could not come, but sent their congratulations. Later, in New York, he was dined at the Century Club. He wrote his mother that "the book is considered a more successful (because more difficult) work than either Longfellow's *Dante* or Bryant's *Homer*. Everything that I have heretofore done, all together, has not given me so much reputation as this one undertaking. People say that no one need ever translate *Faust* again, because no one can surpass my translation."[19] Bancroft, minister to Germany, liked it. Previous translators liked it.

And then his enemies and detractors, for he had them—from Park Benjamin, who said Taylor had traveled more and seen less than any man living, passing the epigram off as Humbolt's, to the Y. M. C. A. secretary, who canceled a lecture engagement Taylor had in Chicago, when a preacher informed him that his speaker was an "immoral" influence! The Springfield *Republican,* in a review of *Faust,* pointed out that one needed to be a poet to translate poetry, that one needed also the gift of "inspiration," which

19.  Taylor-Scudder, 2-5-71., *op. cit.,* II, 549.

had been denied Taylor The St. Louis *Republican* commented in like fashion, adding that all translation is futile.

These unfavorable opinions were all massed together, conveniently, by Miss Juliana Haskell in a Columbia dissertation. Starting with the premise that no German translation into a language predominantly of Latin origin can be successful,[20] she proceeds to prove, most neatly, that Taylor's translation is not successful. She registers a number of corollary complaints: Mrs. Taylor was probably the guiding spirit in the work.[21] Taylor is "in his Preface, twice guilty of fallacy, by implication."[22] Taylor "labored" over the work, and great poetry is always written without premeditation. Other quaint demurrers are urged, and this lady (who answers the question: Was Taylor a poet? by quoting some dozen opinions of his contemporaries and immediate successors, selected for their unfavorableness) is driven, by inexorable logic and a profound degree of nonsense, to her stern Q. E. D: "I hold therefore that it is an inadequate translation."[23] What is adequate to her no doubt chaste judgment one never is able to guess. She concludes by confessing her inability to understand either "how it has 'usurped the position of standard'" or the esteem it enjoys with "certain German authorities." Thus scholarship, of a sort, in 1908.

Such scholarship seems really of little importance in this world. What *is* important, rather, is the fact that

20. *Op. cit.*, p. 39.  22. *Ibid.*, p. 35.
21. *Ibid.*, p. 15.  23. *Ibid.*, p. 89.

Taylor's translation took its rightful place among the great ones in America, that it remains to this day one of the best in English, that leaning upon the ample strength of Goethe, supplied for once with a depth that was foreign to him, Taylor did a thing which will probably keep his memory alive, winnowed though most of his other work may be now to a scant dry dust, to "the unenviable status of documents."

# STORIES

## XVI

TAYLOR wrote frequently for the *Atlantic,* and some
of his sketches are interesting. A number of them
appeared later in volumes, as we have seen. He collected them as often as there seemed any chance of a
reissue selling, just as he collected his poems often,
rejecting progressively the more "sensuous," rearrang-
ing, adding the new, hopeful that the development
he was constantly imagining in his art would be apparent to an increasingly cold and vulgar public. Some
of his stories were published in *Beauty and the Beast
and Tales of Home* (1872). Others seemed too ephemeral ever to serve him again, in any fashion. He
probably soon forgot them himself.

He did an article on Thackeray, a year after the
death of the great novelist.[1] "Other pens may sum up
his literary record," he began. "I claim the right to
write of him as a man.... I shall repeat no word of
Thackeray's which he would have wished unsaid or
suppressed."

He recalled his introduction to the Englishman in
New York, ten years before. He was a delightful fellow,
delighted with America. What delighted him most was
the American's capacity for culture. A man can rise
from nothing here and yet become an individual of

1. *Atlantic Monthly,* XIII (1864), 371-9

great assurance. In England, by contrast, a new arrival most often "feels like a flunkey." Taylor explained this fact to his friend's entire satisfaction: He recalled Goethe's story of the boys of Venice. They were clever and graceful because each one realized that he might one day become the Doge.

Thackeray complained that his two big "dragons" were Indolence and Luxury. But Taylor added that his friend's virtues of Courage and Generosity eclipsed these faults. For instance, Thackeray was condemned by the press in Canada and England, because of his speeches in this country about the four Georges; yet he returned to London and spoke even more severely on the subject. Emerson's *English Traits* was published in 1856. Emerson is too severe with us, said a distinguished member of Parliament. Emerson is too laudatory, replied Thackeray. In 1857, during a visit at Thackeray's home, Taylor complained of financial conditions in America and added, mostly in jest, that he might soon run short of money. His host hurriedly checked his accounts, announced that he had £200 available, and insisted that Taylor take the entire sum.

And this man was so broad, so willing in the interest of truth to discard an earlier, false opinion! "Thackeray understood neither the real nature nor the extent of the [American] conspiracy, supposing that Free Trade was the chief object of the South, and that the right to secede was tacitly admitted by the Constitution. I thereupon endeavored to place the facts of the case before him in their true light." Taylor did so, but according to the light, not of truth, one fears, so much as of the Abolitionists. But Thackeray was impressed. He wanted Taylor to write an article on the subject for the *Cornhill Magazine*. Taylor wrote the article, but the editor turned it down, saying that, in fairness, a rejoinder would be necessary. Thackeray's enthusiasm was not chastened. The article was taken to the *Times*, and left there. Yet somehow it never achieved the sanctity of print. Taylor was vexed: "It was a careful, cold, dispassionate statement."

"The Strange Friend"[2] threatened to be mystery fiction. It treats of Lord Dunleigh's family, who come to a Quaker settlement with a forged "certificate of fellowship" from another Society at Islip. The family name is changed to Donnelly. They all live in rigid economy, not a well favored lot to their neighbors, until the son, who has been on the point of rebelling against the denial of his luxuries, is killed by a fall from his horse. Thereafter the Quakers of the place shower them with sympathy.

Taylor keeps the antecedents of the Donnellys hidden until late in his narrative. A servant, O'Neil, comes to them at length, discloses their exalted identity, declares that their Irish castle, which they were about to lose through domestic extravagance, is now free of debt. A wealthy cousin has also given them added moneys. Lord Dunleigh rejoices, yet leaves the kind Quakers with a sigh. This narrative was entirely historical, Taylor declared.

"Travel in the United States"[3] might well have been

2. *Ibid.*, XIX (1867), 54-65.
3. *Ibid.*, XIX (1867), 477-84.

written originally as a lecture. It is an intelligent essay, the fruit of more than a decade of often harrowing experiences. "Migration at home," he declared, "has become so general a habit that cases of strong local attachment are almost exceptional. To have visited Europe is one of the understood requirements of our conventional gentility." The fact of the voyage is accepted as implying a higher degree of culture.

This may well be the case: Taylor will not argue it, but it is certainly true that in our own country traveling facilities have not kept pace with the public's demand for them. Our railroads are overcrowded. Conductors behave surlily. Systems do not compete with one another; combinations are effected. Officials are insolent, bloated with power and privileges.

In America "we are swift in all things, but we are thorough in very few. We are practical. . . . up to the demands of our most pressing necessities, but beyond that point chaos begins." We simply have no conveniences on the railroads. "Our rule seems to be that a hastily built road may be carelessly managed." There is great delay at all stations. Time-tables are worthless. There are far too many accidents. Travelers are often actually manhandled by conductors, who realize that their road is too rich to be prosecuted, and that the judges who would try them have been bribed and corrupted.

Railroad seats are "torture screws" (Taylor, remember, was six feet tall). Pullmans are fairly satisfactory, but too expensive. Food is wretched at depots, but we lack the courage to protest. An occasional day coach is kept fairly clean, for the ladies and for married people. "In others, the refined and the brutal, the clean and the filthy, the invalid and the swearing, tobacco-squirting rowdy are packed together. Some of these coaches in winter, when one's feet rest in an ice bath of bitter air and one's head reels in a burning disoxygenized atmosphere, can only be compared to one of the outer circles of Dante's Inferno." And in these holes, even in fine weather, we sit quietly. We have clamored for arrangements which allow a great number of people to crowd together, but once this end is achieved "we become silent and uncommunicative." "Americans are gregarious, not social."

He broadened his discussion, still writing intelligently and with force. "Corporations, with us, are controlled by a few individuals, and we endure in all the practical relations of life an amount of tyranny which would not be tolerated a single day, were its character political. Our corporations are more despotic, dishonest, and irresponsible than in any other country of the civilized world. Our politicians, of whatever party, repeat the old phrases indicative of mistrust of corporations: yet we find the latter controlling entire states, electing their own legislatures and members of congress, demoralizing voters, and exercising other dangerous privileges, in utter defiance of the public interest. We are silent under impositions which would raise a popular tempest in many countries of Europe.

"Whatever our theory (it is doubtful indeed whether we have any), our practice appears to be based on the idea that the corporations into whose powerful hands are confined our travel and the facilities of our business are not the servants, but the benefactors, of the people. We are swift to create them, we generously load them with privileges, and we require a mere shadow of obligation in return. Sometimes, when a specially frightful accident occurs, we establish a single rule whereby that particular form of accident may be prevented, but we neglect the comprehensive legislation which would protect the public against dangers and impositions of all kinds. The shock of a catastrophe makes but a temporary ripple on the swift, seething, impetuous current of our life. The competition upon which our legislators fondly relied for our protection is slowly transforming itself into a gigantic system of combination, in the railroad, telegraph, and express business, against which the public is powerless. It is time that the balance were restored. Except in the case of the Pacific railroads, the need of encouraging. . . . these great physical enterprises is past, and those which have been built by a confiding generosity should be called upon to fulfill at least their most obvious duties."

Taylor did not stop with the corporations—indeed, the title of this essay does not begin to indicate its breadth. He deplored the architecture of the midnineteenth century. "Most of our inland cities and towns have as yet only a material interest; they are simply so many evidences of growth. They have neither history, monuments, nor individual peculiarities. The smaller towns look as if one individual had built them all, on contract, at the same time. The age of a place may be instantly determined by a glance at its dwelling houses. The Grecian portico indicates thirty years; the (so-called) Swiss cottage, of clap boards, twenty; the square block, with square box on top, fifteen years; the bracketed, towered irregular mansion, ten; the mansard roof, today. The towns imitate and intensify the monotony of the landscape about them. . . . Yet those who are familiar with the railroads of Belgium know how charming those dead Flemish levels have become, through varied cultivation and traces of the changing habit of centuries." Taylor does not consider, apparently, that the cause of much of the lack of picturesqueness he deplores was traceable —still is—to the fact of our newness, to the fact that "the changing habits of centuries" had had no chance to operate in America. But neither does Mr. Lewis Mumford, for that matter. To say this, of course, is to urge no brief against Taylor's dislike of standardization in architecture. On this point he wrote ably— much more ably, perhaps, than later, more venerated critics have written.

"Jacob Flint's Journey"[4] is a typical success narrative. The hero is a shy lad, incredibly given to blushing. His friends at school ridicule him, especially since his rash prediction that he will one day make a journey and come back rich. After being offended at a party by certain belles of his village, he does make a journey; yet he comes back, not rich, but engaged to Susan, a farmer's daughter. His father consents to the wedding. Later, we learn that the father had been en-

4. *Ibid.*, 24 (1869), 313-25.

gaged to Susan's mother and would have married her, had not another lady lured him away. Out of spite, after his wedding to the temptress, he placed all his money in trust for Jacob. Jacob inherits this fortune, and with part of it buys the fine Whitney place, shaming the neighbors who had once made light of his prophecy. The story indicated, said Taylor, "the good fortune which sometimes follows honesty, reticence, and shrewdness." It also indicates the sad depths to which his work often fell, when he was financially compelled to write, but had nothing to write about.

"Twin Love"[5] is another short story, rather suspicious in its implications. It is concerned with twin brothers, David and Jonathan, the children of their parents' middle age. They look precisely alike, and are inseparable. Their father, dying, senses a more than normal intimacy between them, and compels them to promise to live for a time apart. They are as unhappy as separated lovers can possibly be. David meets Ruth, is interested in her, but goes away. When Jonathan calls on her, she mistakes him for his brother and marries him. After three children are born, she dies; but not until there have been prayers that David may return. These prayers are answered, the brothers are reconciled and sleep together, hands clasped, lips often meeting, as tenderly as ever.

I don't think Taylor would have been a fair subject for the Freudians. These supremely clever gentlemen, had they troubled themselves to consider one so low in the scale of accepted values, would probably have

5. *Ibid.*, 28 (1871), 257-64.

distorted his life past recognition. He wrote constantly to his mother, asking her advice, and relying on her confidence in practically every important decision he meditated. This fact would have given the Freudians their text. The sheriff, his father, would next have been seized upon. They would have made him out as a brute who thwarted Bayard's essentially feminine ambitions, who compelled him to dig in the ground occasionally, after Taylor had said himself that as a youth he had "a constitutional horror of dirty hands." This would have impelled him irresistibly toward that grotesque misnomer, the Oedipus complex. But the Quaker and the Purist in his blood would have been, subconsciously, of course, in constant revolt against this abhorrency: hence his great affection for cousin Frank; hence his passionate desire to get away to a New England school. Then Boker would have come into his life, another thwarted and tender personality, and the letters about their fervent love for each other would have been shrewdly explained, with the skill and terminology for which writers of Freudian psychographs are notable. Then crowning evidence, Mary Agnew would have died, Taylor's great love for her unconsummated. There would have been no saving him then. Only the seeming dormant Quaker in him: filling him with disgust—wholly superficial, wholly a defense mechanism—toward Swinburne, whom he feared, toward Whitman, whom he feared also, in both instances because had he liked them (in his weakness, he knew it) he would have been compelled to throw over the traces completely. And this fear was without doubt what ruined him. Had he dared, he might have become the Oscar Wilde of America!

Next they would have quoted, from *Joseph and his Friend,* what would have been, perhaps, to them, the most savory passage available in all his works. Joseph and Philip "took each other's hands. The day was fading, the landscape was silent, and only the twitter of the nesting birds was heard in the boughs above them. Each gave way to the impulse of his manly love, rarer, alas! but as tender and true as the love of woman, and they drew nearer and kissed each other. As they walked back and parted on the highway, each felt that life was not wholly blind and that happiness was not yet impossible."[6]

Finally, his numerous letters to men whom he esteemed would have afforded more evidence; the dominant rôle of passion in his verse would have offered still more; the quarrels with Stoddard could thus be deductively accounted for. The stark simplicities of this method are endless.

They are also somewhat tedious, not a little disgusting. The truth is that Taylor was quite healthy, quite safe, and for his day quite normal. Indeed, one of his most pronounced personal traits, as has been suggested, was a gusty, cheerful athleticism that won friends for him almost everywhere.

"Studies of Animal Nature" is one of the most curious things Taylor wrote. He begins by defending Darwin. The theory of this scientist is "not degrading to man; it simply raises the animal world in dignity."

6. P. 217.

Then he quarrels with zoölogists generally. "They are more interested in the skull of an elephant, the thighbone of a bird, or the dorsal fin of a fish than in the intelligence or rudimentary moral sense of the creature."[7] Since these specialists have ignored any study of these latter points, Taylor adds, they have naturally not pre-empted them for the layman. He believes that animals do have a moral sense; at times he has noted amazing evidence of his belief. He will give his observations:

"I have a horse who is now not less than *forty-one* years old.[8] It is possible that he is a year or two older; for thirty-eight years ago he was broken to use." This horse once picked up with his teeth six boxes which were stacked on the oats bin; then he began, leisurely, to munch oats. *Very definitely* the horse was taking small mouthfuls; Taylor was peeping through the door at him. Suddenly he burst into the stable. The horse "opened his jaws to their fullest extent, thrust his muzzle deep into the box, and gravely walked back to his stall with at least a quart of oats." Obviously, the beast was seized with a conviction of sin!

This uncommon animal—called Ben, very commonly—had a habit of playfully snapping at Taylor's arm when being harnessed. It was a very old habit, very fixed. Once Ben bit him, accidentally. Taylor looked at Ben and said, quietly, "Never do that again." And he never did!

7. *Atlantic Monthly*, 39 (1877), 135-42.
8. I am informed by a gentleman skilled in such matters that the average horse lives only to the age of about twenty years. But, of course, Ben was not an average horse.

Ben once stopped in the road and began to twist about, in extraordinary fashion. "What's the matter, Ben?" Ben held up his foot. A shoe was off. Taylor sympathized, but Ben still twisted, quite unaccountably. At length, pitying the obtuseness of his master, he shook a hind foot for some moments. The shoe rattled, was extremely loose. Again Taylor sympathized. Ben trotted on, satisfied.

And then there was Mrs. Kirkland's parrot, in the Chicago fire of 1871. A lady rushed in for a final snatch at the moveables. She saw only the parrot and the Bible. Well, God came first with her then, for she was terrified. She seized the Word. "Good Lord deliver us," screamed the bird. She dropped the Word.

Barnum in his museum kept a broad-backed hippopotamus. Taylor spoke to it once, in English. No response. Then he said to it softly, in Arabic: "I know you. Come here to me." The hippo came to the bars of his cage and allowed Taylor to stroke his head.

A famous poet was once walking near London with the novelist, Charles Kingsley. Suddenly a "fierce mastiff" beset them. Kingsley talked to the dog, very quietly, and it returned to its kennel. Taylor had a similar experience in San Francisco. He went to the home of a friend, and after ringing the doorbell, another fierce mastiff beset him. Taylor, too, began talking, quietly but fluently: "I shall ring once more. If there is no answer I shall go away. You may stay and watch me. I am not afraid of you." His ring was not answered. "I see there is nobody at home, so I shall go, as I told you I would." The dog stopped growling.

"When I had closed the front gate, he turned away with a single dignified wave of the tail, which I understood as a combined apology and farewell."

Taylor had subdued bellowing herds of cattle, purely by doing the unexpected. While on a picnic near Brandywine creek, hundreds of them, "wild," thundered down upon his party. Death appeared imminent. Taylor mastered their savagery by sitting down on the ground and folding his legs. They stopped short, departed in awe. He explained their odd behavior by saying that the men they had seen in the past had all been on horseback.

He kept a peacock at Cedarcroft. The bird was incredibly vain. "I have often watched John spreading his tail before a few guinea fowl, who were so provokingly indifferent to his royal splendor that he invariably ended by driving them angrily away." Taylor wrote at a table, near a bay window. "As soon as I took my place there, after breakfast, the peacock flew upon the window sill, and whenever I failed to notice him, the sharp tap of his bill upon the glass reminded me of his presence. Then I turned, and as in duty bound, said 'good morning, John,' after which he continued to sit there, silent and content, for two or three hours longer."

Finally there was a toad, at Cedarcroft, which developed a fancy for the Taylors. When Bayard and Marie would sit out on the lawn, in summer starlight, almost always the toad would visit them, hopping to its rest on his shoe, or upon the corner of his wife's gown. And doubtless this innocent unknowing thing would awaken for them some rather cosmic reflections, concerning the great peace of the darkness, and its greater intimacies—bringing as it did the basest and the most exalted of God's creatures into a pulsing communion, unspoken but holy.

# CALAMITIES

## XVII

THE financier of the Civil War, Jay Cooke, probably thought very little about Bayard Taylor. He had probably not read even one of Taylor's many books. Busy with over-reaching secretaries of the treasury, with selling government bonds, at nice profits, when the government seemed unable to sell them itself; busy, further, with thrusting a railroad line into the uncharted northwest, in the name of civilization and in return for close to fifty million acres of land grants; busy, finally, with perfecting a system of salesmanship that brought churchmen, hack writers, lawyers, and even a vice president into the messianic chorus that hymned the blessedness of his vision—busy with all these things, Taylor probably was to him little more than a name, a lesser star in a firmament of no importance.

Yet once this deacon-faced wizard had need of Taylor's services, and though the service was slight intrinsically, it seems indicative of something that may not be slight at all. Cooke formed a "pool" to build the Northern Pacific Railroad, and concerned himself with selling bonds in the United States and abroad. He subsidized thirty newspapers in Germany. He stressed the patriotic nature of his enterprise, one which would carry the immeasurable blessings of civilization into the far Dakotas and Montana and Oregon. He would lay open to the poor the limitless, rich wheat lands of the prairies; he would surrender to them, at a mere six to ten dollars an acre, the depthless mineral wealth of the Rockies; the incalculable timber resources of the Puget Sound territory he would give them; he would annex western Canada by benevolent absorption. It is our patriotic duty to buy these bonds; it is our one great chance of opulence. Manifest Destiny spreads her broad wings to enfold us!

Now Cooke was a realist as well as a dreamer; he was a stubborn Sam Johnson as well as a Colonel Sellers. This being true, he was not slow to perceive that unless confidence in this particular enterprise was established, the money which was to make it possible would remain, idly and stupidly, in his countrymen's strongboxes. He began, therefore, as early as 1869 to advertise his project in the *Times* and the *Tribune*. He distributed stock judiciously among editors, preachers, and congressmen. He sent a fishing-rod to President Grant's little son, Jesse. He took the President himself in quest of trout. He shipped cases on cases of wines— made from the grapes in his own vineyard—to gentlemen who could extol publicly his noble schemes for the public good. He was extremely shrewd.

And in the summer of 1871, probably, he heard of Taylor, another man who in his small way had been for a long time now very busy also. Why not let this man—who, it is said, has a sizeable following with the public—write, as so many others are doing, in praise of his benevolent plans for the country?

Cooke managed this detail in characteristic fashion. He ordered a special train and planned a tour. Dana of the *Sun* was invited, D. G. Croley of the *Tribune,* and many other editors and reporters from the leading journals of New England and Chicago. The train would carry these men from Buffalo to the end of the line, at Duluth, Minnesota. Then by coach they would be driven through the wheat lands of the Red River Valley, then on to Winnipeg, Canada. Only one request was made of them: They were to report what they saw. Naturally, they would see what was pleasant. Naturally, they would praise their host, Mr. Cooke, and Mr. Cooke's fine schemes for the nation's development. And naturally, Mr. Cooke himself reasoned, they would do a great deal to shape public opinion favorably: they would persuade the congressman of their section that Mr. Cooke's request for a revised land grant belt of 120 miles in the territories through which his "proposed" road would run should be approved. And this would mean that Mr. Cooke's company, at its own terms, could dispose of this land to settlers, could amass a fortune such as no one else in America had dreamed of.[1]

Taylor made the trip, and he wrote delightfully about what he saw. But a little later—taking orders no doubt, as before, from those who controlled his income—he did another thing which perhaps did not please Mr. Cooke even slightly. The St. Paul and

1. See, on the preceding two pages, E. P. Oberholtzer, *Jay Cooke, Financier of the Civil War* (Phil. 1907), II, 225-238-346. Also see V. L. Parrington, *Main Currents in American Thought,* III, 31-43.

Sioux City Railroad had emerged as a rival to the Northern Pacific. It, too, desired a renewal of its land grants, which were about to expire. And the thing of importance, with respect to Taylor, is the fact that Ezra Cornell had endowed his university, at Ithaca, with properties which this line controlled.

Taylor had been invited again to lecture at Cornell.[2] He was being paid well. And since he was well-known in Pennsylvania, Mr. Cornell requested that his lecturer go to Washington as a lobbyist, that he try to influence certain congressmen of his native state into voting against the ruthless schemings of Mr. Cooke. Cooke had offered to buy out the company of his rival; he was denouncing its unfair methods, its "injurious and unmodified competition"; Taylor had received a considerable favor from Cooke. But he was also receiving favors from Cornell. He was pressed for money, sorely pressed, bitterly pressed. What could he do? He went to Washington.

As is well known, Cooke had his way in Congress, but his company was wiped out in 1873 when the

2. The titles of these lectures indicate that Taylor was giving a very sane and commendable partial survey of his subject. He stated the titles to Prof. Willard Fiske, of the Cornell faculty, in a letter of May 11, 1871, and concluded by saying that he hoped to add to the subjects at the rate of twelve a year. The titles follow: (1) "The Beginnings of German Literature," (2) "The Minnesingers," (3) "The German Epics of the Middle Ages," (4) "The Nibelungenlied," (5) "The Literature of the Reformation," (6) "The Literature of the Seventeenth Century." *Unpublished Letters of Bayard Taylor* (Huntington Library Pub., J. R. Schultz, ed.).

Franco-Prussian war destroyed his bond market in Europe. But this matter is hardly pertinent here.

What is pertinent is the fact that with the beginning of the 1870's Taylor saw his last wisp of freedom and leisure swept away from him, saw himself reduced to the status of a slave who must obey commands, no matter how fundamentally at variance with his private convictions they might be. The slavery he had abhorred in the South was gone. But that, he was beginning to realize, did not mean that all slavery had been ended. It seemed to mean anything but that. He hated a monopoly, so long as it went unregulated. It should be made, he thought, to minister to the people. Corporation officials are, by nature, public servants. Selfish exploitation was villainy to him, and in lecture after lecture, in city upon city, he said so with courage, and emphatically.

But that, alas, was before the world was darkened. That was in a delicious foretime, when people read good literature, when royalties and newspaper dividends made him close to independent, when intelligent audiences paid well to hear his lectures. Now they wanted Pike humor, vulgar humor, the cheap barbarism of Whitman. The sun was in eclipse. Savagery was on the land.

One must bide his time, waiting for the new day which in his enduring faith he knew would come. Meanwhile, for the sake of one's family and position, one must occasionally stoop to some rather sordid enterprises. God has willed it so. God has driven one to a denial of his convictions, into a hated servitude.

But this will pass. Truth will win out. "I look to the future with confidence."[3]

## 2

The *Diversions of the Echo Club* began to appear serially in the *Atlantic* in January, 1872. Their publication, as we have noticed, brought on a fresh misunderstanding with Stoddard. But Stoddard at length forgot this unpleasantness, and in 1895 edited the collected *Diversions* for Putnam. He told how these verse combats started, in the early 1850's, when all the participants were very young, very ambitious, very much devoted to poetry, convinced that even toying with the Muse was better than discussing the profoundest political or economic matters in prose.

The combats "began in my rooms and were continued in his [Taylor's] rooms, neither of which bore the least resemblance to the Bohemian resort which he described in his settings to the different nights, more I am sure, from the report of others than from his own knowledge, for I am sure he never crossed its threshold. Careful of his conduct and choice in his friendships, he respected himself too much to royster among his inferiors in a beer cellar."[4]

The *Diversions* follow in a loose way the plan of the *Decameron*. There are eight nights. About four authors are satirized or parodied each night. There is also a suggestion of Dryden's *Essays on Dramatic Poesy* in the use of typical characters to express certain rather standard points of view: Thus, The Ancient, represents "the calmer, judicial temper"; Zoilus, the

3. Letter to J. McEntee, 4-29-71. Taylor-Scudder. *op. cit.*, II, 558-60. See also letter to McEntee, 4-7-72. *Ibid.*, II, 588.
4. Introduction, p. xxii.

"carping, cynical, arrogant critic"; Galahad, the "young, sensational, impressive element in the reading public"; and The Gannett, "brilliance, without literary principle, the love of technical effect."

Of the three important participants in these diversions, Taylor and Stoddard have already been noted. Fitz-James O'Brien, the last, was born in Ireland in 1826. He inherited £8,000, and ran through it in two years. He came to New York to earn another fortune at hack writing, edited the forgotten *Lantern* for awhile, turned next to free lance journalism, contributing prose and poetry to the best periodicals of his day. His mystery tale, "The Diamond Lens," brought out in the first volume of the *Atlantic*, made him fairly famous. He was named an officer at the outbreak of the war, and died from wounds in February, 1862. One might term him, in many ways, the Richard Steele of nineteenth century American literature. Certainly, like Captain Dick, he was dashing, brilliant, often in debt, a delightful person to know.

These young gentlemen would put names in a hat, and draw them out simultaneously. If one drew out Browning's name, he was expected to write a parody of Browning's verse in the Browning manner. The winner of the contest was he who finished first. Taylor and O'Brien in general divided honors. They had uproarious evenings, topping them off, usually, with a dozen oysters, fried or raw.

What appear now more important than the parodies are the criticisms which Taylor wrote, to accompany them in their published form. Many of his judgments, it is true, seem merely prose repetitions of the rhymed estimates of Lowell's *Fable for Critics*. Yet even these may be of significance in any effort to classify Taylor's literary judgments; they may show, among other things for example, the still surviving if effete conventions of the Brahmins—the critical atrophy which New England had induced in him.

He begins with Poe, then dead and mostly forgotten. "There are two men in him. One is a refined gentleman, an aspiring soul, an artist among those who had little sense of literary art." The other "built his nest with the birds of night." In Taylor, there was no appreciation for a man who failed to conform, even when the age which demanded conformity had no place in its scheme for the artist.

He was displeased with Browning's *Sordello*, and with other obscurities in his work. Of course, even here he was saying nothing new. Tennyson had complained on the same score, so had Carlyle; so had any number of critics. "Now I call this [*Sordello*] perplexity, not profundity. Wasn't it the Swedish poet, Tegner, who said, 'The obscurely uttered is the obscurely thought?'" Browning had written, in a dedicatory letter to a new edition of his poem, that he had taken pains to make of it something "which the many *might* instead of the few *must* like," but that, after all, he decided not to publish the revised draft. This attitude, declared Taylor, was arrogant and inexcusable. "The *must* which he flings at the few is far more offensive than utter indifference to all readers would have been."

On Swinburne he declined to pass judgment. "I have been waiting for his ferment to settle, as in the case of Keats and Shelley, but there are no signs of it in his last volume. How splendidly the mind of Keats precipitated its crudity and redundancy, and clarified into the pure wine of *Hyperion!* In Shelley's case the process was slower, but it was steadily going on. You will find the same thing in Schiller, in Dryden, and many other poets; therefore, I mean to reserve my judgment in Swinburne's case and wait, at least until his next book is published."

The point in his parody of Aldrich centered "about a mistake Aldrich made years ago, in the color of crocus. He called it *red*, and there may be red crocuses, for aught I know; but yellow or orange is the conventional color. Of course, we didn't let the occasion slip." Zoilus wrote the following:

> *I walked in the garden, ruffled with rain,*
> *Through the blossoms of every hue;*
> *And I saw the pink, with its yellow stain,*
> *And the rose with its bud of blue.*

He was kind to Stoddard. "I always find in Stoddard a most true and delicate ear for melodies of verse, and I thoroughly enjoy his brief snatches, or 'catches' of song. When I disagree with him, it is usually on account of the theme rather than the execution.... He seems to have wandered down to us from the days of Charles the First."

Then he quoted "The Cantalope," written in Stoddard's favorite manner.

*Side by side in the crowded street,*
*Amid its ebb and flow*
*We walked together one autumn morn*
*('Twas many years ago).*

*The market blushed with fruits and flowers*
*(Both Memory and Hope)*
*You stopped and bought me at the stall*
*A spicy cantalope.*

*We drained together its honeyed wine,*
*We cast the seeds away.*
*I slipped and fell on the moony rinds.*
*You took me home in a dray!*

*The honeyed wine of our love is drained;*
*I limp from the fall I had.*
*The snow flakes muffle the empty stall*
*And everything is sad.*

*The sky is an inkstand, upside down,*
*It splashes the world in gloom*
*The earth is full of skeleton bones*
*And the sea is a wobbling tomb.*

He discussed the author of *Leaves of Grass.* "There
are splendid lines and brief passages in Walt Whitman;
there is modern, half-Bowery-boy, half Emersonian
apprehension of the old Greek idea of physical life,
which many take to be wholly new on account of the
singular form in which it is presented. I will even

admit that the elements of a fine poet exist in him, in a state of chaos. It is curious that while he proclaims his human sympathies to be without bounds, his intellectual sympathies should be so narrow. There never was a man at once so arrogant and yet so tender towards his fellow man."

Thus spoke Zoilus. The ancient agreed: "You have very correctly described him. The same art which he despises would have increased his power and influence. He forgets that the poet must not only have somewhat to say, but must strenuously acquire the power of saying it most purely and completely. A truer sense of art would have prevented that fault which has been called immorality, but which is only a coarse, offensive frankness."

These are not the only authors whom Taylor considers: He wrote a harmless parody of Whittier. He mentioned Boker, praising especially, "the grave sustained measure" of his sonnets. He was saddened by Bryant's withdrawal from the literary movements of the day, by his "iceolation." He called Stedman, in effect, a literary curiosity, our one broker who was also a poet. He referred with deep respect to Longfellow, citing him as one who amid the chaos of his age had stood "a sweet, clear, and steady" symbol of the good life. He criticized himself ("a genuine poet is always the best judge of his own works, because he has an ideal standard by which to measure whatever he does"): rhetoric, he said, was at once his strength and his weakness. It has often "led him away from the true substance of poetry." He "has too many irons in the fire." But there are "signs of some new form of development in his later poems."

In the *Diversions,* as published, there is an irritating timidity, a constant evidence of the fear that someone with whom he is personally on cordial terms will be offended by his playful references to him. As soon as he writes an unfavorable (but quite honest and true) line, he hastens to overemphasize an obvious virtue, appealing to his subject to remember that all is said in sport and imploring him to consider, further, that "it is an evidence of a poet's distinct individuality when he can be imitated." When he quotes his parody of Whittier, he said, fawningly conciliatory: "I'll agree to start with you for Massachusetts by tomorrow morning's express train and lay before the poet what I've written. If he doesn't laugh heartily on reading it, I'll engage to come all the way back afoot."

The result of such extreme solicitude for the sensibilities of his friends is that the *Diversions* are practically worthless as criticism. All that Stoddard had said about the difference between himself and Taylor, as critics, is there glaringly evident. Taylor was simply too thin-skinned for criticism, the most callous of all the professions in Art. He published the *Diversions* because he needed money. If a decision was necessary between saying the truth and deflating his friends, or saying the pleasant and flattering them, he chose to remember the delightful evenings he had spent in their company. He chose to be kind. Had they not encouraged him from the beginning of his career? Was he not, really, very much as they were? Would not an indictment of them, therefore, be in a large measure an indictment of himself? His was the way of the Brahmin world, of that world with which in many ways he longed so desperately to be identified. It was the way of nearly all American literary criticism of the Gilded Age. Perhaps it is also the way of much American criticism, even now.

3

Several very untoward events befell Taylor in the year 1872. The first of them was, more than anything else, simply vexing—the kind of thing which dashed his vanity. It concerned Browning—who in earlier years, before the cult of his worshippers spoiled him, had been as cordial as anyone might ask. Boker was sent to Constantinople by the government; he was to be minister to Turkey. He went by way of London, and Taylor gave him a note of introduction to the great man of English poetry.

Boker was "dreadfully disappointed."[5] "When I met him he was endeavoring to play the fine gentleman, and as he has not had the early breeding necessary for that rôle, he broke down deplorably at every turn. Under the circumstances anything like fellowship between us was impossible, as Browning was flippant, nervous, ill-mannered, foolish, and oh how boastful of himself and his qualities. In short, I saw the idol in the midst of his idolators, and the spectacle was far from pleasant. If Browning were not one of the greatest of living men, as in my soul I know

5. *Cornell Mss.*, Boker to Taylor, 7-28-72.

him to be, I should have said, here is a vain, shallow little man, whose head has been turned by some accidental good fortune. He had never heard of me as a poet, which is quite natural; but then he told me so, which was far from polite. I bore him no grudge for that, however, as I have no vanity to offend; but as he continued to talk at me, rather than to me, I drew myself up as a great 'swell' and affected to look down upon him as a little 'cave' [*sic*] who amused me. This attack from the social side of the position really seemed to flatten him out, with all his genius to back him; for I really believe that Browning has such social ambitions that he really envied me my ability to play the languid, insouciant 'swell.' All this was very sad and painful to me.... I have made this long explanation, but if you had seen such a man as Browning playing the *petit-maitre*, boasting of his acquaintance with this and that titled person, you would have shared in my disgust."

Now this note was very interesting, but it did not disclose the primary cause of Boker's unhappy opinion. Before he would make that known, even to Taylor, he must learn what his friend thought about Browning, as a man. Apparently Taylor had had reason not to think too well, because in his next letter Boker left nothing unsaid.

It all centered around a discussion of Taylor's *Faust*. "I did not know that you would not consider me to have been a damned fool for what I said of Browning .... Now that you have reason to agree with me in my opinion of his manners, let me tell you that anger on your account was at the bottom of my presumptious conduct toward that really great man, and let me confess that all I did to nettle him I did with tears in my heart. He is, among living poets, absolutely my idol, and I would rather cut off my own right arm than harm a hair of his illustrious head.

"But to my story—when I presented your letter to him, he said with a contemptuous sniff: 'As I have already been presented to your Excellency (he rolls all titles under his tongue as a sweet morsel, and as though he were proud of the duty performed by that member), I need not look at this letter; and he put it, unread, into his pocket. 'Taylor, Bayard Taylor,' he continued, with an air of supercilious thoughtfulness. 'Yes,' said I quickly, fearing that he might say something to offend me, 'my best and oldest friend.' 'Ah,' continued Browning, 'I believe that I lately received a big book from him.' 'Perhaps his admirable translation of *Faust*,' I said. 'I don't know,' replied Browning; 'I have not opened it. I shall never look at it. You know, I read my *Faust* in the original.' 'So do many people who have found a pleasure in Mr. Taylor's translation,' I rejoined. 'Ah, indeed?' said Browning. 'Well I am satisfied with *Faust* as Goethe left it.' 'That is very good of you,' I retorted, and left him in disgust.

"My reply seemed to open his eyes as to the kind of man with whom he had been talking, and during the evening he seemed inclined to make friends with me but I————[6] the great diplomatic swell over him

6. One word of Mss. illegible to me.

from the height of my eyebrows and answered him in monosyllables. Have you ever noticed what an advantage height gives over a small man when you wish to treat him coldly? I believe that Browning, in spite of his great intellect, was vexed at my conduct, because it made him cut a poor figure before the company. I tell you the man is an innate snob, with his worship of mere rank, and his boastfulness about his aristocratic associates, and I do not care ever to see him again."[7]

Things were coming to a damnable pass. This petty cockstrutting from the greatest living poet in England! Tennyson was lost to him; now Browning had turned prig—Browning, whose wife had been so rare a creature that merely to have known her made one, in some unaccountable way, more civilized and decent.[8] His attitude was inexplicable. Taylor would not forget it.

Nor did he forget it, even after three years, and many bitter changes of fortune. Browning's *The Inn Album* came out in the fall of 1875, and Taylor reviewed it.[9] He was not very kind, though of course it would be hardly fair to attribute this fact entirely to

7. *Cornell Univ. Mss.*, Boker to Taylor, 10-23-72.
8. Browning's attitude on this occasion is, indeed, hard to explain. When Taylor recovered from his illness at Casa Guidi, Florence, in 1867, he wrote Browning about a vision—how in spirit Mrs. Browning came to him and enjoined his nurses, "He has worked enough. He must now rest." Taylor also wrote a poem about the experience, which he enclosed with the letter. See *Unpublished Letters* (Huntington Library Pub., J. R. Schultz, ed.).
9. *International Review*, III, 342 ff.

the letters from Boker. The review is written in imitation of the original verses:

> Reflect, tis Br! he neglects prepense
> All forms of forms; what he gives must we take,
> Sweet, bitter, sour, absinthean, adipose,
> Conglomerate, jellied, potted, salt or dried
> As the mood holds him, ours not to choose.

Taylor is irritated especially at the monotony of Browning's plot formula:

> Here's Browning's receipt: take heaps o' hate,
> Take boundless love, hydraulic, pressed in bales,
> Distilments keen of baseness and of pride
> And innocence and cunning; mix 'em well
> And put a body round 'em, add the more
> O'this or that, you have another story!
> The sex don't count; make female of the male,
> Male female, all the better; let them meet
> Talk, love, hate, cross, till satisfied. Then kill!

Finally he complains that Browning's context is obscure:

> The meaning ask you, O ingenious soul?
> Why were there such for you, what then were left
> To puzzle brain with, pump conjecture dry
> And prove you little where the poet's great?
> Great must he be, you therefore little. Go!
> The curtain falls, the candles are snuffed out;
> End, damned obliquity, lugubrious plot.

When Taylor received the first of these annoying letters, he was in Europe. He had sailed with his family in June, 1872. He was editing a series of travel books for Scribner and Armstrong. He was writing a school history of Germany for Appleton. Cedarcroft had been leased for three years, he thought to a gentleman who was entirely trustworthy. Mr. Greeley was running for president against Grant. The times were stirring; he was busy, but not too busy.

He had gone abroad, this time, to prepare for the greatest work of his life. He was to do a thing now which would dwarf even his *Faust*. He was planning no less than a combined biography of Goethe and Schiller. He would become the great interpreter of German literature for the English speaking world. He was amassing no end of material. He was in his "prime." He was confident.

And then the storm of reversals that swept down upon him, almost at once, as if by divine premeditation! The family at Gotha were all together. But poor Bufleb was far gone. He was paralyzed. He was helpless. He spoke incoherently. All that formerly had impressed him seemed meaningless. Twenty years ago he had been so young, so alive, so fresh in his reactions to the world! Ten years ago, even five, he had been the same. Now he waited—this man who had meant more than even a brother to Taylor—for darkness and death. How could a thing as incalculably stirring as life take on with such awful inevitable finality the complexion of wretchedness and decay? Here perhaps, but by the grace of God, was Bayard Taylor.

And other news—disgusting him, flinging his plans to the unheeding winds. "The man who took my house threatens to break his contract; the gardener has given me notice of the termination of *his;* an arrangement I made for my parents has been spoiled by the neglect or bad memory of the friend who offered to see it carried out; the money I have been expecting from four different quarters does not come.[10] And the *Tribune* passed its quarterly dividends. And his old friend Putnam died. And Greeley was defeated for the presidency. And then Greeley died, suddenly—this man who had held the *Tribune* together, this miracle among editors.

When Taylor heard this last news, casually announced at a dinner, it struck him, for a moment, speechless. He left the table. What else would happen now, what else *could* happen? Here had been a certain minimum income upon which he was able to depend always, no matter what else wavered. His assurance was gone. The future stretched before him, clouded with unbroken toil. He must become a reporter again. He must take orders from a superior, as he had done when New York first attracted him. There was no freedom in the world anywhere. His titanic quest of it, the overwhelming effort of twenty-five years which had gone into his heart-crushing payment for it, had come at this date, neatly, to nothing.

10.  To J. McEntee, 10-18-72. Taylor-Scudder, *op. cit.,* II, 601.

# CENTENNIAL

## XVIII

AND now began his enthrallment by a world whose dizzying revolutions he would never again simplify, his lasting struggle with an indecipherable alphabet, the beginning of his dissolution, the end of his wistful, sweet longing for peace. Henceforth there would be no time that remained his own, no time for longing even, only incoherent protests, only weak rebellions drowned in the deluge of unpredictable, mountainous, but always mounting, labor.

In the fall of 1872 he worked on *Lars.* "The story is not only highly moral, but religious!!!" Do not mention the matter publicly yet. Do you like the title? Why not? No title can be fatal to a good poem. I think *Lars* rather better than the average title.[1] Fancy names have been used too much. It runs to more than 2,000 lines. It is too late to publish anonymously. The secret can't be kept now. I'll add *A Pastoral of Norway* to the title. I have worked hard on this poem. And I have lectured on American literature in German. And I have gathered much material about Goethe. And I have traveled extensively. I am a little run down, a little tired.

He was busy ten hours a day, through the winter,

1. To Osgood and Aldrich, 1-26-73. Taylor-Scudder, *op. cit.,* II, 615.

with his school history of Germany. It was a most tedious affair. He had to know facts; a fluent fancy would not serve him. But he had no regular income anymore. It was necessary to do other things, many other things; it was imperative that he be at all times alert to developments from which he might wring a news story for the *Tribune,* a short story for the *Atlantic,* a sketch for *Harpers,* a review for the *International.*

With spring came orders from Whitlaw Reid, Greeley's successor, that he go to Vienna and write descriptive articles about the Great Exhibition, then ready to open. He was there for a month, all other of his plans left dangling. He did a thorough job. At a newspaper dinner, attended by representatives of all important journals in the world, he spoke eloquently for the American press, in German. He coined a new word, *Weltgemüthlichkeit.* It was taken up by German editors and praised as expressive of the cosmic good will which the Exhibition had awakened. Herr Taylor was much publicized.

The history kept him grinding until August. Then he found himself annoyed again with "a bronchial difficulty." It had first beset him more than two decades before, and a trip to Egypt had been necessary to cure it. Well, he must go to Egypt again. He proposed that he manage it by writing for the *Tribune,* as always, that Reid pay him a thousand dollars for letters which he would do rather frequently.[2] Reid could think it over.

2.  *Ibid.,* 7-23-73, II, 627.

Meanwhile he continued to sift Goethe material. "I have carefully read all the *German* biographies, and recently Lewes over again, with a most encouraging result." He found what every biographer finds who has planned to interpret the life of the world's elect: "The man and poet, Goethe, is not clearly or fairly drawn in any of them."[3] Later he was told that Lewes, Goethe's best known English commentator, had "pumped lackeys and old servants while in Weimar, and took no pains to get acquainted with the intelligent friends of Goethe."

He was also writing a long drama, *The Prophet.* Maybe we can publish this anonymously. It runs to 3,400 lines. The action begins in New England and moves quickly to the Western States. "The history of the Mormons is a background to the poem.... It is a two-edged sword, cutting the fossilized Orthodox to the heart no less than the Mormons. It is full of passion and intrigue.... My suggestion is this: I will send the Mss. by mail in the spring. During the summer the work may be heralded by mysterious hints of a new author. (If need be I will write two or three poems in some striking manner, to be used.)" The hero David Starr "is a Hamlet nature, and the germs of his final fate are in him from the first."[4]

*The Prophet* was not his only concern in the fall of 1873. Lillian, his daughter, was seriously ill. Mrs. Taylor was "run down," but ready to start for Egypt as soon as the child's health would permit. For weeks

3. *Ibid.*, To Stedham, 10-14-73, II, 630.
4. *Ibid.*, To Osgood and Aldrich, 11-30-73, II, 634-6.

they awaited her improvement. Taylor was restless. He wrote for the *Atlantic* one of his worst stories, "Who was She." In an article for the *Tribune* he sketched the highly important excavations Schliemann was undertaking at the site of ancient Troy. But these were merely the activities of single days. Meanwhile, winter had come. His plans were upset. His boredom increased. *The Prophet* was finished, and he was left unoccupied.

In February they left Gotha, went to Rome, to Naples, to Alexandria, to Cairo. The weather was wretchedly cold. He wrote only eleven letters—hardly a third of the number he expected to do. By the first of May they were back in Gotha, exhausted. Mrs. Taylor had been taken ill at Florence. And he had hardly reached his German home when news came informing him, woefully, that the Appletons would not publish his history for another year, and that they could allow him nothing in the way of advance royalties. Soon after that letter he received a note from Reid, requesting that he go to Iceland, to report for the paper "the one thousandth anniversary of the first settlement of the island."

He went. It was his Alma Mater who commanded him, and her command, to one who has known no other allegiance, was "like that of the trumpet unto the warhorse." Before he had settled with his family at Cedarcroft the fall of 1874 was upon him.

But, once home, it seemed that the degenerate age in which he was living was far on its way again to civilization. His letters about Egypt and Iceland had made him famous anew. He was rushing them, in collected form, through the presses. There were news stories about him, nearly all of them pleasant. And finally, surest sign of all that sweetness and light were once more ascendant, invitations to lecture were pouring in upon him, invitations from everywhere, and on excellent terms. And how sorely he needed the money! The man to whom he had leased Cedarcroft had all but ruined the place. Nobody would buy it, in its present condition. It was practically falling to pieces!

Yet he planned to live there himself no longer. The reluctant confession he had made his mother was unforgettable: he could not afford it, no matter how inviting the prospect. "I mean to keep Cedarcroft (until there is a good chance of selling) as a home for my parents, my sister and family." He could do this without the necessity of maintaining it in the grand manner. He meant to move to New York. He was going to work regularly for the *Tribune*: he had to, however melancholy the thought, however opposed it seemed to the philosophy of perpetual progress wherein lay his deepest faith.

He passed up no opportunities to speak. He addressed the Delta Kappa Epsilon fraternity at the University of Virginia. He prepared a lecture on "Ancient Egypt," and gave it wherever it was asked for. The routine began as of old, running from October through March. It was "the severest winter since 1841." He spoke one hundred and thirty times. He traveled fifteen thousand miles. He cleared eleven thousand dollars. He paid four thousand dollars on old debts.

Then he lectured at Cornell. Then he wrote "summer letters" for the *Tribune*. Then he revised *Faust* for "a cheap popular edition."[5]

But why would the the damned reviewers persist in misunderstanding his *Prophet?* My design was not to represent a phase of Mormon history. "The original conception was totally unconnected with any actual events; the features which suggest the Mormons were added long afterwards. . . . . It is the most steady, conscientiously elaborated, and uninterruptedly carried out work of my life. The main lesson of the drama— the (to me) most tragic element—has not yet been perceived by any critic."[6] At least his German friends should know the truth. He wrote the editor of the *New-Yorker Staatszeitung*, explaining his sources, his purpose, his attitudes: He was simply pointing out the inherent tragedy in a blind acceptance of every word of Scripture. He had not written the work to be acted. He didn't care about its popularity. "I only ask that the readers may be made acquainted with the author's intention."

Many other things were happening. His *Home Pastorals, Ballads, and Lyrics* were brought out in the fall. "A thousand thanks for the new volume," wrote Holmes. I have read it through. I like many of the poems. The lines I quote here are delightful. "There should be twelve Home Pastorals, instead of three, praised Longfellow—one for every month of the year.

Mr. Longfellow, you have cheered me once more!

5. *Ibid.*, Taylor to G. H. Yewell, 7-31-75, II, 669-71.
6. *Ibid.*, Taylor to P. H. Hayne, 10-29-74, II, 664.

"Last night at the Century Club, a man whose poetic instinct is marvelous for one not a poet said to me, 'You should go on and write more of the *Pastorals,* filling out the design already indicated, by other pictures of life and nature.' Here was your thought again, and, to be frank, my own secret hope, waiting to be justified by the verdict of a friend."[7] Only the judgment of poets is reliable. Two stupid reviewers have said that these poems resemble "Locksley Hall!"

And the old, old rumor about an appointment to the Consular service—that was rife again, fretting his hopes.[8] "There was a strong effort made by prominent men in Washington (including two members of the cabinet) to have me appointed Minister to Russia.... I was told last night that the same friends are determined that I shall have an appointment two or three years hence."

7. *Ibid.,* 10-14-75, II, 675.
8. There had been some talk, during the winter of 1873, of Taylor's being appointed minister to Switzerland, but he did not greatly encourage it. "Do not, I beg of you, *urge* the Swiss mission upon the President," he wrote his friend, Calhoun.... "If the propriety of the appointment is not evident to him, let there be an end of the matter." The only temptation to accept the place, if offered, was that it would "be a convenience to me in regard to my Goethe researches." But Taylor knew that President Grant was aware of his connection with the *Tribune,* the paper founded by his campaign opponent, Greeley. "Hay (between ourselves) writes to me that if Grant supposes the appointment agreeable to the present proprietors of the *Tribune,* he will certainly *not* make it." Nothing ever came of the matter. Letter of 1-22-73. *Unpublished Letters of Bayard Taylor* (Huntington Library Pub., J. R. Schultz, ed.).

Meanwhile, in his hurried, harried way, he was writing rather often to Sidney Lanier, then in Baltimore, tardily recognized as a musician, yet to be recognized as a poet. "I am heartily glad to welcome you to the fellowship of authors, so far as I may dare to represent it; but knowing the others, I venture to speak in their names also. When we meet, I hope to be able to show you, more satisfactorily than by these written words, the genuineness of the interest which each author always feels in all others; and perhaps may be also able to extend your own acquaintance among those whom you have a right to know."[9] The next month Taylor wrote him again. Lanier seemed willing to wait for his success. He had the true poetic "morale." "Be of good cheer," my friend. Think not of the low popular meaning of success. Have courage! Remember the ideal, never attainable, but always calling us, in clarion tones, to our grandest achievements.

Later he was able to do Lanier a sizable service. He was able to bring to him, in a way, even that vulgar success which true poets despised. The United States Centennial Commission had asked Taylor to write either the Hymn or the Cantata, or both, for the opening day of that great event. Taylor decided to do the former only. He advised the Commission to select Lanier for the Cantata. Lanier must consent. But he must seek to express "the general feeling of the nation," rather than any individual ideas.

Lanier did consent. That was fine. He would represent the South, vanquished but now reconstructed, re-

9.  Taylor-Scudder, *op. cit.*, 8-17-75, II, 669.

generate. Yet Taylor saw fit to warn him again. "One dare not be imaginative or particularly original." By all means that *must* be remembered.

Lanier was inexpressibly happy. For many years poor, for many years neglected, he was being shown now, by the Laureate of the age, the most marked favors, the most courteous attention. His gratitude was profuse, more profuse really than the Laureate had time to acknowledge. "I have sent you my thanks very often," he wrote once to Taylor. "I hope they don't become monstrous to you. Your praise has really given me a great deal of genuine and fruitful pleasure. The truth is, that as for censure, I am overloaded with my own; but as for commendation, I am mainly in a state of famine; so that while I cannot, for very surfeit, profitably digest the former, I have such a stomach for the latter as would astonish gods and men."[10]

But a greater fortune had come to Taylor, a challenging and significant new offer. The most important literary distinction connected with the Centennial was, of course, the privilege of delivering the Ode. And here, in spite of its importance, the Commissioners met with trouble. They invited Longfellow first; Longfellow declined. They applied to Lowell, they applied to Holmes, they applied to Whittier, they applied to Bryant. Still the honor went begging. One pleaded his advanced age, another "neuralgia in the head," still another illness of another sort. The probable truth is that the older generation was played out. But Taylor

10. *Ibid.*, 11-24-76, II, 693-4.

was not played out! He had no false pride. He would not let the call go unheeded. When the perplexed board turned to him, therefore, he withdrew his earlier contribution and accepted. It was a fine-spirited thing to do.

Reid had sent him to Philadelphia anyhow, to report the occasion for the *Tribune*. July 4 dawned, fiendishly hot. The Continental Hotel swarmed with a curious jostling rabble. All the state governors were there. Taylor marched in the great procession, with his wife and daughter, mounted the immense platform that ran the length of Independence Hall, oblivious to the many greetings of friends, rapt in the ecstacy of his mission.

He used no notes, no manuscript. He recited his Ode eloquently. Even the restless spectators who had climbed nearby precipitous trees were stilled by the inspiration of his utterance. It was a triumph for Poetry, for that rare, fine art which, more than all other arts together, he had loved throughout his life with the measureless passionate love of his measurelessly passionate nature. The applause was thunderous. And later, when he attempted to slip away, wild hands seized his hands, earnest eyes stared at him, and excited voices cried hysterically: "That's Bayard Taylor! That's the poet! Hurrah for our poet!"[11]

The next day he was back at his desk at the *Tribune*. Congratulations came in. Cynical allusions to the inadequacy of his Ode came in also, maddening him. He was obviously overworked. In addition to a full

11. *Ibid.*, II, 687.

day's employment at the paper, he was editing *The Echo Club* for publication as a volume; he was editing *Boys of Other Countries*, a series of sketches written some time before; he was doing occasional letters for the *Cincinnati Commercial*. And he was carrying on in a feverish way such a private correspondence as few men ever bothered with.

These letters are depressing to contemplate. Written to friends though most of them were, how rarely are they personal, how rarely do they reflect anything but the furious desperate hurry of his life! Lanier wanted to discuss the philosophy of composition with him. Another friend wanted to discuss blank verse. Still another was curious about a phrase of Shakespeare. But Taylor had no time to reckon with the imponderables. He had no time to think. He could only hasten through a record of his activities, in cold, impersonal, pitiful narrative. "Drudgery, drudgery, drudgery"[12] was all he knew now, the senseless coming and going of his days, the utter exhaustion with which he fell asleep.

Why the original compulsion of this drudgery; why could he never rest? The question is complex, but important. Of course it all revolves around the eternal problem of money; and as early as 1859, it is plain, the details of that problem, as they affected Taylor, had long been known to his more intimate friends, to Boker especially. In July he asked Boker for a loan of five hundred dollars. "I refrain from borrowing in this neighborhood [Kennett Square] because my brother's affairs are in hopeless condition, and my own credit

12. *Ibid.*, To Lanier, 3-12-77, II, 698.

would be suspected if I were to do so."[13] What this brother's hopeless affairs actually were is not known. We do know that he was a doctor, and we have seen that his name was Howard. Also we know that he had a family. For at least twenty years, one feels safe in saying, Taylor more or less supported that family, assuming the responsibility for Howard's debts,[14] until even his friends were disgusted with him. Boker wrote in 1875: "I somehow heard that your brother the doctor is again in trouble. . . . Do you still continue to sustain the body of *that death*, and to make yourself poor and anxious for the sake of one who never, brother as he is, has treated you with distinguished gratitude?"[15] Then there was brother Fred's commission, as we have also seen, and Fred's debts, and his father's debts—"for which I am responsible." Just what *they* were is, again, not clear at all, but that they oppressed Taylor is obvious. "I have done all my duty toward my family, and if one has gone to ruin in spite of me, I have saved the rest."[16] This was written in March, 1861. The following week he informed Boker that during the past twelvemonth he had paid $4,000 to his creditors, and that in two more years, at a similar rate, he would be clear. "But I am tired of this drudgery." And before the year was out he was having to borrow from Boker again: "One hundred dollars for twenty days. Some money I expected failed to come through."[17]

13. *Cornell Univ. Mss.*, 7-14-59.
14. *Ibid.*, See Taylor to Boker, 3-11-61.
15. *Ibid.*, 4-8-75.
16. *Ibid.*, To Boker, 3-11-61.
17. *Ibid.*, 12-31-61.

Then there was the Russian mission. Taylor looked upon it, frankly, as a gamble. To mention again his own statement: "In a word, George, I must make a desperate struggle for the sake of a splendid one. I have made the right beginning here, and if I succeed will be able, in the course of years, to produce my greatest literary work. If I fail, I shall have spent money to no purpose, and will be lucky if I have funds enough to bring me home."[18] But he failed here also, and in 1864 indebtedness was still a vexing question. "I have paid off $9,000 in two years. I have only $5,000 left to discharge."[19] Two years later (after lecturing 600 times and publishing nine volumes during the decade) debts remained.[20] Then, in 1870, he sent his parents to Switzerland, hoping to meet their expenses by the lecture tour in California, which proved, as we have seen, to be one of the most "hideous deceptions" of his career. "Bret Harte assured me that the country is an intellectual wilderness; he can scarcely live in such an atmosphere. The consequence is, I lost instead of earning money, and came back ready to undertake some sort of drudgery—for lecture I will not."[21]

This scattered documentation could be continued at length. Taylor was probably in a sense extravagant; he spent money rather freely when he had it. When he left New York for the Scandinavian countries in 1856, we recall that he took with him his two sisters, his brother, and the sailor Braisted. Yet his mistake, sum-

18. *Ibid.*, 9-28-62.      20. *Ibid.*, To Stedman, 1-6-67.
19. *Ibid.*, 3-11-64.      21. *Ibid.*, To Fields, 1-25-70.

marized, was probably no more than this: though a man of letters, dependent solely upon lecturing and writing for his income, he nevertheless was ambitious enough to want to live well. Such an ambition, on a writer's part, is extremely daring. As a principle, in America, one may even call it foolish.

Taylor once spoke out on this subject—cried out perhaps more truly than he spoke. He asked a question which had troubled him, no doubt, for twenty years, even longer; and the question was important and imponderable, as imponderable in its way as Lanier's Shakespeare question, and also as unanswerable. It was in April, 1877. He had lectured throughout the winter again, and this had probably pointed the question. It had to do with the ultimate worth of the literary career; it faced with honesty the matter of his sense of values. And it suggested, vaguely, the suspicion that his whole life had been misdirected, and futile.

A young friend, Murat Halstead, was beginning to write, and like many another young man of his time, he sought Taylor's advice. The letter he received in answer doubtless proved much more than he had expected. "Have you any idea of the life of a man who has attained a certain amount of name (by which I don't mean fame) in literature? Have you ever considered how many solid claims are made in return for certain very intangible advantages? I should like to enlighten you a little on this point, for within the last year I have seen the comfortable statement repeated in various newspapers that a man has only to do good literary work in order to be appreciated—and rewarded.

"Nothing could be more untrue in this country at this time. The public supposes that the mere knowledge of a man's name is the token of his success. If notoriety were success this would be true; but it is sometimes the reverse. However, notoriety brings with it the same penalties as genuine fame; and a large proportion of the very persons who most worry an author imagine they are cheering him with compliment! When they do this, they boldly assert their claims upon his time and patience. For instance, nothing is more common than for me to receive a package of Mss., accompanied by a letter, beginning in this way: 'I ask of you the same assistance which others gave to you when you were young. Will you read my manuscripts and return them to me with your critical judgment?' The simple fact is, I never had such assistance when I was young. I never sent an article to an author who was not also the editor of a periodical; I never asked another's influence to procure admission into a magazine; and with all the sympathy which I still keep for the hope and uncertainty of beginners, I have never yet found that my frank criticism was of any avail, except to make me enemies when the ardent young poet subsides into the reporter or paragraph writer."

But let us consider this business in fuller detail: "I don't mind requests for autographs—when only one is wanted, and when a stamped envelope is enclosed. But these questioning letters about all sorts of things, the answer to which any fool could discover for himself simply by looking into an encyclopædia! 'Is the Khedive's private income greater than the Sultan's? We want you to decide a little bet for us, out here in Ohio.' And then the requests to deliver orations or poems before colleges, college societies, associations of all sorts, public meetings, charities—they must all be declined—personally, carefully. It dulls and wearies the mind, and for nobody's profit. Sometimes I thus throw away two hours daily, for weeks at a time.

"You can do a great service to literature, my friend, by helping to make people understand that no author not independently rich can possibly respond to a fraction of the claims made upon him. You should make them see that wealth is never attained in this country as a reward for the highest and purest forms of literary endeavor. Let me give you some facts: Emerson is now seventy-four years old; yet it was not until he published *The Conduct of Life*, in 1860, that he received any sizeable royalties from writing. Bryant is in his eighty-third year; yet he could not buy a cottage with all he ever received for his poems. Irving was nearly seventy before the sale of his works at home met the expenses of his simple life at Sunnyside. Now understand me: I have no reason to complain about the way the public has received my books of travel. The point is, these volumes have little if any value as literature. But the translation of *Faust*, to which I gave all my best and freshest leisure during a period of six or seven years—*that work has yielded me only about as much as a fortnight's lec-*

*turing.*[22] I have labored already for almost three years, collecting material for my life of Goethe. I have been trying, for two years more, to amass enough money to afford the leisure in which to write it. I must earn my time in advance. And yet, my dear Halstead, no matter how successful this study may be, I know it can bring me in payment the merest tithe of the amount which drudgery for the common magazine market would afford in the same time. But the matter of money doesn't enter my plans. I only look forward and yearn for the chance.

"Again, don't mistake what I say. I am not really complaining. This is merely an explanation of the artist's problem in America. It seems inevitable with us. I submit to it."[23]

Of course, Taylor might have been blunt about the whole matter. He might have locked his doors to visiting delegations, he might have thrown importunate letters in his waste-basket, he might, in all fairness to his ambitions, have cultivated an exterior of rudeness, even. Others have done it in the name of Art.

But in his case this solution would scarcely have been effective. He did have a public, which paid him for lectures. If he offended that public, the cost in diminished invitations would probably have made itself felt, soon and harshly. In other words, he probably realized that as long as the damned public supported him, the damned public must needs to some extent be humored. Moreover, the reputation of the *Tribune*

22. Biographer's italics.
23. Taylor-Scudder, *op. cit.*, II, 701-4, 4-16-77.

was in a way at stake, and he owned stock in the *Tribune*. And then one could never know but that, were effrontery practiced, the individual affronted might be intimate with a senator—a senator whose industrious opposition might well destroy his chances of a place in the consular service. Taylor was interested in politics; he had been a diplomat, for a time, already. And the thought of becoming one again was not untenable.

Another consideration ought to be mentioned. Taylor was kind, even tender. He had retained his sensibilities in spite of all his travels. He hated to give pain. Could it not have been, then, that his nature simply rebelled at the thought of insulting this stupid public, this public that was so unreasonable in its demands, but that, after all, was fundamentally good, well meaning, only blind, only pitifully human? Could not pity have flooded his contempt, washing away the poison of it and leaving him only exasperated, beaten? His generosity, one thinks, proved his undoing here. But to have lacked generosity would have been a sadder thing still.

Whatever the explanation for his tolerance, the strain of maintaining it and of doing his work was breaking him. Late in May he rushed off to Cornell, to lecture again on the writers of Germany. Then he hurried to Providence, to read a poem, "Soldiers of Peace," before the Grand Army of the Potomac. Abstraction was habitual with him now. Often when Mrs. Taylor would speak to him, he would not hear. He would stare before him, vacantly, at vacancy. All of his earlier liveliness was gone. A celebration was being held in Chester County. He was implored to come there, to deliver another poem. This time he refused, with a frankness that was disarming: "Both last year and this, I have been severely taxed, and I feel that I cannot and ought not to undertake a new labor."

Instead, he went, as he should have done long before, to White Sulphur Springs, Virginia. He would rest awhile. He painted, he walked in the forest, he drank the restorative waters. But other disturbing rumors about possible appointments reached him even there. He was to be sent to Russia. He was to be sent to Belgium. Well, he wouldn't go to Belgium, that was final. Why did no one think of sending him to Germany? That was the logical mission for him. He began to suggest as much to his solicitous friends in Washington.

Another stirring thing happened to him at the springs. Months before he had written part of a lyrical drama," *Prince Deukalion*. It was to give the world his philosophy of religion; it was to clarify, for all time, the question of his faith. The critics, who thought him conservative; the Quakers, who thought him an apostate; the public, who thought him indifferent—they would all be silenced by the grandeur of his vision.

Yet somehow, in the middle of this poem, his fluency had played out. He toiled at it to no purpose. The well of his inspiration seemed unaccountably dried up. He was palpably worried, at times even alarmed. And then in this calm retreat, inspiration came surging back, overcoming him "like a summer cloud." In no time, almost, *Deukalion* was finished.

Its completion left him exhausted. He hurried to Cedarcroft. He hurried for a few days rest to Newport, he hurried to Mattapoisett, he hurried to Cohasset, he hurried back to New York. Though he had gone to the coast for a vacation, he returned with an agreement to translate Schiller's *Don Carlos* for the tragedian Lawrence Barrett. This was in September. The next month he was busy with a series of lectures on German literature at the Lowell Institute, Boston. He was working his full day at the *Tribune*. He was writing articles for the *North American Review*. "I am staggering on the brink of mental and physical exhaustion."[24]

Thus ended his fifty-second year, ended as had the five years before it, in a bewildering, whirling round of activity that seemed madly to get nowhere, in spite of his heroic efforts to shape it. There was material here for tragedy, for a tragedy so poignant that *The Prophet* would have appeared, when likened to it, a flaccid irrelevant legend. His world was dehumanizing him; it had destroyed his capacity for leisure; his spirit was dead. Within two weeks he would have another birthday. Fifty-three years. What had they meant? Where was the peaceful afternoon of his dream, the day declining to its close, imperceptibly, even, and calm? Where was the quietude he had sought? Where was anything that seemed really beautiful—beautiful and at the same time possible? Win-

24. *Ibid.*, Letter to Boker, 12-29-77, II, 713.

ter was on the land. Winter was in his heart. And farther and farther away from him, like the strange mirage he had first seen in Africa, stretched the delectable waters of a youth now inconceivably dim and remote—the waters of a once resplendent desire, the glassy cool translucent wave.

# DRAMAS

## XIX

ONE might well be curious about the nature of those long poems and dramas which Taylor wrote during the last six years of his life. So different they seemed from what he had done before that he thought of them as belonging, almost, to another life, to a richer revelation. The world, for all its darkness, would not willingly let them die. Had not his wisest friends assured him of that? Had not Whittier likened *Deukalion* to "the grand Dramas of the Immortal Greeks?"

*Lars:A Pastoral of Norway* was published in 1873. In uninspired but characteristic blank verse it recounts the sublimation of "Berserker rage" in the spiritualities of Quakerism. Lars is a silent man of Norway, in love with Brita. Brita has another suitor, Per, "gay with laughter of [the] seas which were his home." The village pastor urges her to hasten her decision between them. Lars proposes, but is put off. Later, Brita is with Per in a boat when the brooch of her grandmother falls from her dress into the sea. It is an ill omen.

The omen is soon verified. The rivals meet at a wedding and have angry words. In the fight which follows, Per is slain, and the vacillating Brita decides, as he expires, that it is he whom she loved, Lars whom she hates.

Disconsolate, Lars comes to Pennsylvania, where it was rumored an ancestor had settled years before. He meets Ruth and agrees to work for her father. He is obviously attracted by this lady, but there is Abner to be reckoned with, a man "rigid in the sect," rich also, and sneering. Lars studies English with Ruth and seems interested in salvation when Abner learns of his past and taunts him with it. The old rage of the Norseman blinds Lars: he would have killed this rival also had he not escaped.

Ruth then, in patience, sets out to purge the evil in Lars' breast. She takes him to meetings. Her father tells him of God's surpassing love, and Lars, in tears, feels his wild spirit calmed. He will find the way. He will bear his cross in peace.

The story does not end here. Lars becomes a Quaker, after confessing the murder to Ruth. He changes his name from Thorstensen to Thurston. He marries Ruth, and their devotion deepens. With the death of Ruth's father, Lars takes his wife to Norway. The influence of their gentle manners spreads. A Society springs up, a "brotherhood of earnest seekers for the Light." But the brother of Per plans to avenge his death. Lars goes to meet him, and is stripped and armed by the crowd.

But the weapon of darkness falls from his hand: he cannot hold it, nor can Per's brother bring himself to fulfill his duty. And while the natives labor with the unusualness of this circumstance, trying to understand it, Lars begins to preach. He tells his old friends that murder is sinful. He regrets that blindness once led him into it. The conventional pastor terms Lars' talk heresy, and is about to persuade the crowd to share his opinion. But Brita's brooch is washed up before them. It is a good sign. Brita goes away with Ruth and Lars, to become a Quaker.

The poem was dedicated to Whittier. As a narrative it is developed with clarity. There are several stirring passages in it—in particular, the account of Lars' fight with Per. And yet even the pastoral tradition of simplicity cannot quite excuse the monotonous sweetness of Ruth, or make more than slightly interesting the undefended dullness of Taylor's account of Quaker mannerisms and prejudices. Fundamentally, *Lars* does not come to life; there is no high quality in its verse to reedem it. Longfellow, to name no one else, had done this kind of thing much more ably in *Evangeline*.

*The Prophet*[1] was more labored than *Lars*, but by no means as readable. It is a lyrical drama in five acts, treating the rise and eclipse of the Prophet, David Starr. David's beginnings in religion date from the time he announced to the camp revivalist that he had no sins to confess. His bride, Rhoda, believes in him; so do many others, who persuade him that he should preach. He does so, works a miracle, collects a zealous but motley following, and goes West, to a place oddly like Utah.

Sin soon discovers his whereabouts, and begins in a devious way to work his undoing. Livia, "a woman of the world," has joined his band and affects him strangely. They are prospering, and building a city,

1. *Dramatic Works*, pp. 1-164.

but desire a sign from heaven. For a while the spirit does not move David, but the visitation comes: Livia falls heir to the gift of tongues; she talks Dutch, French, and Cherokee with ease. The people are happy, all except Rhoda, who senses her husband's growing indifference.

Much plotting goes on: A conspiracy within the Council of Twelve is slowly developing. And an idea which saddens the women is developing too: it is that a man may have as many wives as he chooses, that the Prophet, for example, may have both Rhoda and Livia. This practice is adopted. News of it and of other unconventional actions by the flock stirs Colonel Hyde, of "the Gentiles," to an investigation. He learns that David has planned to kill one of his own followers, whom he suspects of treason. Other followers are trafficking with the Colonel. When he marches against them, however, they sally out to fight, led by Livia. David waits idly by for the sign which never comes, for he is corrupted now; his prayers "rebound" from Heaven. He can think only of the past, of his innocence, and of Rhoda when they were young together. "The Gentiles" are victorious; David is mortally wounded and dies before he can utter the ultimate revelation to his people.[2]

Taylor said, as we have seen, that he regarded this work as "a two-edged sword, cutting the fossilized orthodox to the heart no less than the Mormons." This former class seem represented mainly in Act I,

2. *Ibid.*, V, 7, 164.

where the author, in a convincing scene, describes the
exhortations of a preacher:

> *Oh there are more among ye shall be plucked*
> *As brands from out the burning! By the hair*
> *I'll seize you—even by the single hair*
> *That holds you from the pit!My hands are singed*
> *With loosening the Devil's grip on souls;*
> *And you, who should strike out with fists and feet,*
> *Leave me the fight, the cowards that you are!*
> *You think the Lord can't see you: even so*
> *The ostrich sticketh in the sand her head*
> *To save her gay tail feathers: pull them out*
> *And cast them from you! Though you hide your-*
>    *selves*
> *Under the mountains, it will not be long*
> *He'll send you wiggling forth, as mean as mice;*
> *And though you dive down in the deepest sea*
> *He'll haul you to the surface like a whale,*
> *Harpooned and spouting blood.*[3]

Later, in the same scene, Peter attempts to persuade
David to preach. There have always been preachers,
he declares; we are used to them; people say that
things would go to rack without them.

> *But I wish*
> *They'd yell and bang and thunder less. Somehow*
> *The text is friendly, smooth, and innocent*
> *As seems a flint; yet soon they knock from it*
> *Thick sparks of hell-fire, and the sulphur-stink*
> *Goes to men's heads, and sets them raving wild.*

3. *Ibid.*, I, 3, pp. 9, 10.

It is probable, again, that Taylor had the "fossilized orthodox" in mind when he sent Rhoda to the New Testament, looking for an injunction against her husband's doctrine of polygamy, and pointed out that her search was a failure. His opinion was, apparently, that not every wrong is labelled in scripture. He was even careful to suggest the Old Testament's sanction of the practice.

But the Mormons are much more obviously indicted. Prophets, he seemed to believe, are with us no longer; we have only our good sense to guide us, Edward Irving, Carlyle's early friend, was the prototype of his hero, Taylor once declared. Irving had preached the doctrine of the miraculous renewal of the gifts passed on by the apostles to the early Christians.[4] This was false doctrine, the poet thought. Those so-called miracles which do occur are either natural accidents or perhaps the work of the Devil. One cannot trust them. When the miracle is most needed, it fails us.

Considered more broadly, Taylor's complaint with the Mormons, and with sects generally, is the complaint of perversion. It was quite permissible for Colonel Hyde, officer of outraged respectability, to break up their brotherhood. Abnormalities of all sorts can fester within the narrowness of a sect. He had seen it happen in Kennett Square.[5] One needs breadth,

4. *Ibid.*, p. 327 (Notes).
5. Consider, likewise, his comment on the Temperance question. "I confess," he wrote to an unknown friend, "that I cannot yet understand the extreme impatience which the Temperance people show towards all who do not

varied contacts, the challenging fresh influence of radically different minds. One needs also to remember that religion is not the only problem with which human nature is compelled to reckon. So read his message.

Yet the ideas in this message, while sensible, are scarcely distinguished. They represent little more than the conviction of any educated person of Taylor's day. One fears, none the less, that they represent also the one redeeming glimmer from a work that is otherwise as dull as any he ever wrote.

In the "National Ode" Taylor had a good deal to say: America, "Liberty's latest daughter," stands acknowledged and strong, and free now; "the menace is dumb that defies her, the doubt is dead that denies her."[6] But the older nations of the world are querulous. . . . . What claims to greatness can we make? they ask.

Taylor answers that we have conquered a wilderness. We have driven our plowshares through "the thousand-centuried sleep" of the prairies. We did not pause in our conquest of nature until we had "channeled the terrible canyon," and built our homes "on the strand of the world wide sea," the Pacific. Nor is this all. We have not been made barbarians in the

wholly accept their views. True culture is so much more important, for it includes and insures Temperance! If a Prohibitory law could weaken the original vice out of which intemperance springs, I would gladly advocate it; but no law can touch that. The vice itself is kept alive by the narrowness and bitterness of the virtue." 4-11-70. *Unpublished Letters of Bayard Taylor* (Huntington Library Pub., J. R. Schultz, ed.).
6. *Poems*, p. 342.

process. "Crowned conscience and tender care, Justice that answers every bondsman's prayer—" all these things have been preserved in us, he implies.

America is a composite:

> *In her form and features still*
> *The unblenching Puritan will,*
> *Cavalier honor, Huguenot grace,*
> *The Quaker truth and sweetness*
> *And the strength of the danger girded race*
> *Of Holland, blend in a proud completeness....*
>
> *'Twas glory, once, to be a Roman:*
> *She makes it glory, now, to be a man!*[7]

For all this blessedness America must thank God, and her sons who died in her defense. She cannot ignore "the burden of her debt,"

> *When for a captive race*
> *She grandly staked and won,*
> *The total promise of her power begun*
> *And bared her busom's grace*
> *To the sharp wound that only tortures yet.*[8]

Those who died that this eloquent consummation might be realized, are enskied and ensainted now, bending over their great Mother, with hands clasped in benediction. Let us recrown our country's head, with the radiant blessing of these men—her heroes. Let no iconoclast arise to question their achievement, "to make a blank where Adams stood," to spoil the

7. *Ibid.*, p. 344.        8. *Ibid.*, p. 345.

crowns we have laid on Jefferson and Franklin, to "wash from Freedom's feet the stain of Lincoln's blood." So much for our past.

As for our future, there are two things worth remembering. The first is that in our blood we should preserve "some force unspent, some essence primitive, to seize the highest use of things."[9] Fate does not employ kings as the instrument of Progress with us. It employs, rather, the average man, whose responsibility to his country is therefore greater than is the case under despotisms. The second caution he suggests is that while we "look up, look forth, and on," we should never forget that our garments must be kept pure:

> *Pluck them back, with the old disdain*
> *From touch of hands that stain!*
> *So shall thy strength endure."*[10]

The Ode, it must be confessed, is hardly inspired. One thinks that the poet's responsibility on this occasion, and his opportunity as well, was rather sweeping and important. He was charged with speaking for a nation that for a hundred years had known but one hesitant interlude in its dazzling rise to world eminence. Things had happened in this land, momentous things, events that were not within the compass of pretty stanzas that are Pindaric in form only, events which, for good or evil, had done much to shape the destiny not only of a continent but of a hemisphere.

But Taylor seems not to have been aware of this, seems not to have been able to reckon with it. He did

9. *Ibid.*, p. 347.       10. *Idem.*

not lose himself in the sensuous imagery of his oriental poems; there is no talk of passion or about physical beauty; but neither is there anything satisfying to replace this absence. Taylor was simply out of his element. He could only write in vague, often turgid and incoherent, language concerning our progress and our forebears; he could only suggest, weakly, his far-from-weak awareness of our significance in the world, the promise of our future. But this future is not adequately previsioned, just as our past is not adequately bespoken. The Ode is a failure, as anyone by comparing even Lowell's "Harvard Commemoration Ode" must admit. Dr. Pattee has called it "one of the greatest failures in the history of American Literature."[11] Perhaps this distressing judgment is not very far from the truth.

Though both true and distressing, however, it had been often anticipated. It was anticipated, in a general way, with almost every successive publication that bore Taylor's name. Yet these criticisms, as long as friends remained faithful, were things which one might largely ignore, or explain away on the count that they were written by jealous and prejudiced, or by ignorant, reviewers. But one estimate he received could not be thus interpreted. It came from Boker, who was quoting Lizzie Stoddard.

Ostensibly, Boker was trying to account for his own recent indifference to poetry. Yet the letter implied much more: "Lizzie, Dick, and one or two others and myself were sitting together one night in the rooms of

11. F. L. Pattee, *History of American Literature*, p. 121.

the Pythoness [a frequent name for Lizzie] when suddenly she broke forth in her usual oracular manner. 'George, you, Dick, Bayard, Stedman, Aldrich, Read, the whole lot of you youngsters, have all been dreary failures as poets. Not one of you has won even a third class position as a poet. There is not one of you who can justly lay claim to popularity, in any true sense of the term. You have not even attained to such a position as is held by that weakling Longfellow, for whom no one can challenge more than a third class place, as compared with the mass of English poets. Since you began to write, a half dozen English poets—Swinburne being an example—have arisen and secured the fame to which you in vain aspired. It was not time that you lacked therefore to become known, but poetic ability. The world is not unappreciative of real genius, as you flatter yourselves is the case, only you are not up to the required standard. You are all failures, and the sooner you stop writing the things that no public will read, the better for your peace of mind. Is not this the truth,' she said, turning to me very sadly. 'God's truth,' my lips and my conscience cried with one voice. 'God's truth,' echoed poor Dick, with his heart's sickness in his face. 'I, you know, have given up writing verses with any hope of success. My poems are jobs now.' 'Damned bad jobs!' muttered our comforter. . . .

"I have no more respect for Lizzie's opinion than you have, but once in a while her poisoned shafts hit the white. . . . I do not judge for the others whom Lizzie included in her catalogue of failures; but in my own relation to her words, I must acknowledge their utter truth. 'Knocked over by a woman,' you say: 'You of all men.' No, dear Bayard, not by a woman. Forget the instrument of heaven. The same truth might have fallen from the lips of babes and sucklings, and would have been, no less, the holy truth which we worship."[12]

Taylor saw only one copy of *Prince Deukalion*. A month after it reached him he was dead. It was, as we have seen, a statement of his faith, and in the light of this fact is important. In historical scope, the drama is comprehensive indeed. Act I occurs in the fourth century A. D., Act IV in a future that for the twentieth century is still remote.

In the early scenes one finds Deukalion and his betrothed, Pyrrha, seeking Prometheus and Pandora in Hell. The Fire Bringer is Deukalion's father; Pandora is Pyrrha's mother, and it appears that both must approve their marriage. The act closes with the parental command that the lovers are to return to the Earth and wait, are first to fulfill their destinies.[13]

The lovers return and encounter Medusa, symbol of Catholicism. Like his father, Deukalion is concerned with man's welfare. He asks the sorceress what she can do for the race. Does she tread it down, lest it grow beyond her, or can she offer peace for its "illimitable questions and desires?" Medusa does offer peace, but only "through obedience." She demands reverence from man, yet extends to him no reverence in return. Deukalion is not satisfied with her. Her opposition to error

12. *Cornell Univ. Mss.*, 7-30-74.
13. *Dramatic Works*, I, 6, p. 226.

is questionable, because she knows no more than he who commits error. She is man-made and, therefore, like all else so made, frail. Pyrrha decides that Medusa has lured man through her knowledge of sex: "sexless thyself, the secret of the sex is lightly caught by thee." Later, additional complaints are urged against her: she suspects the muses. Art is not free under her despotism. Passion she terms revolt. Poetry is "the music if illicit minds."[14] Science is a serpent. Deukalion defies her; she will perish as all things mortal perish, but he, the immortal in man, will live on.[15]

Deukalion turns against Calchas, the High Priest, as well as against Medusa. The Priest would also keep men puppets. He has but one purpose toward which to point Humanity, to whom all purposes should be disclosed. He lacks faith in man. The single anchor which Calchas offers Man will drag him down: "give Man room," Deukalion cries, "Yea, room to doubt." Expose him to "sharp denial's gust, that makes all things unstable." Do not deny him the right to investigate Science. In his wide-ranging quest for Truth is Freedom and Dignity.

And Pyrrha is equally insistent:

> *Give up*
> *Dead symbols of the perished ages: doff*
> *The trappings of a haughty alien race*
> *Whose speech was never thine: keep but the spark*
> *Of pure white Truth which nor repels, forbids,*
> *Nor stings, but ever broading warms the world. . .*

14. *Ibid.*, II, 2, p. 237.
15. *Ibid.*, II, 4, p. 249.

*Be all where thou art but a part—*
*Be all, teach all, grant all, and make thyself*
*Eternal.*[16]

And with this speech, and others like it from Deukalion, Prometheus appears to the lovers and tells them that their wisdom is as great as his own, and that he can guide them no further.

Taylor does not surrender blindly to the gospel of Science, even though he defends that gospel against the fetters of Catholicism. Urania, who is Science, cannot comprehend either the First Cause or the Last Cause. Science is not God. "Almighty Love, lord of intelligence, anointed Prophet of Eternity, lives" even as Science lives; and the laws of science cannot destroy Love. When Agathon, who seems to be Taylor, declares this conviction, Urania asks, a little sadly, "Why, to flatter life, wilt thou repeat the unproven solace?"

The answer to this question involved Taylor's faith in immortality: Immortality is not an unproven solace. It is proven by our need of it. It is proven, again,

*By fates so large no fortune can fulfill;*
*By wrongs no earthly justice can atone;*
*By promises of love that keep love pure;*
*And all rich instincts, powerless of aim,*
*Save chance, and time, and aspiration, wed*
*To freer forces, follow. By the trust*
*Of the chilled Good that at life's very end*
*Puts forth a root, and feels its blossom sure.*[17]

16. *Ibid.*, III, 3, p. 276.          17. *Ibid.*, IV, 2, p. 299.

No purpose, in other words, is ever fully realized in this life; there must be another, a freer life, in which to complete it. Our need of immortality is our warrant that it is a reality.

Meanwhile, unending Progress is our destiny. Even the symbol of the Cross may in time be supplanted by "some diviner type." Certainly the advice of Buddha, that we seek Deity through renunciation, is unacceptable. Life is good and should not be renounced! There is "gladness" in it, "health, clean appetite, and knowledge, beauty, aspiration, power."[18] And to Medusa's declaration that she does not change, and to her further declaration that only youth believes otherwise, Taylor replies that her belief is rooted in darkness, that she is a "sorceress caught fast" in her own toils, that a thousand years have swept by without her knowing, that her theology is low and tribal, and is being supplanted by one that is universal. The drama ends with Prometheus' blessing upon Deukalion and Pyrrha; they shall go forth to redeem the world.

Of all Taylor's original works, *Prince Deukalion* appears, to me, to be his wisest and most important. For once he has content to sustain him. He has something of high significance to say, and he says it well. The drama indicates no hastily conceived reflections. He rarely talked about religion wth his friends, but the fact implied no indifference to it. Its meaning, he seems rather to have thought, was simply a private matter. Transcending, as it does, the limitations of reason and experience, it transcends at the same time

18. *Ibid.*, IV, 3, p. 304.

the limitations of argument. To discuss it is futile. Besides, the discussion of it might lay bare the sources of a man's faith, which to him, were not for the world to know. They took him back to his memory of Mary, and that memory was too sacred for speech. It was one of the few experiences which the world had not made sordid. He had kept it from the world. He would keep it so forever.

# MINISTER

## XX

IT was January, 1878, and the immediate future seemed as cheerless as the past. He was doing, as always, his piece of hack work, he was writing, as always, his polished verses, he was carrying on, as always, his heavy correspondence, and, as always, he was tired, was looking now only vaguely toward that change for the better which had been often rumored, but which in the end, just as often, had fallen away to nothing.

And then, in late February, it came—the reward that, of all rewards, was most perfectly at one with his intended labor and desire. President Hayes named him Minister to Germany. Everywhere, it appeared, there was approval. The government had hit upon the popular will this time, it seemed, with rare success. Telegrams overwhelmed him. Strangers wrung his hand in the street. Letters poured in upon him. He answered one hundred and fifty in four days. "There is a rewarding as well as an avenging fate," he declared to Lanier;[1] and to Hayne, in lines the most pitiful he ever wrote, he confessed his open amazement and his gratitude: "If you knew how many years I have steadily worked, devoted to a high ideal, which no one seemed to recognize, and sneered at by cheap critics as a mere

1.   To Lanier, 2-19-78. Taylor-Scudder, *op. cit.*, II, 723.

interloper in Literature, you would understand how incredible this change seems to me. . . . I was right in my instinct: the world *does* appreciate earnest endeavor in the end."[2]

Later began the nightly round of banquets and speeches that was not to end until he sailed in April, then already broken past curing, worn out in mind as well as body. The Goethe Club wined him and dined him. He was frank with them: "I hope," he declared, "to secure at least two hours out of each twenty-four for my own work [on Goethe], without detriment to my official duties, and if two hours are not practicable, one must suffice. I shall be in the midst of the material I most need, I shall be able to make the acquaintance of the men and women who can give me the best assistance and, without looking forward positively to the completion of the task, I may safely say that this opportunity affords me a cheerful hope of being able to complete it."[3]

Members of the Century Club gave him a breakfast. Sixty of them were there—notable among them, Bryant, to send happily on his way this beloved fellow poet. Stedman arranged another grand affair, a public dinner at Delmonico's. It was a triumph for literature, exalting that art "in the eyes of our unæsthetic countrymen."[4] He hurried to Washington to talk to Secretary Evarts, to enjoy the courtesies the German Minister

2. *Unpublished Letters of Bayard Taylor* (Huntington Library Pub., J. R. Schultz, ed.).
3. Taylor-Scudder, *op. cit.*, II, 725.
4. *Ibid.*, To Stedman, 3-6-79, II, 726.

had arranged in his honor, to rush again to New York, before they were over. On his return he wrote Hayne that "every evening until we sail [the date was four full weeks off] is pre-engaged for dinners and receptions."[5] At times the multiplying demonstrations frightened him. They all bespoke, so plainly, the magnitude of America's trust in him. But the cynics remained— his old enemies—to talk, editorially and vexingly, of the number of dinners with which our Minister Plenipotentiary was fortifying himself against the strenuosities of his office.

Yet, though these cynics did vex him, their cheap and envy-nourished jest was drowned in the libations of his countless well-wishers. Even the natives of Kennett were thawed by the nation's warmth toward him, and at neighboring West Chester he was also honored. He had brought fame to the section. His literature had immortalized it. They called him Friend Bayard; his home was a show place.

Of all these dinners, perhaps a certain one at Delmonico's proved most elaborate. His "friend and humble servant" Bryant presided. Literature, Art, the learned professions, commerce—they were all represented. Table decorations, in confectionery, pictured scenes from *Lars,* "The Bedouin Song," "The Quaker's Widow," and from his other poems. Taylor spoke to the many guests as though they were all his intimate friends. His conception of his duty was generous: "It is a mistake to suppose that a minister is merely a political representative, whose duties cease when he

5. *Ibid.,* 3-13-78, p. 728.

has negotiated a treaty of commerce. . . . Our age requires of him larger services than these. He ought also to be a permanent agent for the interchange of reciprocal and beneficient knowledge, making nations and races better acquainted with each other; an usher, to present the intelligence, the invention, the progressive energy of each land to the other; always on hand to correct mistaken views, to soften prejudices, and to knit new bonds of sympathy. Finally, as a guest, privileged by the government which receives him. . . . he must never forget that every one of his fellow citizens is honored or dishonored, justly or unjustly judged, by the action of him who represents the country."[6]

At midnight the company passed from the tables into the parlors. Taylor went to a balcony and looked out. The street was crowded; there was a torchlight procession going on in his honor, and a band was leading it. The musicians stopped beneath the window and played a tender serenade. Then a rich chorus of men's voices sang for him. It was the German Liederkranz, come to wish him farewell. He spoke to them from the balcony, in German.

A week later he sailed. His friends were at the dock to see him off. Many went aboard, planning to return in a tug, well stocked by the German Consular-general with stimulants to be drunk in his honor. But the fog and the rain and the swell were so heavy that the ship was not to be approached. The tug steamed off. His well-wishers had to wait on board until morning. But long before morning Taylor had gone to his state-

6. *Ibid.*, II, 731-2.

room, exhausted with the many drains upon his strength, wracked with "brain fever," and drugged by the doctors into a sleep that could in no normal way be summoned, despite his torturing, lamentable need of it.

2

Stopping for a few days in London he visited the aged Carlyle. They talked about Goethe, and as was meet, he let the Scotchman do most of the talking—the grand old man, who had read the great German before Bayard Taylor was born. They parted with affection. And even after Taylor had turned to go, Carlyle called him back, to shake his hand again: "I'm verra glad you've come to see me; we may never meet agin, and I want to say to ye that I desire yer prosperrity."[7]

They hurried to Paris, to do the intensive shopping necessary to keep up the dignity of his position. Five days they were there, "and very fatiguing days they were." A parade was staged during his visit, in honor of the opening of the French Grand Exhibition. Taylor had a "fearful time" at it—"lost my carriage, had no umbrella, tramped three miles on foot to the hotel in rain and mud, and narrowly escaped being killed in crossing the boulevard." At General MacMahon's Palace that night were the former King and Queen of Spain, the Prince of Wales, the Crown Prince of Denmark, "a Nevada Bonanza lady, and what not, all mixed up together." When Taylor arrived with his family, there was no one to announce him. He intro-

7. *Ibid.*, Taylor to Reid, 5-7-78, II, 737.

duced himself to the Marshall-President of the Republic; it was the only thing left to do. But he was glad to leave France. The only pleasant memory of his visit was an evening he spent with Victor Hugo. "I was delighted. . . . He was amiability itself, and even hinted at giving me a dinner, if I could remain long enough. The man is much better than his preposterous *pronunciamentos*. His manners are those of an old school gentleman, and his French the purest and most delightful I ever heard in my life. I stayed to a queer midnight supper with him.[8]

By May he was in Berlin. "We are very busy paying the round of formal visits which is required of us." Think, mother, I have already left one hundred and fifty calling cards! I have ordered three hundred more to be printed. The Crown Prince welcomed me "with the greatest friendliness. He came up to me with outstretched hand, saying in English, 'Oh, I know you already! My wife was talking about your *Faust* only a few weeks ago.' The entire diplomatic corps is aware of my hearty reception by the imperial family. It has made the other Ambassadors very polite to me. My two secretaries are very efficient and take all the bother off my hands. My mulatto man, Harris, is gorgeous in his gold-banded stove pipe hat. No one else has a colored footman except Prince Karl, and Harris adds immensely to our respectability."[9]

Yet for all the cordiality of his reception, he was plainly a sick man. Fiendish pains in his stomach

8. *Idem.*
9. *Ibid.*, To his mother, 5-18-78, II, 743-4.

tortured him. He consulted a physician. The advice
he received did not alarm him, the prescription he received did not seem severe. He was told to work very
little, to sleep nine hours, to walk one hour, to take
light wines with brandy and seltzer, and a tonic to
restore his appetite. "I feel eager for my task, and a
fortnight will not go by before I write the opening
chapter of my biography of Goethe."

Germany's leader at this date was Bismarck, and
Taylor began to make use of the fact at once. "Saturday I had an hour's talk with him in the garden behind
his palace; he was accompanied by a huge black dog,
and I by a huge brown bitch. I tell you, Stoddard, he is
a great man! We talked only of books and birds and
trees, but his deepest nature opened now and then,
and I saw his very own self." Taylor had written an
essay on the Chancellor the year before. Of the six
great European statesmen of the century (Pitt, Stein,
Metternich, Cavour, Gorchakov, and Bismarck), he
regarded the last named as easily the most important.
He freely told why: All such leaders should be ap-
praised in the light of "that grasp of mind which never
fails to consider passing events in their broadest relation to all history. . . . He [Bismarck] bears down ob-
stacles from impulse. He has an almost phenomenal
capacity to see all life and all history apart from his
inherited intellectual tendencies."

Taylor compared him in appearance to our own
General Winfield Scott, "but his face has nothing of
the vanity and petulance which characterized the latter's." Socially, the German is attractive, he added;

he enjoys repartee and is, in personal matters, uniformly generous. Only in statecraft is his brutality evident, though in debate he often becomes furious with his opposition. Afterwards, however, just as often, he apologizes.[10]

Summer was a stirring season in Berlin. Attempts had been made to assassinate the Emperor. The Social Democrats were fighting for power. The Eastern question was warmly debated in a world congress at the capitol. And, finally, to increase Taylor's concern with his office, word came that General Grant and a large party were to visit in Berlin. Should he ask the General to stay at the legation? And how should he entertain him? And should he present him to the Emperor? And why hadn't the General informed the Minister of his plans?

He was seeing much of the great men of Europe. "Gortchakoff" greeted him as an old friend. "Beaconsfield is very cordial: he refers to me as *Sans peur et sans reproche!*" I now seem to have known Bismarck for years."[11]

But there was no doubt about it now, something physically serious was wrong with him. The Grants came and departed; problems of etiquette proved of small moment, but at the dinner given the General at Potsdam, Taylor was unable to eat anything but asparagus and soup. He was forced to stand for hours at formal receptions. At the marriage of the Crown Prince he stood for five hours. When Grant came he

10. *Two German Giants*, edited by John Lord (New York, 1894).
11. See letters, Taylor-Scudder, *op. cit.*, II, 751-4.

had made a tedious journey to meet him, and had returned with high fever. Later he suffered "from furious muscular cramps, pains in the stomach, spells of vomiting, and a persistent feeling of sea-sickness which made food repulsive." He had lost thirty pounds.

He went to the mountains to rest, and for a time was restored. But only for a time. Physicians examined him again and advised that he take the waters at Karlsbad. He wouldn't do it. It would involve asking permission of Evarts to leave the country, and he had not been in Germany long enough to feel free to venture the request. He went, instead, to Friedrichroda, stayed a few days, and returned to Berlin.

His illness had not wholly saddened him. With the loss of weight, he looked "almost graceful." I carry a small ebony cane, have my moustache waxed into sharp points, and slightly powder my face to give me an aristocratic paleness. But I am not proud. When the guards at the Brandenburg gate rush out to present arms, I slightly wave my hand, as if to say, 'I do not exact it!' and they retire abashed."[12]

But what was happening to him really this while? The doctors decided that he had constipation of the liver. Then they decided that he had dropsy as well. He had written to his parents for the last time, thankful that they had lived to see their sixtieth anniversary. The leaves outside his window turned from green to dull brown. They were dry and withered, and the wind scattered them, the wind was now sharp, they said, and merciless, as so often the winds of his life had

12. *Ibid.*, To Samuel Bancroft, Jr., 9-15-78, II, 758.

been merciless. He was in constant pain. The doctors operated. He was still in pain.

But daily, in spite of pain and warnings, he would order himself dressed, and he would go to his library. There were his Goethe volumes before him, piles upon piles of them, crowding the room. In a corner stood a mask of Goethe's face, made from life. He would sit down to write. But he could not; he had not the strength, not even the strength for a single line.

Yes, this was the end of him, and he knew it. He had seen Orange Blossom and Apple Blossom dance in warm Egyptian moonlight, he had seen the glittering bazaars of Constantinople, he had seen the surging millions in London. Everywhere he had seen life; everywhere *was* life, and young love speaking, as always, the immemorial language he had sought to capture in poetry.

But speaking it, alas, no more for him to know. He was now to march to a different counting, to a sterner music than lovers were meant to hear. He who had striven all his life, "in the direction of a broader and higher human culture"[13] for his countrymen, to whom poetry had been, always, the "serious passion"[14] of his days and nights, was worn out and broken irrevocably. And yet, how could he leave it all? It did not matter, greatly, that his body was suffering. It did not matter that the illusion of sleep was lovely to him of late, lovelier by far than the heavy illusion of waking.

13. *Unpublished Letters of Bayard Taylor* (Huntington Library Pub., J. R., Schultz, ed.).
14. *Ibid.*, To J. J. Piatt, 5-2-66.

There was still his unfinished Goethe. And while that remained true, his life was unfinished. This work the world would never let die Give him time to complete that, and he would go resignedly.

The favor was not granted. The wasted man, almost unrecognizably broken and old now, would have to forego it. Yet not in apathy. It was December 19, and he sat in his chair, staring at his wife, and Lillian, and the doctor. "I want—oh you know what I mean—*that stuff of life.*" He became quiet and slept. Two hours later, still sleeping, he died—a martyr to the American way of life.

Honors were paid him in Germany. His body was left there until March. It was brought next to New York, where further honors were paid him. Then it was taken to Cedarcroft. The following day, at Longwood, he was buried, amid his blue remembered hills. And by his side slept Mary, to make kinder the coming snows.

THE END

# BIBLIOGRAPHICAL NOTE

The important sources of information about Taylor are, of course, his own works—set down chronologically on the following pages; his letters, collected at Cornell University and at the Huntington Library; and the manuscripts of fourteen of his lectures, now in the possession of the town library at West Chester, Pennsylvania. The collection at Cornell approximates 3,200 letters, the Huntington collection 500 more. Dr. J. R. Schultz, of Allegheny College, is publishing an edition of the latter, to appear as a Huntington Library Publication. To him, and to Dr. Ferrand, of the Huntington Library, I am greatly indebted for permission to examine this material.

There have been three previous biographies. Conwell's (1879) hardly deserves notice. It was rushed into print for purely commercial reasons, and is obviously the work of an opportunist who had no access to original documents. The *Life and Letters* (2 vols. Houghton-Mifflin, 1884), by Marie Hansen Taylor and Horace Scudder, is a thorough and conscientious study, scarcely critical in any real sense, but amply factual. A. H. Smyth's *Bayard Taylor* (American Men of Letters Series, Houghton-Mifflin, 1896) is over-slight and marred by pedantic discursiveness. I found it useful chiefly for its bibliography.

In preparing my own volume I have naturally been led to read rather widely in nineteenth century American literature. When it appeared necessary, I have cited, in the notes proper, references based upon that reading. The following bibliography, in so far as it relates to this phase of my study, is selective, of course, though all the important works I have used are indicated. The bibliography of Taylor's writings, however. is complete to the best of my knowledge.

# BIBLIOGRAPHY

## TAYLOR'S WORKS

*Ximena, or the Battle of the Sierra Morena, and other Poems.* Philadelphia, Herman Hooker, 1844. 12mo. (suppressed later).

*Views Afoot; or Europe seen with Knapsack and Staff.* With a preface by N. P. Willis. In two parts. New York, Wiley & Putnam. 1846. 12mo.

*Rhymes of Travel, Ballads and Poems.* New York, Geo. P. Putnam. 1849 (actually published December, 1848).

*Eldorado, or Adventures in the Path of Empire.* With illustration by the author. In two volumes. New York. Geo. P. Putnam. (May) 1850. London, Richard Bentley. 1850. 12mo.

*A Book of Romances, Lyrics and Songs.* Boston, Ticknor, Reed and Fields. 1851. 16mo.

*A Journey to Central Africa, or Life and Landscapes from Egypt to the Negro Kingdoms of the White Nile.* With a map and illustrations by the author. New York, G. P. Putnam & Co. (August) 1854. 12mo.

*The Lands of the Saracen; or Pictures of Palestine, Asia Minor, Sicily, and Spain.* New York, G. P. Putnam & Co.; London, Sampson, Low & Co. (October) 1854. 12mo.

*Poems of the Orient.* Boston, Ticknor and Fields. (October 27) 1854. 16mo.

*A Visit to India, China, and Japan in the year 1853.* New York, G. P. Putnam & Co.; London, Sampson Low, Son & Co. (September) 1855. 12mo.

*Poems of Home and Travel.* Boston, Ticknor and Fields. (Nov.) 1855. 16mo.

*Views Afoot.* Revised edition with a new preface. New York, (Nov.) 1855. 12mo.

*Cyclopædia of Modern Travel.* Cincinnati, Morre, Willstach, Keys & Co. 1856. 8vo.

*Northern Travel: Summer and Winter Pictures of Sweden, Denmark, and Lapland.* New York, G. P. Putnam; London, Sampson Low, Son & Co. 1857. 12mo.

*Travels in Greece and Russia, with an Excursion to Crete.* N. Y., G. P. Putnam; London, Sampson Low, Son & Co. 1859. 12mo.

*At Home and Abroad: A Sketch-Book of Life, Scenery, and Men.* N. Y., G. P. Putnam; London, Sampson Low, Son & Co. (Nov.) 1859. 12mo.

*Cyclopædia of Modern Travel.* Cincinnati. 1860. Revised and enlarged edition, 2 vols.

*At Home and Abroad.* II Series. N. Y., G. P. Putnam. 1862. 12mo.

*The Poet's Journal.* Boston, Ticknor and Fields; London, Sampson Low & Co. (December) 1862. 12mo.

*Hannah Thurston, A Story of American Life.* N. Y., G. P. Putnam; London, Sampson Low, Son & Co. (Nov.) 12mo.

*The Poems of Bayard Taylor.* (Blue and Gold edition.) Boston, Ticknor & Fields. (October) 1864. 12mo.

*John Godfrey's Fortunes: Related by Himself. A Story of American Life.* N. Y., G. P. Putnam; London, Sampson Low, Son & Co. (Nov.) 1864. 12mo.

*Poems.* Cabinet ed. 1865.

*The Story of Kennett.* N. Y., G. P. Putnam; London, Sampson Low, Son & Co. (March) 1866. 12mo.

*The Picture of St. John.* Boston, Fields, Osgood & Co. (Oct.) 1866. 12mo.

*Colorado: A Summer Trip.* New York, G. P. Putnam & Son. (Jan.) 1867. 12mo.

*The Golden Wedding.* A Masque. Privately printed. Philadelphia, J. P. Lippincott & Co. 1868. 16mo.

*By-Ways of Europe.* N. Y., G. P. Putnam & Son. 1869.

*Views Afoot.* New edition. Revised by the author, for Low's copyright cheap editions of American Books. London, Sampson Low, Son, and Marston. 1869. 12mo.

*Joseph and His Friend.* N. Y., G. P. Putnam. (Nov.) 1870. 12mo.

*Faust.* A Tragedy by Johann Wolfgang von Goethe. Part I. Translated in the original meters, by Bayard Taylor. Boston, Fields, Osgood & Co. (Dec.) 1870.

*Translation of Faust,* Part II. Boston, James R. Osgood & Co. (March 25) 1871. Q.

*Faust,* Parts I and II. London, Strahan & Co. (July) 1871. 8vo.

*Faust,* Part I. Leipzig, F. A. Brackhaus. (Nov. or Dec.) 1871. 8vo.

*The Masque of the Gods.* Boston, James R. Osgood & Co. (April 10) 1872. 12mo.

*Lars: a Pastoral of Norway.* Boston, James R. Osgood & Co. (Mar. 1) 1873. London, Strahan & Co. (March 8) 1873. 12mo.

*The Prophet.* A Tragedy. Boston, James R. Osgood & Co. (Sept. 13) 1874. 12mo.

*Egypt and Iceland in the Year 1874.* N. Y., G. P. Putnam's Sons. (October) 1874. 12mo.

*A School History of Germany:* from the Earliest Period to the Establishment of the German Empire in 1871. With one hundred and twelve illustrations and six historical maps. N. Y., D. Appleton & Co. 1874. 8vo.

*Home Pastorals, Ballads, and Lyrics.* Boston, James R. Osgood & Co. (Oct.) 1875. 12mo.

*Faust.* Kennett edition. Boston, J. R. Osgood & Co. 1875.

*The Echo Club and other Literary Diversions.* Boston, J. R. Osgood & Co. (July) 1876. 16mo.

*Boys of Other Countries;* Stories for American Boys. N. Y., G. P. Putnam's Sons. 1876. 8vo.

*The National Ode,* in facsimile. Boston, J. R. Osgood & Co. 1876. 8vo.

*Faust.* Part II. Leipzig, F. A. Brockhaus, 1876. 8vo.

*Prince Deukalion.* A Lyrical Drama. Boston, Houghton Mifflin, Osgood & Co.; London, Trubner & Co. (Nov.) 1878. 8vo.

*Studies in German Literature.* With an introduction by George H. Boker, N. Y. 1879. 12mo.

*Critical Essays, and Literary Notes.* N. Y., G. P. Putnam's Sons. 1880. 12mo.

*The Poetical Works of Bayard Taylor.* Household edition. Boston, Houghton, Osgood & Co. 1880. 12mo.

*The Dramatic Works of Bayard Taylor.* With notes by Marie Hansen Taylor. Boston, Houghton-Mifflin & Co. 1880. 12mo.

*A History of Germany from the earliest times to the present day.* With an additional chapter by Marie Hansen Taylor. N. Y., D. Appleton & Co. 1894. 8vo.

# SELECTED SECONDARY SOURCES

## BOOKS

Adams, J. T., *The March of Democracy*, Vols. I, II, New York, 1932-3.

Adkins, Nelson F., *Fitz-Greene Halleck*, New Haven, 1930.

Aldrich, Mrs. T. B., *Crowded Memories*, Boston, 1920.

Applegarth, A. C., *Quakers in Pennsylvania, Johns Hopkins Studies in History and Political Science*, Baltimore, 1892.

Beard, Charles, and Mary, *The Rise of American Civilization*, New York, 1927.

Beers, H. A., *N. P. Willis* (A. M. L. S.), Boston, 1885.

Belden, E. Porter, *New York, Past, Present, and Future*, New York, 1851.

Branch, E. Douglas, *The Sentimental Years, 1836-1860*, New York, 1935.

Child, Mrs. Lydia Maria Francis, *Letters from New York*, London, 1879.

Conway, M. D., *Thomas Carlyle*, New York, 1881.

Conwell, R. H., *The Life, Travels, and Literary Career of Bayard Taylor*, Boston, 1879.

Damon, S. Foster, *Thomas Holley Chivers, Friend of Poe*, New York, 1930.

Dayton, A. C., *Last Days of Knickerbocker Life in New York*.

Derby, J. C., *Fifty Years Among Authors, Books, and Publishers*, New York, 1876.

Dickens, Charles, *American Notes and Pictures from Italy*, London, 1903.

Disturnell, J., *New York As It Was and As It Is*, New York, 1876.

Duyckinck, E. A., and G. L. *Cyclopædia of American Literature* (edited to publication date by M. L. Simons), Vols. I, II, Philadelphia, 1875.

Faxton, F. W., *Literary Annuals and Gift Books*, Boston, 1912.

Finley, Ruth E., *The Lady of Godey's: Sarah Josepha Hale*, Philadelphia, 1931.

Firkins, Oscar, *W. D. Howells*, Cambridge, 1924.

Greeley, Horace, *Recollections of a Busy Life*, New York, 1868.

Greely, A. W., *Explorers and Travelers*, New York, 1902.

Greenslet, Feris, *Thomas Bailey Aldrich* (A. M. L. S), Boston, 1908.

Griswold, R. W., *Poets and Poetry of America*, Philadelphia, 1852.

Haight, Gordon S., *Mrs. Sigourney, The Sweet Singer of Hartford*, New Haven, 1930.

Haskell, J. C. S., *Bayard Taylor's Translation of Goethe's Faust*, New York, 1908.

Holder, Chas. F., *The Quakers in England and America*, Los Angeles, 1913.

Horner, C. F., *Life of James Redpath*, New York, 1926.

Howells, Mildred (ed.), *Life and Letters of W. D. Howells*, Vols. I, II, New York, 1928.

Minnigerode, Meade, *The Fabulous Forties*, New York, 1924.

Mott, F. L., *A History of American Magazines*, 1741-1850, New York, 1930.

Mumford, Lewis, *The Brown Decades*, New York, 1931.
————, *Sticks and Stones*, New York, 1924.

Nevins, Allan, *The Evening Post, A Century of Journalism*, New York, 1922.

Oberholtzer, E. P., *A Literary History of Philadelphia*, Philadelphia, 1906.
————, *Jay Cooke, Financier of the Civil War*, Philadelphia, 1907.

Pancost, Charles, *A Quaker Forty-Niner* (Anna P. Hannum, ed.), Philadelphia, 1930.

Parrington, V. L., *Main Currents in American Thought*, Vols. I, II, III, New York, 1927-30.

Rourke, Constance M., *Trumpets of Jubilee*, New York, Harcourt Brace and Company, 1927.

Seitz, Don C., *Horace Greeley*, Indianapolis, 1926.

Smyth, A. H., *Philadelphia Magazines and their Contributors*, Philadelphia, 1892.

Smyth, A. H., *Bayard Taylor* (A. M. L. S.), Boston, Houghton-Mifflin, 1896.

Stoddard, R. H., *Recollections, Personal and Literary*, New York, 1903.

Stedman, E. C., *Poets of America*, Boston, 1885.

Tassin, Algernon, *The Magazine in America*, New York, 1916.

Taylor, Bayard, *The James Bayard Taylor Verse Book*, West Chester Library Mss.

Taylor, Marie Hansen, *On Two Continents*, New York, 1905.

Taylor, Marie Hansen and Scudder, Horace, *Life and Letters of Bayard Taylor*, Boston, Houghton-Mifflin, 1884.

Wells, Carolyn, *A Satire Anthology*, New York, 1905.

White, Stewart Edward, *Forty-Niners*, New Haven, 1921.

*Who's Who in the Lyceum* (Introduction by Anna L. Curtis), Philadelphia, 1906.

Woods, Daniel B., *Sixteen Months at the Gold Diggings*, New York, 1852.

Wyman, Mary Alice, *Elizabeth Oakes Smith*, Lewestón, Maine, 1924.

## ARTICLES

Beatty, R. C., "Bayard Taylor: A Mind Divided," *American Review*, III, 77-95 (April, 1934).

————, "Swinburne and Bayard Taylor," *Philological Quarterly*, XIII, 297-9 (July, 1834).

————, "Bayard Taylor and George H. Boker," *American Literature*, VI, 316-27 (November, 1934).

Lanier, H. W. (ed.), "Letters Between Two Poets; the Correspondence of Bayard Taylor and Sidney Lanier," *Atlantic Monthly*, LXXXIII, 791-807 (June, 1899).

Lieder, F. W. C., "Bayard Taylor's Adaptation of Schiller's *Don Carlos, J. E. G. P.*, XVI, 27-52 (January, 1917).

Maybe, H. W., "Bayard Taylor: Adventurer," *Bookman*, XLIII, 51-9 (March, 1916).

Schultz, J. R., "New Letters of Mark Twain," *American Literature*, VIII, 47-51 (March, 1936).

Stedman, L., "Bayard Taylor," *North American Review*, CCI, 904-7 (June, 1915).

Stoddard, R. H., "Bayard Taylor," *Critic*, V, 169-74 (October 11, 1884).

Warnock, R., "Unpublished Lectures of Bayard Taylor," *American Literature*, V, 123-32 (May, 1933).

Warnock, R., "Bayard Taylor's Unpublished Letters to his Sister Anne," *American Literature*, VIII, 47-55 (November, 1935).

# INDEX

Hansen, Peter A., 209.
Harvard, 82.
Haskell, Juliana, 279.
Hawthorne, N., 14, 91.
Hayes, R. B., 351.
Hayne, P. H., 264-5, 353.
Heidelberg, 367.
Hemans, Mrs. Felicia, 29, 93.
Hewitt, Mrs. Mary, 59.
Hoffman, C. F., 53.
Holbrook, Josiah, 24-5.
Holmes, O. W., 322.
*Home Pastorals*, 319.
Howells, W. D., 104-5.
Hunt, Leigh, 208.
Hugo, Victor, 356.
*India, China, and Japan*, 132-7, 170, 182.
Irving, Washington, 8, 106, 204, 211, 271, 329.
"Jacob Flint's Journey," story by Taylor, 287-8.
Jerusalem, 122-3.
*John Godfrey's Fortune*, 234-7.
*Joseph and His Friend*, 240-2, 290.
Kennett Square, 13, 15, 220, 229, 368.
Kirkland, Mrs., editor of the *Union Magazine*, 60.
Lanier, Sidney, 221-2, 324.
Lapps, 197.
*Lars, A Pastoral of Norway*, 314, 335-7.
"Life in Europe and America" (Taylor's lecture), 161-4.
Lincoln, 223, 228.
Lind, Jenny, 84-5.
Ling-Branting, gymnastics course, 207.
Lockhart, 45.
London, 36.
Longfellow, 10, 11, 28, 46, 47, 95, 204, 245, 255, 271, 278, 322, 345.
Lowell, J. R., 25, 28, 46, 63, 91, 96, 103, 245, 251, 253-4, 344.
Lyceum, 25, 146, 211-12, 219, 268-9.
Lynch, Anne, 59.
Macaulay, 101.
"Man and Climate" (Taylor's lecture), 153.
Marshall, John, 102.
McClellan, General, 223.
Melville, Herman, 86.
Mendelssohn, 38, 58.
Mendenhall, Benjamin, 13.
Mesmer, 1.
Milan, 40-1.
*Mirror* (N. Y. paper), 10.
Murray, London publisher, 42, 45.
Nevins, Allan, 57-8.

BAYARD TAYLOR, Laureate of the Gilded Age, by RICHMOND CROOM BEATTY, has been composed on the linotype in 10 point Elzevir No. 3. This typeface is commonly called "French Old Style," or "Elzévier." The best form of the letter, according to D. B. Updike, appears to be that brought out by Mayeur of Paris, about 1878. Although styled "Elzévir," it has a great resemblance to the *types poétiques* cut by Luce in the eighteenth century. Linotype Elzevir No. 3 appeared in 1919, produced under the direction of Mr. E. E. Bartlett. The name which it bears is a derivation of general trade custom, and not intend to imply that the face is copied from those actually used by the Elzevir printing house in the seventeenth century.

THE PRINTED PAGE IS  EVERYMAN'S UNIVERSITY

UNIVERSITY OF OKLAHOMA PRESS

NORMAN

F